Asian Journal of Pentecostal Studies Series
1

Series Editors

Wonsuk Ma
William W. Menzies
Joseph R. Suico

APTS Press
Baguio, Philippines

David Yonggi Cho
A Close Look at His Theology and Ministry

Wonsuk Ma, William W. Menzies, Hyeon-sung Bae

Editors

WIPF & STOCK · Eugene, Oregon

Wipf and Stock Publishers
199 W 8th Ave, Suite 3
Eugene, OR 97401

David Yonggi Cho
A Close Look at His Theology and Ministry
By Ma, Wonsuk and Menzies, William W.

ISBN 13: 978-1-4982-9480-5
Publication date 6/15/2016
Previously published by APTS Press, 2015

This edition is published by Wipf and Stock Publishers
under license from APTS Press.

CONTENTS

INTRODUCTION

THEOLOGY

PRAXIS

PROSPECTS

FOREWORD

Samuel Huntington recently predicted that the church in the South will shape the new-century's global Christianity. Earlier, Harvey Cox convincingly argued that Pentecostalism would epitomize the twenty-first century Christian spirituality. This is not simply theory, but has been happening for some time.

The Pentecostal churches of Asia are in the spotlight of international observers and Korea has been one of the epicenters of this powerful spiritual move. At the center is Dr. David Yonggi Cho. My companionship with David in life and ministry for almost one half century is a living testimony. I was only a young schoolgirl when Cho and my mother, Rev. Jashil Choi, began a humble tent church in poverty-stricken post-war Seoul. I never imagined that this young and energetic preacher was one day going to be my own husband. The rest is history.

However, this is only the beginning. Cho's legacy should never be preserved in a museum, but live on as a dynamic and evolving tradition, raising up hundreds of other "Chos" in future generations throughout the earth. This book is a tribute to this future heritage.

As we mark a critical sister-school relationship with Asia Pacific Theological Seminary, this book, co-published with Hansei University Press signifies a godly synergy which will nurture and grow unique spiritual traditions like Cho's. This volume also demonstrates an approach to serious scholarly reflection whereby any spiritual tradition can be studied. The hard work of the editors deserves appreciation from all of us, and from future generations.

Sunghae KIM

Dr. Sung-hae (Grace) Kim, President
Hansei University
Goonpo, Korea

FOREWORD

Strategic alliances are one of the vital indicators of vibrant organizations. Having forged such an alliance to further the Kingdom cause of Spirit-anointed training and academic excellence, Asia Pacific Theological Seminary and Hansei University take joy in presenting this volume on the life, ministry, and practical theology of David Yonggi Cho. It is fitting that as the first concrete demonstration of this relationship, these two premiere Pentecostal schools in Asia can jointly present this publication. It is with great enthusiasm and satisfaction that we recommend this volume dedicated to the literature, work, and ministry of one of the truly outstanding churchmen of our time.

As the contributions of Dr. Cho have impacted the church in Asia and the world in the twentieth century, so these sister-schools will continue that impact in the twenty-first century by training a new generation of Pentecostal theologians and practitioners who will take their place alongside the pioneers and builders who have paved the way in building the Kingdom of God through dedicated and anointed evangelism, church-planting, missions, and theological training.

Wayne E Cagle

Dr. Wayne E. Cagle, President
Asia Pacific Theological Seminary
Baguio, Philippines

PREFACE

In several ways, this book signals a fresh breakthrough in the study of Asian Pentecostalism. First, this is a serious Asian attempt to reflect on various aspects of the Asian Pentecostal movement. Compared with other non-western continents, it is quite evident that there are very few books available on the subject. Only this year, the friends of Birmingham University, following the epoch-making work of Walter Hollenweger, publishes the very first book on the subject of Asian Pentecostalism. Secondly, this title signals the launch of the AJPS Series. The strategic contribution of the *Asian Journal of Pentecostal Studies* has been noted throughout the world and the inauguration of its monograph series has been anticipated. The time has come. The journal editors have chosen as its first title David Yonggi Cho, the pastor of Yoido Full Gospel Church, the largest single congregation in the world. Arguably, there is no single individual in the Asian Pentecostal circle who has made a greater contribution than Cho. He stands out in the Asian and the global Pentecostal movement and thus deserves the honor. Thirdly, this project is undertaken jointly by APTS Press and Youngsan Theological Institute of Hansei University in Korea. The enthusiastic support of this cooperative undertaking has been rather encouraging. Various levels of university leadership warmly welcomed the editors' proposal for the joint publication. In fact, during a recent short visit to the Philippines, Dr. Sung-hae (Grace) Kim, the president of the university, Dr. Kee-ho Um, the chair of the university's board of trustees and Dr. Hyeon-seong Bae, the director of the institute, warmly endorsed this joint arrangement.

For this first effort to come forth, as in many works of this nature, the process began much earlier than even the editors realized. Three conferences supplied the bulk of the current collection: the Youngsan International Theological Symposium (2002 and 2003) and the Youngsan International Church Growth and Leadership Conference (2003). The former events were organized by Dr. Hyeon-seong Bae, also serving as the director of Youngsan Theological Institute, Hansei University, Gunpo, Korea, and the latter by Dr. Young-gi Hong, the director of the Institute for Church Growth, Seoul, Korea. Footnotes indicate the conference where the original version of a chapter was presented. The editors acknowledge the gracious permission of the organizers. However, most of the presentations went through an extensive process of revision, and some of them were published in *Asian Journal of Pentecostal Studies* 7:1 (2004).

The editors express our deep appreciation to the contributors for their hard and tedious work to bring this important volume to light. In addition, the strong commitment of the two schools, Asia Pacific Theological Seminary and Hansei University, to the advancement of Asian Pentecostal studies is extremely encouraging. The two institutions also committed their financial resources to this project. In addition, the Boys and Girls Missionary Crusade through the Asia-Pacific Regional Office (director: Rev. Russ Turney), Assemblies of God World Mission, Springfield, MO, USA, has extended financial assistance to this publication. The same fund, administered by the Northern Asia Region (director: Rev. Ron Maddux) provided funds toward the Faculty Publication Assistance Fund of Asia Pacific Theological Seminary. Their invaluable assistance is gratefully acknowledged.

A few people deserve our special note of appreciation. My (Ma's) secretary Barbara dela Cruz extended her diligent assistance in communication and indexing. Kathy Baxter and Judy Cagle read the entire manuscript several times, particularly to improve the writings of non-English speakers. Their efforts make this truly a community work.

Several comments on this volume are necessary. Throughout the chapters, Asian names follow the western order, that is, the first name, middle name (if any) followed by the family name. The editors express our apology to those who have customarily written their names otherwise. The contributors have been instructed to minimize references to Korean works by or about Cho, although an extensive use was unavoidable in several contributions. For non-English titles, their Roman transliterations are given along with their English equivalences. In their subsequent citations, however, the abbreviated English equivalences are provided. Books authored by Cho are often referred to without the author's name specified. The author index does not include Cho's writings as they are referred so frequently that indexing them simply does not serve a good purpose.

It is the desire of the editors and publishers that this volume would serve as an encouragement to Asian Pentecostal churches and emerging scholars as they work diligently to preserve the Spirit's work in our continent and reflect theologically. This effort will certainly enrich our understanding of the spiritual tradition of the Asian church, contribute to the future development of the movement, and ultimately provide the global Pentecostal circle with a valuable resource.

The Spirit enabled us to bring this publication into the light. Thus, to God be the glory.

Editors
Easter, 2004

CONTRIBUTORS

Allan ANDERSON (D.Th.), a South African Pentecostal, Reader in Pentecostal Studies, University of Birmingham, UK.

Hyeon-sung BAE (Ph.D.), Dean of Graduate Schools and Director of Youngsan Theological Institute, Hansei University, Goonpo, Korea.

Simon K. H. CHAN (Ph.D.), a Singaporean Pentecostal, Earnest Lau Professor of Systematic Theology and Dean of Studies, Trinity Theological College, Singapore.

Young-Gi HONG (Ph.D.), Associate Pastor of Yoido Full Gospel Church; President, Institute for Church Growth, Seoul, Korea.

Chang-soo KANG (Th.M.), a Korean Pentecostal, part-time faculty, Asia Pacific Theological Seminary, Baguio City, Philippines.

Sam-hwan KIM (Doctorat), Associate Pastor, Yoido Full Gospel Church; Director, International Theological Institute, Seoul, Korea.

Young-hoon LEE (Ph.D.), Associate Pastor, Yoido Full Gospel Church, Seoul, Korea.

David S. LIM (Ph.D.), Executive Director, China Ministries International-Philippines (CMI-Phil.), Quezon City, Philippines.

Wonsuk MA (Ph.D.), a Korean Pentecostal, Vice President for Academic Affaires, Asia Pacific Theological Seminary, Baguio City, Philippines; Co-editor, *Asian Journal of Pentecostal Studies.*

William W. MENZIES (Ph.D.), Chancellor, Asia Pacific Theological Seminary, Baguio, Philippines; Co-ditor, *Asian Journal of Pentecostal Studies.*

Myung Soo PARK (Ph.D.), Professor of Church History and Director of Korea Evangelical Holiness Church Historical Research Center, Seoul Theological University, Bucheon, Korea.

Chris SUGDEN (Ph.D), Professor of Theology at Stellenbosch Theological Institute, University of Stellenbosch, South Africa.

HWA Yung, (D.Miss.), a Malaysian Methodist minister, Director of Centre for the Study of Christianity in Asia, Trinity Theological College, Singapore.

INTRODUCTION

THE LIFE AND MINISTRY OF DAVID YONGGI CHO AND THE YOIDO FULL GOSPEL CHURCH

Young-hoon Lee

As the Korean church grew explosively in the 1970s, one congregation attracted the attention of the churches of the world. Yoido Full Gospel Church (YFGC) pastored by Rev. David Yonggi Cho had the largest congregation in the world with a membership of 700,000 by the end of 1994. Cho founded YFGC in 1958 and has pastored the church since. Many view YFGC as the base of the Pentecostal movement in Korea. This paper will discuss the history, development, characteristics, and influence of this church in relation to the ministry of Cho.

1. The Life and Ministry of Yonggi Cho[1]

It is impossible to understand YFGC and its ministry without considering the man behind it—David Yonggi Cho. Cho was born on February 14, 1936 in a small town in Wooljoo county, Kyung-nam Province in the southern part of Korea, while the country was under Japanese occupation. From the time that Japan invaded Manchuria and started a war with China (1931), the Japanese exploited most crops and requisitioned Koreans to harvest them. It

[1]His story was published by an American reporter, Nell L. Kennedy, *Dream Your Way to Success: The Story of Dr. Yonggi Cho and Korea* (Plainfield, NJ: Logos International, 1980). See also Woonhak Nyo, *Chooyo Tutdaero Iroososuh* [Thy Will Be Done: World Mission and Yonggi Cho] (Seoul: Kyujang, 1982).

was in this devastating situation that Cho spent his childhood. The country was liberated in 1945 but divided into south and north by American and Soviet forces: the north became a communist country and the south a democratic one. But South Korea was still going through major chaos both politically and socially.

Cho's father, Doo-Chun Cho, ran for election to Congress on May 30, 1950 but failed. The Cho family was suffering financially. Less than a month later the Korean War broke out, Yonggi Cho witnessed the destruction and suffering caused by the war. In spring of 1953, when Cho was a sophomore in high school, he was injured in the chest while exercising. He gradually became weakened. Since it was still during the war and his family was poor, he could not get proper medical treatment. Later he was diagnosed as having a terminal case of tuberculosis. Without proper treatment, he became severely weakened and close to death. On what was thought to be his deathbed he was visited by a Christian girl who was a friend of his sister. His Buddhist parents had forbidden her to visit their home, but she persisted and gave Cho a Bible, preaching the gospel to him. Soon Cho became a Christian and his health began to improve dramatically.

He happened to meet Kenneth Tice, an Assemblies of God missionary, and began to interpret his sermons for him and another missionary, Lou Richards. Richards taught the Bible to Cho. While Cho was reading about divine healing in the Bible, he was touched by it and repented for not having fully believed it. He prayed and fasted for three days. On the third day he had a vision of Jesus in which he was called to dedicate his life to preaching the gospel.[2] After this experience, in 1956, he moved from Busan to Seoul and enrolled in the Full Gospel Bible College, which belonged to the Assemblies of God denomination. Although he was not in very good health, he managed to continue his studies. As his Christian faith grew deeper, his health also gradually improved. During these years of study, Cho met Jashil Choi, his classmate and a former registered nurse, who took care of him. She later became his associate pastor and mother-in-law.

---

[2]Kennedy, *Dream Your Way*, 118–21.

Cho started a tent church in 1958. Its 38-year history, although it assumed different names as the church moved from one location to another, may be divided into three periods. The first is the pioneering period (1958–196[3] in which YFGC was the instrument of the Pentecostal faith's taking root in Korea by its strong Full Gospel message and divine healing. The second is the developing period (1961–1973) when the church took the leadership in the Pentecostal movement of Korea and spread the Pentecostal faith in the Korean church. The third is the current period of expansion (1973–). The church has taken the lead in the Holy Spirit movement of the entire Korean church, has become mature enough to show its concern for Korean society, and has greatly expanded the Holy Spirit movement.

2. History of the Yoido Full Gospel Church

2.1 The Pioneering Period (1958–1961)

Cho, a new seminary graduate, put up a tent in a slum area of Daejo-dong, Seodaemun-ku, Seoul on May 18, 1958 with Mrs. Jashil Choi and her three children. The tent church that had started with only five grew rapidly as Cho's powerful message and healing ministry, with his ardent prayer and street evangelism, made a great combination. Many who had various diseases came and were healed. The news of the work of the Holy Spirit at this tent church spread among the people, and by 1961, the church had a membership of 600.

The primary characteristic of this pioneering period was its ministry among city slum-dwellers. This was a post-war time of devastation and most people despaired in emptiness and

---

[3] International Theological Institute, *Yoido Kyohoeui Shinanggwa Shinhak* [The Yoido Full Gospel Church: Its Faith and Theology], vol. II (Seoul: Seoul Books, 1993), 96. Hereinafter, ITI stands for International Theological Institute.

frustration.[4] To these city slum-dwellers in Daejo-dong, Cho preached the good news of hope. He proclaimed that they could gain not only spiritual blessing but also material and situational blessings from God if they came to Jesus Christ and lived by the word of God. Cho's message of salvation in body and spirit gave enormous comfort and hope to people who were poor and suffering.

The second important characteristic of YFGC was the experience of Spirit baptism and divine healing. Cho preached Pentecostal faith, which emphasized Spirit baptism and the subsequent signs such as speaking in tongues, based on the prophecy of Joel that God would pour out His Spirit in the last days. The most outstanding manifestation of God's power in Cho's tent church was divine healing. Many were healed from various diseases. Cho's sermons penetrated the lives of city slum-dwellers. Divine healing and Spirit baptism were the driving forces behind the growth of the church. The explosive growth of YFGC was not only because of divine healing however, but also because members who were changed by God's power, went out, and preached the word of God to others.[5]

The third was powerful prayer. The early apostolic church was born by the descent of the Holy Spirit upon the disciples, as they devoted themselves to prayer in the upper room.[6] Cho stressed prayer and devoted himself to it. He prayed at dawn, fasted and prayed, and prayed through the night.[7] Prayer became one of the most important elements of his ministry.

---

[4]Kyung-bae Min, *Hankook Kidokkyohoesa* [Church History of Korea], rev. ed. (Seoul: Christian Literature Society of Korea, 1982), 470.

[5]Yonggi Cho, *More than Numbers* (Waco: Word, 1984), 87.

[6]Acts 1:14; 2:1–4, 42–47.

[7]Dawn prayer was initiated at Changdaehyun Church in Pyungyang, during the 1907 revival meeting and expanded by Sun-joo Gil. Fasting prayer and all night prayer were expanded by Yonggi Cho and Jashil Choi.

2.2 The Developing Period (1961–1973)

Cho interpreted the sermons of Rev. Sam Todd, an American evangelist, during revival meetings held for one month in September, 1961, at Seodaemun rotary. A great number of people came to these meetings and experienced God's grace. Many received Jesus and many were healed. After the meeting, Cho decided to establish a second church and held an opening worship service on October 15, 1961. "Full Gospel Revival Center" was the name of his second church. He started construction, and finished it on February 18, 1962. Cho was ordained as a minister on April 26, 1962. On May 13 of the same year, he changed the name of the church to "Full Gospel Central Church." The membership reached 3,000 in 1964.

Cho overworked to the point of fainting and suffered quite some time from bad health. One Sunday, while he was administering baptism to hundreds of people,[8] Cho collapsed and spent a week in a hospital. A week later, he returned to the pulpit to preach but collapsed again. He was hospitalized. While reading the Bible in the hospital, he received revelation from Exodus 18 and used it to organize a cell-unit system,[9] which has become a trademark of YFGC.

Cho appointed women as cell-unit leaders, a revolutionary attempt in the tradition of the Korean church or any Korean society with a strong Confucian background. Until then, the position of women in Korean society was not well recognized, if at all. The cell-group system brought liberation to the status of women in Korea. These women leaders devoted themselves to the growth of the cell groups by effective home visitations and street preaching. Cell units conceived as sub-churches grew rapidly having worship services, prayer and fellowship. The growth of cell units thus made a significant contribution to the growth of the church. Meanwhile, various departments of the church were

---

[8]The Assemblies of God churches approve nothing but baptism by immersion, following the traditions of the apostolic church in the New Testament and also the traditions of Anabaptists.

[9]ITI, The Yoido Full Gospel Church: Its Faith and Theology, 185–86.

organized, including men's and women's mission and service groups. The church started publishing a Christian monthly magazine *Shinanggye* [The World of Faith] in 1967 in order to expand the Holy Spirit movement based on the word of God.

The primary characteristic of this period was the work of the Holy Spirit experienced in the community. If the work of the Holy Spirit in the pioneering period wasindividual experience, the work of the Holy Spirit in this period was the revival and renewal of the church as a community. The outpouring of the Spirit restored the Christian lives of a discouraged people of God. By this experience, the church could follow the model of the church presented in the book of Acts. When the church acknowledged and worked with the Holy Spirit it became Spirit-filled and this partnership brought with it the rapid growth of the church.[10]

The second characteristic of the period was the cell-group structure. Other churches had neglected cell-group structures but as employed in YFGC cells proved to be a great turning point. All members joined the cell system. Cho educated and trained the cell-group leaders so that they could take care of their groups. The structure of the cell-unit system contributed greatly to the effective training and pastoral care of the new members. With the help of this system, Cho could minister to the 700,000 members of his church. This subject will be discussed further.

2.3 The Expanding Period (1973 to the present)

Since the church could not accommodate the rapidly growing numbers, it decided to build a new church and started construction in Yoido, an island with nothing but sand. Despite economic depression, opposition and hardships, they finished construction and dedicated the new church on September 23, 1973. Church growth accelerated after moving to Yoido. Its membership reached 100,000 in 1979; 200,000 in November 1980; 500,000 in 1985;

[10] Yonggi Cho, "Naega Chehumhan Siljiljuk Kyohoesungjang" [The Practical Church Growth That I Experience], *Church Growth* 2 (Seoul, 1985), 136-53 (147-49).

and 700,000 in 1992.[11] During this time, the church built a prayer mountain (1973), opened a publishing company (1976), and started a weekly newspaper, *Full Gospel News* (1978). To propagate Pentecostal faith and for the effective training and education of its members, YFGC established the Institute for Full Gospel Education, which became the International Theological Institute (ITI) in 1993.

YFGC also fully supports the Full Gospel Bible College to educate Christian leaders. The college later became Hansei University with full accreditation from the government.[12]

The primary characteristic of this period was the explosive growth of the church. Some try to explain such growth in relation to the sociological, economic and political backgrounds in the 1970s.[13] The following factors contributed to the growth: the message and the leadership of Cho, divine healing, the baptism in the Holy Spirit, and the proper training of the church lay leaders by the Holy Spirit movement leadership.[14]

Second, the church began to take the primary role in the Holy Spirit movement of the Korean churches. In this period of expansion YFGC has dispersed the Holy Spirit movement all over

---

[11]Church Growth International, *Church Growth Manual*, No. 7 (Seoul: Church Growth International, 1995), 145.

[12]Full Gospel Theological Seminary later became Hansei University, a Christian university fully accredited by the Korean government. Its undergraduate school consists of the Departments of Theological Studies, Journalism, Computer and Information Management, Business and Management, History, Industrial Design, and Music. Its graduate school confers Master and Ph.D. degrees in Theology and Music. Hansei University, *2003 Hansei University Catalog* (Gunpo: Hansei University, 2003).

[13] Joon-shik Choi, "Hannkukeui Jongkyojuk Ipjanguesuh Barabon Kidokkyo Tochakhwa Shinhak" [Intercultural Theology from Perspective of Korean Religions], *Shinhaksasang* [The Theological Thought] 82 (1993), 96-128 (126–28).

[14]ITI, The Yoido Full Gospel Church: Its Faith and Theology, 111.

the country and contributed greatly to the spiritual movement of the Korean church.[15]

Third, the Pentecostal movement of YFGC expanded into the world. Since the 1970s, YFGC has facilitated women workers and stirred a revival movement through the cell-unit system. They have brought the Pentecostal movement to thousands by concerted prayer, person to person evangelism, publications and broadcasting.[16] Pentecostal mission theology puts stress on eschatological expectation and the realization of the kingdom of God.[17] YFGC has made every effort to further the Holy Spirit movement with its eschatological expectation, thereby to fulfill the vision of the Lord Jesus: to evangelize the world before the end comes by reviving the church.

Fourth, it emphasized the renewal of the church and its participation in society. Realizing that the church must go before modern society to continue its growth, YFGC has concentrated on church renewal since 1993.[18] They practiced Christian love by broad charity work for the lower class and the underprivileged.[19] The current operation of YFGC is as follows.[20]

---

[15]ITI, The Yoido Full Gospel Church: Its Faith and Theology, 125-26.

[16]Young-hoon Lee, "Hankuk Kyohoewa Sungrungwoondong" [Korean Churches and the Holy Spirit Movement], *Shinanggye* (October 1995), 134-39 (137).

[17]L. Grant McClung, Jr., "Truth on Fire: Pentecostals and Urgent Missiology," in *Azusa Street and Beyond*, ed. L. Grant McClung, Jr. (South Plainfield, NJ: Bridge, 1986), 47-54 (52).

[18]ITI, The Yoido Full Gospel Church: Its Faith and Theology, 139-40.

[19]The charity work of YFGC includes: providing cardiac operations to children with heart disease; donating blood; "bread of love" (distributing food to the hungry); giving relief to foreign refugees; a sharing movement; the establishment of a training institute, and so on. For detail, see ITI, *The Yoido Full Gospel Church: Its Faith and Theology*, vol. II, 141-44.

[20]Statistics are as of December, 2003.

2.3.1 Worship services

There are seven worship services each Sunday, three each Wednesday, and two each Saturday. The seven Sunday services have different focuses: Cho preaches in two services; executive assistant pastors preach in three worship services; one is with an emphasis on praise and worship; and one is a healing service. There are also daily early-morning prayer meetings and all-night prayer meetings. Sunday schools and various mission groups have their own worship services on Sundays.

2.3.2 Organization

Centered on the leadership of Cho, its senior pastor, the church has ten departments and subordinate branch departments. There are 20 regional chapels, 20 large districts, 309 sub-districts, 4,374 sections, 11,214 cell units, and 700,000 members.

2.3.3 Education

The Department of Pastoral and Theological Studies of the International Theological Institute takes care of the continuing education and training of pastors and lay workers. A lay education institute ministers to the needs of lay people. Sunday schools and various mission groups have their own education programs.

2.3.4 Evangelism and world mission

Various mission groups and committees participate in evangelical programs. The Mission Department supports Cho's foreign campaigns, sends missionaries and establishes and supports foreign Bible schools. As of 2003, YFGC has sent 600 missionaries, established seven Bible seminaries [21] and one university, and expands its missionary work in the Two-Thirds World.

---

[21] As an effective missionary strategy, YFGC builds up Bible seminaries in the mission fields and raises native pastors and Christian leaders to evangelize their own countries. There are seminaries and Bible colleges in Malang (Indonesia), Nairobi (Kenya), Chimkent (Uzbekistan), Hong Kong (China), Tel Este (Bolivia), Osaka and Tokyo (Japan).

3. Unique Features of the Holy Spirit Movement of Cho and YFGC[22]

Cho claims that the Holy Spirit movement can bear fruit when it is accompanied by the fullness of the word, prayer and the Holy Spirit. If one is neglected or overly emphasized, the dynamic work of the Spirit will be impossible.[23] Since the Holy Spirit movement of YFGC has been established and developed through the ministry of Cho, a discussion of Cho's message, prayer, Spirit-baptism and speaking in other tongues, divine healing and cell unit system is in order.

3.1 Message

The distinguishing elements of the Holy Spirit movement of YFGC are: salvation of the spirit; faith centered on the word of God; experience of the Holy Spirit; and world evangelization.[24] They are made concrete by Cho's messages.

Jin-hwan Kim described Cho's message. "It is positive and hopeful with stress on Bible-centered genuine faith and on the work of the Holy Spirit."[25] Karen Hurston has said, "Cho does not prepare his sermons exclusively by his own planning but by calling on the Holy Spirit."[26] E. J. Peterson wrote: "A preacher

---

[22]Dr. Daniel J. Adams, a professor of systematic theology at Hanil Theological Seminary in Korea, published a brief theological research report on the Yoido Full Gospel Church. Daniel J. Adams, "Reflections on an Indigenous Movement: The Yoido Full Gospel Church," *The Japan Christian Quarterly* (Winter 1991), 36–45.

[23]Yonggi Cho, *Sunggongjuk Kyohoesungjangeui Yulshue* [A key to Successful Church Growth] (Seoul: Seoul Books, 1976), 40-44.

[24]Young-hoon Lee, "Hankukkyohoe Sungrungwoondongeui Naah-galgil" [Suggestions for the Holy Spirit Movement of Korean Churches], *Sungshinsaegye* [The World of the Spirit] 1 (1992), 26-27 (27).

[25]Jin-hwan Kim, *Hankukkyohoe Buheungwoondongsa* [The History of the Revival Movement in the Korean Church] (Seoul: Seoul Logos, 1993).

[26]Karen Hurston, *Growing the World's Largest Church* (Springfield, MO: Gospel Publishing House, 1994), 153.

who is called by God and possessed by the Spirit becomes a powerful tool of God."[27] Cho's Bible-based and positive sermons have contributed not only to the growth of YFGC but also to the expansion of the Holy Spirit movement.

The framework of Cho's sermons is the fivefold gospel and threefold blessing. The fivefold gospel consists of: the gospel of salvation; the gospel of the fullness of the Holy Spirit; the gospel of divine healing; the gospel of blessing; and the gospel of the second coming of Jesus Christ.[28] The threefold blessing is based on 3 John 2 and describes the blessing that Christians receive by the work of the cross of Jesus Christ. It consists of spiritual blessing, physical blessing and the blessing of circumstances.[29] Cho emphasizes that only with the help of the Spirit can such a message effectively reach people[30] and change them to trust in Jesus completely.[31] Hence, Cho's Holy Spirit movement is based on the word of God and is a movement to proclaim Jesus. Since the Spirit testifies about Jesus (John 15:26), it is a "Jesus-witnessing movement," because Christians testify about Jesus when they are filled with the Spirit.

3.2 Prayer

Cho is a man of prayer, saying that he learned in the early days of his ministry, that he himself should pray before telling

---

[27] Eugene James Peterson, *A Theology of Church Growth* (Grand Rapids: Zondervan, 1981), 47.

[28] The structure of the fivefold gospel is similar to that of the fourfold gospel of the Holiness church. The Holiness church stresses regeneration, sanctification, divine healing and the second coming of Christ.

[29] See Yonggi Cho, *Ojoongbokeumg-wa Sambakjachookbok* [The Five-fold Gospel and Threefold Blessing] (Seoul: Seoul Logos, 1983) and ITI, *The Yoido Full Gospel Church: Its Faith and Theology*, 13–141.

[30] Yonggi Cho, *Nanun Iruke Sulgyohanda* [I Preach This Way] (Seoul: Seoul Logos, 1989), 173.

[31] Cho, I Preach This Way, 174.

people to pray.[32] Cho has stressed that Christians must learn how to pray, discipline themselves to pray, and devote themselves to prayer, for prayer is a hard and long process.[33]

The 120 disciples of Jesus devoted themselves to prayer before the descent of the Holy Spirit on the day of Pentecost (Acts 1:14). They then received the baptism of the Spirit and became bold witnesses to the gospel. Therefore, any prayer movement is directly connected to the Holy Spirit. Many churches and Christians of other countries have learned the prayer patterns of YFGC and effective methods for running and managing houses of prayer. When they apply them correctly, they experience the power of the Holy Spirit. The Holy Spirit movement of YFGC has thus expanded swiftly.

3.3 Spirit-baptism and Tongue-speaking

According to traditional Pentecostal faith, baptism in the Holy Spirit is an experience distinct from conversion.[34] The disciples of Jesus confessed "Jesus is Lord" by the Holy Spirit (1 Cor 12:3) and Jesus confirmed that they were all clean—that they were already saved except Judas Iscariot, since Jesus had called them (John 13:10). Nonetheless, Jesus said that they should be baptized with the Holy Spirit (Acts 1:4–5). Since Cho emphasized this type of baptism as the second blessing after conversion, churches and denominations with different doctrines have long attacked him.[35] John Wesley's second blessing, which is described as sanctification or as the wholeness of Christ, points to Spirit-baptism.[36] Charles G. Finney, Dwight L. Moody, Reuben A.

---

[32] Paul Yonggi Cho, *Prayer: Key to Revival* (Waco: Word, 1992), 62.

[33] ITI, The Yoido Full Gospel Church: Its Faith and Theology, 119-20.

[34] Yonggi Cho, *Sungryungron* [Pneumatology] (Seoul: Youngsan, 1980), 141.

[35] See ITI, *Sungryungi Nuheiegye Imhasimyun* (When the Holy Spirit Comes upon You) (Seoul: ITI, 1994).

[36] John Thomas Nichol, *Pentecostalism* (Plainfield, NJ: Logos International, 1966), 5-6.

Torrey, and J. W. Chapman have supported this truth.[37] The doctrine of Spirit-baptism is an integral part of the Holy Spirit movement.

There has been a long-running debate on the signs of Spirit-baptism. Cho says that it has various signs, but tongue-speaking is the most common and unique external sign. He also proposes strong testifying to Jesus Christ as an evidence of Spirit-baptism.[38] Cho divides tongue-speaking into two categories: "sign" and "gift."[39]

YFGC encourages people to receive Spirit-baptism, edify the church, and be witnesses to Christ, armed with the power of the Spirit.

3.4 Divine Healing

Healing is an integral part of the development of YFGC and the expansion of the Holy Spirit movement. Cho preached the power of the Holy Spirit in the Book of Acts to the despairing. This brought miracles, signs, and healings of those with various diseases, all contributing to the rapid growth of Cho's tent church. The sick came and Cho provided them the opportunity to listen to the gospel.

We may ascribe the continuous manifestation of divine healing in the tent church to Cho's own experience of healing from the terminal stage of tuberculosis and his faith in the gospel of divine healing. Cho claims that divine healing is the will of God, the prime ministry of Jesus, and the task and command that he gave to us, for God himself has said: "I am the Lord, who heals

---

[37]Donald W. Dayton, *Theological Roots of Pentecostalism* (Grand Rapids: Zondervan, 1987), 101.

[38]Cho, The Five-fold Gospel and Three-fold Blessing, 117.

[39]Yonggi Cho, *Soonbokeumeui Jinri* [The Full Gospel Truth], vol. 1 (Seoul: Seoul Books, 1979), 246-47.

you (Exodus 15:26)."[40] Jesus, moreover, devoted two-thirds of his ministry to healing.

Some advocates of divine healing misused the healing ministry but Cho presented salvation as whole and entire: salvation through the healing of the spirit, the body, and the person's circumstances. He retained a balanced theology in his healing teachings. Problems that arise among advocates of healing are due to a lack of correct understanding of the gospel.

3.5 The Cell System

One of the primary grounds of the explosive growth of the Pentecostal movement lies in the house church movement. This movement has its root in the Christian community of the early church. Meeting in houses was one of the foundations of the growth of the early church (Acts 2:42-47). Christians in the first century, through their small-group house meetings, had fellowship, Bible study and communion service. They may also have shared an *agape* meal, although the evidence on this is not clear.

John Wesley, the founder of the Methodist Church, developed the house church movement.[41] Before John Wesley, the sacraments were at the center of the faith of the church but he wanted to practice the faith patterns of the early church of the New Testament. Wesley emphasized discipleship, small group meetings (classes), and circuit quarterly meetings. It is worth taking note of the circuit quarterly meetings. They were begun in 1748 to promote the unity and fellowship of Methodists. Wesley, or

---

[40] Yonggi Cho, *Shinyouron* [Divine Healing] (Seoul: Seoul Logos, 2001), 22-23.

[41] For the research on the house church movement, see: Arthur L. Foster, ed., *The House Church Evolving* (Chicago: Exploration, 1976); Tony Higton and Gilbert Kirby, *The Challenge of the House Churches* (Oxford: Latimer, 1988); Joyce V. Thurman, *New Wineskins: A Study of House Church Movement* (Frankfurt-am-Main: Peter Lang, 1982); C. Kirk Hadaway, et al., *Home Cell Groups and House Churches* (Nashville, TN: Broadman, 1987).

another leading preacher, was the chairman/leader of the meetings, which were attended by the class teachers and stewards of societies. Leaders discussed the financial support and spiritual activities of the preachers, while the stewards managed financial matters. Wesley wrote "circuit plans" and posted them at the head office. According to the plans, the preachers would become circuit riders and go to the churches and class meetings in their assigned district for a certain period.

Wesley efficiently utilized the system of bands, classes and societies, and believed this type of system was taken from the early church. In their band and class meetings, they discipled edified and helped one another. The class meeting was the first step to becoming a Methodist and served to form well-disciplined and sincere members, leaving out less committed ones.

Such small group meetings made a great contribution to the development of the Methodist Church. The circuit rider system was successfully practiced in the pioneering period of America. Asbury developed it and thus further added to the growth of the American Methodist Church.

Small group meetings also had a significant influence on the holiness revival. In the nineteenth century, they were established weekly and considered important for the promotion of holiness. Phoebe Palmer began regular meetings on Tuesdays. Hence it became "Tuesday meeting."

Also influenced were the revival meetings of Charles G. Finney, D. L. Moody, as well as the twentieth century Pentecostal movement.

Cho reorganized the structure of the small community of the early church into a cell system and made it a "permanent revival center,"[42] so members may experience fellowship, renewal, revival of faith, and engage in evangelical work. In the early stages of the cell system, there were some difficulties because of the lack of places for gathering, the position of women in society (since the majority of the cell leaders were women), and the fact that lay leaders did not have confidence in the cell system. As the

---

[42] Yonggi Cho, *Kyohoesungjang, Jinjungwonhasipnika* [A Secret of Church Growth] (Seoul: Seoul Logos, 1995), 221-42.

problems are being resolved, the cell system is considered an internationally registered mark of YFGC.

People learn the word of God, pray together, and practice a fruitful Christian life through cells. The nature of the cell unit system is described as following.[43]

Five to seven families in the same neighborhood form a cell group, where the strongest spiritual members are the leader and the assistant leader. Metropolitan Seoul is divided into 13 large districts, 20 regional chapels and 150 prayer houses. In each district or chapel, a pastor is assigned as the senior district pastor. Each large district is divided into several sub-districts with sub-district pastors. Currently there are 309 sub-districts. Each sub-district has several sections with sectional leaders. (There are 4,374 section leaders.) In addition, each section has several cell groups and leaders. (There are 11,214 cell groups.)

About five cell groups form a section, 10 to 15 sections form a sub-district and 12 to 23 sub-districts form a large district. Currently YFGC has 634 full-time pastors, who are in charge of districts and other parts of church education and administration.

With their cell group leaders, members pray together and receive spiritual experiences. When a cell group grows to ten families, it is divided into two units, five families for each. The assistant leader of the original cell unit becomes the leader of the new one, and each leader appoints their own assistant leader. This procedure is repeated as the size of the cell grows. The focal point of each cell is its members and his or her needs. In reality it includes not only those already registered in the church, but also those who stand on the fringe of decision.

YFGC consisted of 11,214 home cell units as of December 2003, each of which has its own leader and assistant leader. YFGC has 700,000 members. Home cell group meetings are held once a week at each member's home by turns. They study the Bible in

---

[43]Young-hoon Lee, "The Yoido Full Gospel Church: Its History and Structure" (A report for 95 Alliance World Fellowship [AWF] and World Congress of the Sungkyul [Holiness] Church, Seoul, Sep. 25–Oct. 1, 1995), 3-4, 12-17.

seven steps by themes and each step is a year-long course.[44] This study as a whole is repeated every seven years. At cell meetings, they also pray together for new members, Spirit-baptism, for healing, concerning their personal problems, etc.

This system is the driving force of the unity and fellowship of the church and its growth, following the example of the early church.

4. The Contribution of the Holy Spirit Movement of the Yoido Full Gospel Church

Leading Korean theologians and religionists published a research report on YFGC in 1982. In the foreword of the report, Won-yong Kang pointed out, "The Holy Spirit movement of YFGC attracts the interest of the churches around the world, as well as the Korean churches, both positively and negatively."[45]

I will discuss some effects of the Holy Spirit movement of YFGC and Yonggi Cho and their influence on the Korean church.

4.1 Promotion of the Recognition of the Personhood of the Holy Spirit

Although the Korean church recognized the Holy Spirit as the third person of the Trinity, it was almost ignorant of and uninterested in the ministry of and fellowship with the Holy Spirit. Cho's Holy Spirit movement taught Christians how to minister and work with the Holy Spirit. Consequently, many of the Korean churches recognize the Holy Spirit as a distinct person of the godhead and experience the Spirit's dynamic work. Cho

---

[44]David Yonggi Cho, *Home Cell Group Study Guide*, vols. 1-2 (Seoul: Seoul Logos, 1990); Yonggi Cho, *Guyoksunggunggongbu* [Home Cell Group Study Guide], vols. 1-7 (Seoul: Seoul Logos, 1980-1986).

[45]Won-yong Kang, ed., *Hankuk Kyohoe Sungryungwoondongeui Hyunsanggwa Gujo* [A Study on the Pentecostal Movement in Korea] (Seoul: Korea Christian Academy, 1981), 3-4.

frequently says, "Holy Spirit, we acknowledge, welcome, and trust you."[46]

4.2 Increased Understanding of the Holy Spirit Movement

YFGC had to go through many difficulties due to the lack of understanding of the Korean church of the work of the Holy Spirit. One Presbyterian denomination, in its annual general assembly of 1983, said that Cho had heretical tendencies in his theology and ruled that its members should not have fellowship with Cho. Theological debates on this issue continued for about a decade, which caused increased, widespread knowledge of Pentecostal theology and the faith of YFGC. The publications of the International Theological Institute (ITI) and international seminars on the Holy Spirit, also organized by ITI, have changed the prejudices of the Korean church about the Holy Spirit movement of YFGC and Cho. This has provided the ground for other denominations to understand and accept Pentecostal theology.[47]

4.3 Church Growth

Church growth means spiritual revival rather than just an increase in numbers,[48] and is crucial. It gives glory to Jesus Christ, the head of the church.[49] YFGC is a model church with a rapid growth rate. Cho has introduced the key factors of church growth in and out of Korea and has challenged churches by publishing books and lecturing at meetings and seminars.

---

[46]See Benny Hinn, *Good Morning, Holy Spirit* (Nashville, TN: Thomas Nelson, 1990) and *Welcome, Holy Spirit* (Nashville, TN: Thomas Nelson, 1995). Hinn adopts Cho's conception of the Holy Spirit.

[47]See ITI, The Yoido Full Gospel Church: Its Faith and Theology, 142–205.

[48]Donald A. McGavran, *How Churches Grow* (New York: Friendship Press, 1959), 99.

[49]R. B. Kuyper, *Jundoshinhak* [Evangelical Theology], trans. Su-joon Park (Seoul: Hope, 1980), 113.

4.4 Renewed Thoughts

Cho's sermons are positive and active. Robert Schuller has said that positive thought is just another expression of the faith that Jesus spoke of.[50] Cho presents a positive, active faith to his people and encourages them to practice it daily. This reformed thought has brought changes in many lives.[51] Christians with renewed minds have contributed to the development of society as the country was going through swift changes in its political and economic aspects.

4.5 Indigenization

Indigenization is a process whereby Christianity adapts itself to the culture of a people for greater acceptance. Each country or nation has its own cultural background and traditions.[52] Indigenization combines the harmonious growth of native culture, in the light of the gospel and Christian principles, into a new Christian unity.[53] Cho, with his belief in a good and sovereign God, presented fresh hope to despairing people. He proclaimed God as the One who solves *han* in the present and declared a future life.[54] Balanced spiritual experiences, the prayer movement,

---

[50]Robert H. Schuller, *Your Church Has a Fantastic Future* (Ventura: Regal, 1986), 76.

[51]Sung-hoon Myung, *Gyohoesungjan-ggwa Sulgyo* [Church Growth and Sermons] (Seoul: Seoul Logos, 1992), 70-71.

[52]"Tochakhwa" [Indigenization], in *Kidokgyo Baekgwasajun* [One-Volume Christian Encyclopedia] ed. Young-je Han (Seoul, Christian Literature, 1992), 1446.

[53]Pong-bae Park, "Hankukkyohoeeui Tochakhwa" [The Indigenization of Christianity in Korea], *Shinhaksasang* [Christian Thoughts] (Jan. 1971), 72-81 (81).

[54]ITI, *Osoonjulwoondong-eui Hankukgyohoeye Michin Younghang* [The Influence of the Pentecostal Movement on the Korean Church] (Seoul: ITI, 1993), 69.

cell structure, and lay activities have made it possible for the Holy Spirit movement of YFGC to take deep root into Korean culture.[55]

5. Summary

The Pentecostal movement as led by Cho, (often called the Full Gospel movement), may be positively evaluated in connection with the indigenization of the Holy Spirit movement in Korea. His message of hope has brought hope and joy to the poor and oppressed. Speaking in tongues has contributed greatly to release the *han* in them. By appointing women leaders in the cell-unit system, Cho has acknowledged their capability and thus raised the position of women in society. He has brought spiritual renewal while most churches have been institutionalized.

This Holy Spirit movement may be viewed as a synthesis of the various Holy Spirit movements of Korean church history. Cho's emphasis on prayer and the second coming of Jesus Christ follows the tradition of Sun-joo Gil's Holy Spirit movement; his emphasis on mystical experience through the cross is in line with Yong-do Lee's Holy Spirit movement; and emphasis on healing was also noted in Ick-doo Kim's Holy Spirit movement. Cho's Holy Spirit movement has made the most of the shamanistic background of Koreans to bring rapid church growth. He avoids syncretistic shamanism by adhering to the principles of the Bible.

The Yoido Full Gospel Church and Cho have grown steadily in their thirty-eight year history. During this time, YFGC has been well organized. Harvey Cox points out that order, authority, and responsibility should be emphasized to continue growth in an organization. However, this brings with it the danger of lessening spirituality, Cox warns.[56] Furthermore he suggests that the Korean church may lose its power of ethical critique against Korean

---

[55]ITI, The Influence of the Pentecostal Movement, 52.

[56]Harvey Cox, Fire from Heaven: The Rise of Pentecostal Spirituality and the Reshaping of Religion in the Twenty-first Century (Reading, MA: Addison-Wesley, 1994), 236–37.

society if it takes too much interest in organization.[57] This presents a critical task for Pentecostals: how to balance the work of the Holy Spirit and the operation of organizations.

It is possible to maintain balance only when quantitative growth is accompanied by qualitative judgment. This means that YFGC must broaden its interests to include wider social concern and social reformation. Previous Holy Spirit movements have been more concerned with personal salvation and church growth, and YFGC will have to make a critical choice for its future.

---

[57]Cox, Fire from Heaven, 237.

THEOLOGY

DAVID YONGGI CHO'S THEOLOGY OF THE FULLNESS OF THE SPIRIT: A PENTECOSTAL PERSPECTIVE

William W. Menzies

1. Introduction

I have watched with fascination the remarkable development of the Korean churches in the last thirty years. The Korean War devastated the country. The industrial, transportation, and communications infrastructure was virtually destroyed. Homes and businesses were shattered. Families were torn apart; many died. Few countries suffered in the twentieth century as did Korea. Virtually all had suffered severely. After the war, there was a great spiritual vacuum in the aftermath of this colossal tragedy. Disillusionment and hopelessness prevailed. I remember my first visits to Korea in the early 1970s, less than twenty years after the Truce. Few public buildings were heated in the bitter cold winter; the cities were dingy and dusty. The marks of poverty were everywhere. It was a time of gloom and sorrow for the nation.

And, yet, I shall never forget my first night in Korea. I was hosted by kind missionaries on the campus of the Bible school in Seoul. It was very cold; my room was unheated. Well before daylight, I heard the sounds of feet crunching in the snow, just outside my window. Faithful Korean Christians were gathering in the school chapel for an early-morning prayer meeting—a practice which I learned was common by that time throughout Korea among earnest Christians. The commitment and dedication of Korean believers is one of the great stories of the modern church.

What remarkable changes have occurred in the last generation! Korea has emerged from the ashes as one of the powerful economies of the modern world. The industrial and economic developments have been staggering. Shining cities with efficient transportation and communication are in remarkable contrast to the situation that prevailed just a few short years before. And, even more phenomenal than the physical re-birth of the nation has been the remarkable growth and influence of the Christian church. From a very small minority in the society at the end of the Korean War, Korean Christianity has reached virtually every segment of the population, growing at such a rate that it now comprises, I understand, more than one-quarter of the entire population.

One individual, perhaps more than any other, has been at the center of this noteworthy revival—Yonggi Cho. Cho's personal experience of the Spirit, which he attributes as the source of the empowering, led him to bring together the world's largest church, Yoido Full Gospel Church (YFGC). In addition to his own pastoral leadership, Cho has been a major influence in the shaping of the teaching and life of many of the churches of Korea, certainly within the Pentecostal tradition, but also throughout much of Evangelical Christianity in the country.[1] Several of the mega-churches in the Assemblies of God in Korea are pastored by those mentored by Cho. As the Chairman of the World Assemblies of God Fellowship, Cho has clearly been recognized by Pentecostal colleagues around the world as a major leader having great influence and significance. Therefore, to obtain better insight into the values that mark the Pentecostal churches of Korea, one must include the teachings of Yonggi Cho.

There are some terms that Cho employs and emphases that he champions which are not always clearly understood within Pentecostal churches. It is my contention that it is important to see Cho's theology within the context of Korean social history to avoid misunderstanding his teaching. And, as one reads his

---

[1] Changsoo Kang, "An Analytical Study On the Life of Woon-Mong Na, Indigenous Korean Pentecostal" (Th.M. thesis, Asia Pacific Theological Seminary, 2003), 34.

sermons and other writings, one must bear in mind that all of God's truth cannot be articulated readily in a single setting. Because of the unique history of Korea, and the special circumstances surrounding the beginnings of Cho's ministry, it appears that God raised up Cho at a strategic time in Korean history to highlight several key themes that the people desperately needed to hear—themes of hope, of deliverance, of power, of high expectations. Such themes are certainly not all that God has revealed, but it does seem that God chose to use him to herald a positive message for very discouraged people who needed to hear about the possibilities, the hope that flows from the gospel of Jesus Christ. He must be seen as a man called by God for a special time with a special message. It is with this sense of the importance of context that we now address the teaching of Yonggi Cho on the Holy Spirit.

2. Baptism in the Holy Spirit and Fullness of the Spirit

Let's begin with Cho's own testimony:

> I prayed for an experience with the Holy Spirit whom I had studied and learned about. I asked the Holy Spirit to come and fill me with His power, His ministry and His message for a sick and hurting world. . . . So daily I prayed for the filling of the Holy Spirit. . . . And then it happened. One evening while I was asking the Lord for the filling of the Holy Spirit, I felt His presence draw near. It was a wonderful experience. I was worshipping and praising Jesus aloud, telling Him audibly again and again how wonderful it was to know Him and how much I loved Him. . . . As I worshipped, I felt a warm glow touch my face, then my tongue, then my body, and without realizing it I began to speak new words that came to my mind and my tongue at the same time. . . . My heart was overflowing with praise and worship to Jesus in a new language. . . . That was my initial experience when I was baptized with the Holy Spirit.[2]

---

[2] *The Holy Spirit, My Senior Partner* (Altamonte Springs, FL: Creation House, 1989), 8, 9.

Several things emerge from this brief personal testimony in Cho's own words. First, he recognized that the experience of baptism in the Spirit is separable from new birth. He was already a committed Christian believer. As a student in the Bible school in Seoul, he earnestly desired to serve the Lord effectively. He had been taught to expect a subsequent experience, an "infilling" of the Holy Spirit. Cho acknowledges with appreciation the teaching he received at the Assemblies of God Bible college he attended in Seoul, a school that was the forerunner of today's Hansei University. [3] He was mentored by sympathetic American Assemblies of God missionaries in his early years. Consequently, it should not be surprising that his theology of the Holy Spirit resonates closely with standard Assemblies of God doctrine.

Second, this subsequent experience he recognized, indeed, as a "filling" with the Holy Spirit. We will return to this terminology shortly, since it is central to the later teaching of Cho.

Third, it is crucial to recognize that this experience of the Spirit, baptism in the Spirit, was understood by Cho to be an empowerment for service. This distinguishes Pentecostal teaching from historical Wesleyan or Holiness teaching. The Wesleyan understanding emphasized the role of the Holy Spirit in the sanctifying of believers. The latter quarter of the nineteenth century was punctuated with a strong emphasis throughout Evangelical Christianity of the term, "baptism in the Holy Spirit." Before the birth of the modern Pentecostal movement, Fundamentalists and Holiness exponents freely used this term. The Fundamentalists employed the term to describe an experience of the Spirit subsequent to new birth, understood to be an enduement of power for witness and service, howbeit without tongues. [4] Holiness advocates following the Wesleyan tradition, however, used this popular term in a different manner. By the end of the nineteenth century, many Holiness teachers employed the term "baptism in the Spirit" to speak of an experience commonly called

---

[3]Kang, "An Analytical Study," 2.

[4]A. J. Gordon, *The Ministry of the Holy Spirit* (Philadelphia, PA: Judson Press, 1894; reprinted in 1949), 69.

sanctification.[5] Cho understood this experience clearly to be an empowering for service, clearly identifying with classical Pentecostal teaching—which followed the Fundamentalist teaching on the empowerment of the Spirit for service—rather than the Holiness teaching.

Fourth, Cho recognized that this particular episode was his personal Pentecost, the event in which he was baptized in the Spirit, because it was accompanied by speaking in other tongues. We will return to the matter of tongues-as-evidence later.

At this point, let us compare Cho's understanding of baptism in the Spirit with commonly-accepted teaching among classical Pentecostals. In the recently-issued *New International Dictionary of Pentecostal and Charismatic Movements*, Professor J. Rodman Williams, widely-respected Charismatic Presbyterian leader, outlines several aspects of Pentecostal/Charismatic understanding of baptism in the Spirit by which the reader can readily compare Cho's teaching with that of standard Pentecostals world-wide. First, the term "baptism" is listed as essentially the same as the term "filling," disclosing not only *totality*, but also *abundance*.[6] The term "filling" became the favored term among Korean Pentecostals, including Cho. It should be noted that it is virtually synonymous with "baptism."

J. Rodman Williams makes it clear that Pentecostals distinguish the experience of baptism in the Spirit from salvation: "It is a pentecostal distinctive, therefore, to affirm that salvation precedes baptism in the Spirit or, to put it a bit differently, that one may truly believe in Christ and not yet have received the gift of the Holy Spirit."[7] This is precisely what Cho taught.

Williams readily acknowledges that the purpose of baptism in the Spirit is primarily "power for witness," not a sign of superior

---

[5]Robert P. and William W. Menzies, *Spirit and Power: Foundations of Pentecostal Experience* (Grand Rapids, MI: Zondervan, 2000), 18, 19.

[6]J. R. Williams, "Baptism in the Holy Spirit," in *The New International Dictionary of Pentecostal and Charismatic Movements*, eds. Stanley M. Burgess and others (Grand Rapids, MI: Zondervan, 2002), 355, 356.

[7]Williams, "Baptism in the Holy Spirit," 357.

holiness.[8] This is clearly the teaching of Cho. It is true that some classical Pentecostals follow a "three-stage" soteriology, identifying the initiation into the Christian life as salvation, followed by a crisis experience of sanctification, sometimes called a "second blessing," and finally followed by an experience of being filled with the Spirit. This is the common understanding of that group of Pentecostals who are direct descendants of the Holiness tradition, those who are commonly referred to as "Holiness Pentecostals." Most Pentecostals, however, are classified as "Keswickian" Pentecostals, who understand baptism in the Spirit to be an empowering for service, not a badge of holiness. For them, sanctification begins at new birth and continues throughout one's life in a progressive fashion, even after the event of baptism in the Spirit. The Assemblies of God identifies with the Keswickian understanding. Cho's teaching is in perfect harmony with Assemblies of God teaching on this point.

Pentecostals generally acknowledge speaking in other tongues to be the normative initial sign of Spirit baptism. Williams states, "Whether evidence or sign, the point made is that the distinctive event of Spirit baptism is primarily exhibited through speaking in tongues."[9] The American Assemblies of God employs the term "initial physical evidence" to indicate that the standard biblical sign to be expected as the accompaniment to Spirit baptism is speaking in other tongues.[10] This understanding is articulated in a standard textbook used widely throughout the Assemblies of God, as well.[11] It should be noted that although most Pentecostals adhere to this teaching, not all do. Also, most Charismatics do not emphasize the necessity of speaking in tongues as evidence of Spirit baptism, although many expect that tongues will normally follow.

---

[8]Williams, "Baptism in the Holy Spirit," 358-60.

[9]Williams, "Baptism in the Holy Spirit," 358.

[10]"Minutes of the 49th Session of the General Council of the Assemblies of God, Convened in Kansas City, Missouri, August 7-10, 2001, with Revised Constitution and Bylaws," 92.

[11]William W. Menzies and Stanley M. Horton, *Bible Doctrines, A Pentecostal Perspective* (Springfield, MO: Gospel Publishing House, 1993), 135-38.

Although Cho does not seem to emphasize in his writings what Pentecostals call the "initial physical evidence," it does appear that this is his own testimony and that this is, in fact, what he personally believes. He does state that tongue speaking is "an external, objective sign of the fullness of the Holy Spirit."[12]

Cho seems to prefer the term "fullness of the Spirit" over the term "baptism in the Spirit." There may be an implied nuance of some significance here. The term "baptism" points to a specific event, the initial experience of being filled with the Spirit. However, the term "fullness" points beyond that initial moment to the pattern of life that follows. It seems to speak of the "Spirit-filled life." Chang-soo Kang points out that Cho in later years has chosen to use the term "fullness of the Spirit," a term he feels points more clearly to the pattern of life that follows the initial reception of the Spirit than does the term "baptism in the Spirit."[13] Kang sees this term as the preference among Korean Pentecostals.[14]

In virtually all respects, then, Cho's teaching regarding baptism in the Spirit appears to resonate readily with classical Pentecostal theology, such as is found in the Assemblies of God. His favoring of the term "fullness of the Spirit" does not seem to contradict classical Pentecostal teaching whatsoever.

3. Prayer and Faith

Cho's strong belief in the empowering of the individual for witness and service is anchored strongly in his understanding of the importance of prayer. He writes, "Before the missionary era of the church began, the Holy Spirit revealed to the leaders gathered in Antioch that they should send Barnabas and Saul. Yet, the Holy Spirit only spoke after they had been in fasting and prayer."[15] A

---

[12]*The Holy Spirit*, 114.

[13]Kang, "An Analytical Study," 2.

[14]Kang, "An Analytical Study," 2.

[15]*Prayer: Key to Revival* (Waco, TX: Word Books, 1984), 10.

strong commitment to prayer has marked Cho's ministry from the beginnings in Daejo-dong, an impoverished district just outside Seoul in 1958. He pitched a tent and lived there through the cold Korean winter, "spending my nights in prayer."[16] Soon, others began to join him in prayer, until more than fifty were interceding for God's mighty intervention in their community. Cho learned the value of intercession early in his ministry and has sought to carry this emphasis through in a variety of ways. In this respect, Cho exemplifies what is common practice throughout the churches of Korea—a strong emphasis on prayer, both private and corporate. Only through faithful prayer can one expect the Holy Spirit to operate effectively. This, Cho believes, is the key to revival.

It may be difficult to trace with precision the source of current practices in Korean churches, but common to nearly all is the remarkable schedule of prayer meetings that mark the calendars of the churches, certainly including the Yoido Full Gospel Church. In fact, Cho's church is likely the fountain of influence for much of the prayer meeting schedule in many of the churches. The daily regimen begins with a 5:00 a.m. prayer meeting in the church, to which many laymen and lay women faithfully come. The pastoral staff is expected to be present. On Friday evenings, it is a common practice for the Pentecostal churches (and others, I am told), to feature an "all night" prayer meeting. These begin about 9 or 10 p.m., and run until 2 a.m., or thereabouts. As a visitor to one of these Friday night prayer sessions in one of the daughter churches founded by Cho, I was impressed with the number of men who attended. The pattern seemed to follow a cycle of a time for preaching, a time for congregational singing, and an equal segment devoted to concert, vocal, intense prayer. The meeting was characterized by solemnity and total earnestness. Surely these are the habitations of God the Holy Spirit! Visitors to Korea, looking in upon the disciplined pattern of prayer life, come away with a strong sense that this is the secret of the great growth of the Korean churches. And, certainly this is what Cho has taught for many years!

---

[16] *Prayer: Key to Revival*, 14.

Cho has provided a personal glimpse into his own prayer life. He describes the way he prays, how he prays, and how this impacts the course of his day. It is through this connection with God that the flow of the Holy Spirit rests upon his life.[17] He reports, "How do we get to know the Holy Spirit? We only become aware of His nature as we enter into a life of prayer."[18] He spends time fellowshipping with the Holy Spirit, being renewed spiritually, mentally and physically. "Out of the one hour that I spend in prayer every morning, much of that time is spent in fellowship with the Holy Spirit."[19] Cho says, "The measure of our faith is in direct proportion to our communion with the Holy Spirit."[20]

There is an intimate connection between prayer and faith. In his book, *The Leap of Faith*, Cho illustrates how God works. In 1969, God told him to build a church that would seat 10,000 people. In the providence of God, space for one church had been allotted on Yoido Island, at the edge of Seoul (now it is not too far from the center of the metropolis). From the beginning of construction, many things seemed to go wrong, including the devaluation of the currency and skyrocketing inflation. Many people lost their jobs and the church income suffered. About this time, Cho had felt led to initiate his prayer mountain. Deeply discouraged, Cho joined the group at the prayer mountain. The people of his church had been interceding for Cho. He sensed, all at once, a change in the atmosphere. One poor woman offered all she had—a rice bowl and a pair of chopsticks. Cho, weeping, said he did not want to take these items from the woman, since she had so little. She insisted. One man in the rear of the room heard the conversation. He spoke up and said, "I will buy the bowl and the chopsticks for $1,000." Others joined in the spirit of sacrificial giving. Cho and his wife sold their home and put the proceeds into the building fund. Miraculously, the church was saved from

---

[17] *Prayer: Key to Revival*, 15-17.

[18] *Prayer: Key to Revival*, 43.

[19] *Prayer: Key to Revival*, 45.

[20] *The Holy Spirit*, 18.

disaster and the new building was completed. Prayer was the key that produced faith, and faith prevailed![21]

It is appropriate to acknowledge the legacy of the great revival in Pyongyang in 1906. The Presbyterians had established the practice of gathering each morning for prayer. Revival broke out. Christians confessed their sins. "As a result, Koreans were converted in all parts of the country as the spirit of prayer prevailed."[22] Cho would readily acknowledge that the pattern of prayer which has characterized the Korean churches really began in the great revival of 1906. He has been a faithful steward of that legacy.

4. The Fivefold Message of the Gospel

In a popular document prepared in honor of thirty years of Cho's ministry, titled *Ordeal and Glory through the Thirty-Year History of Yoido Full Gospel Church*,[23] an outline is provided that captures the special emphases in Cho's preaching and teaching. What Cho calls the "fivefold message" is a listing of the "four cardinal doctrines" of the Assemblies of God, plus a fifth one he has added: "blessing." The four cardinal doctrines, borrowed from American Evangelical Christianity, are: salvation, the baptism in the Holy Spirit (what Cho calls the "fullness of the Spirit"), divine healing and the second coming of Christ.

3 John 2, a scripture passage that is central to understanding Cho's ministry, is emblazoned on the wall in the reception area of the great Yoido Full Gospel Church. This verse is the Apostle John's expression of desire that those to whom he wrote would "prosper and be in health." It is critically important to keep in mind, as one evaluates the teaching of Cho, the situation into which he came. The Korean nation had suffered terribly. The

---

[21] *The Leap of Faith* (South Plainfield, NJ: Bridge Publishing, 1984), 56-59.

[22] *Prayer: Key to Revival*, 13, 14.

[23] YFGC, *Ordeal and Glory through the 30-Year History of Yoido Full Gospel Church* (Seoul: YFGC, 1988).

Christians had suffered. Many were very discouraged and had lost all hope. It was into the dark night of post-war Korea that God raised up Yonggi Cho to elevate the horizons of his people. His message was the announcement of hope, of the victory there is in Christ, of the available empowering of the Holy Spirit. He saw the practical blessings of salvation embracing not only the spiritual dimension of mankind, but also the physical and the material dimensions, as well. It was this emphasis that caused Cho to be criticized, not only by non-Pentecostal Evangelicals, but by many Pentecostals, as well.

In the United States, excesses in the "salvation-healing" crusades of some evangelists led to a reaction to those who proclaimed what was called the "prosperity gospel." And, certainly a case can be made for the need for a balanced presentation of truth so that God's desire for the prosperity of believers is not construed to mean that faith will guarantee paradise here and now with no suffering to be encountered by those with sufficient faith. However, an equally strong case can be made for the need to raise the horizons of deeply-discouraged people to dare to believe for God's divine intervention into dark circumstances. It is in this context that Cho's teaching on "the fivefold message of the gospel" must be understood.

The influence of Oral Roberts is clearly evident in the teaching of Cho. One theme of Roberts with which Cho resonates is "God is a good God." In a animistic Buddhist culture, in which works-righteousness is mixed with fear of the supernatural, Cho preached that God is a God of love, a God of grace, and that he intends for good to happen to those who will trust him. Jesus came to bring life and that more abundantly![24]

Based on 3 John 2, Cho sees three dimensions of God's intended blessing for his people. The first is "as your soul prospers." His primary focus is on the salvation of the individual, new birth. However, Cho moves beyond entrance into the family of God to the fullness of the Holy Spirit.

---

[24]*Salvation, Health and Prosperity* (Altamonte Springs, FL: Creation House, 1984), 11-18.

> The fullness of the Spirit includes: 1) speaking in other tongues under the control of the Spirit as a sign that we have received the fullness of the Spirit; 2) an overflowing blessing which touches the lives of others as we live for Him.[25]

Cho moves beyond the initial reception of the Spirit, emphasizing that believers should seek to be filled daily. Instructive in this teaching is that the purpose of the fullness of the Spirit is to bless others. Spirit-filled believers are empowered to bring deliverance to others, to enrich and to bless.

Cho refused to limit the blessing of God to the spiritual realm. He boldly challenged Korean believers to expect God to bless their lives materially. He stated,

> The prosperity God wants to see in our lives applies to the whole picture of living: child-rearing, our jobs, businesses, human relationships, the necessities of life, the stability of life, joy and so on. Consequently, if we are made whole in our spirits, souls and bodies, the natural outcome is that we should prosper in every area of our lives. Jesus shed His precious blood and made out a deed—a certificate of title—calling for our prosperity in all things. The remaining work for us now is to exercise the rights and privileges that have already been given to us in order to obtain those provisions.[26]

Again, we must bear in mind that this message was delivered to people who needed to hear that God, indeed, loved them and wanted his children to raise their vision to greater expectations. Critics could charge that this was a one-sided message, since no qualifications seem to be stated to allow for the difficulties and disappointments that come into every life. However, at the time this was delivered, Cho wanted to bring a strong message of hope to Christians who had been systematically taught to bear suffering and to expect suffering in this world.

In the last generation, an extreme form of positive thinking abounded in the West, commonly labeled the "positive

---

[25] *Salvation, Health and Prosperity*, 49.

[26] *Salvation, Health and Prosperity*, 55.

confession" movement. Advocates of this teaching promulgated the overly-simplistic belief that merely articulating a desire would put God into the position of having to supply whatever wish the individual expressed. It was taught, for example, that if one wanted a fine, large automobile, he or she should cut out a picture of the object and put it in a conspicuous place where the person could remind God of the need for him to fulfill the desire by granting this wish. This promoted a view of God as little more than a "cosmic bellhop." It promoted materialism and self-centered living. Against such extreme teaching, it was felt necessary in the American Assemblies of God to produce a position paper on this matter, titled "The Believer and Positive Confession." The document states,

> God's Word does teach great truths such as healing, provision for need, faith, and the authority of believers. The Bible does teach that a disciplined mind is an important factor in victorious living. But these truths must always be considered in the framework of the total teaching of Scripture.[27]

Cho did not allow his teaching to descend to that level of abuse. One must remember that his mission was to pull discouraged people out of the depths of despondency.

Cho supplies this insight into his self-understanding about poverty and what God wanted him to do about it:

> I once thought that poverty had great moral value. In Korea ministers used to preach that poverty was a blessing, that the poor were those who reaped the most from life's experiences. However, these same ministers were also continually asking their congregations to give more and more money to the church. Teaching the value of poverty, they also preached the merit of increased contributions. This contradiction bothered me. When I became a minister myself I volunteered to pastor in a slum area of the city of Seoul. People in that community lived lives of poverty, mostly eating only one meal a day. Children were sick

---

[27] "The Believer and Positive Confession," in *Where We Stand* (Springfield, MO: Gospel Publishing House, 1997), 131-144 (144).

> from malnutrition, and many were starving to death. It was then that I read the Bible anew, searching for a solution. I wanted to know God's will about poverty.[28]

It is clear that Cho was addressing a very definite crisis need in the Korean situation. Certainly he emphasized strongly one dimension of the Christian faith—the possibilities for a better life. He should not be faulted for not tempering his message with all the qualifications that can be cited in a balanced message, since in the crisis of that time, he understood what emphasis was most desperately needed.

In Cho's understanding of 3 John 2, he also saw implications for the Christian and physical health. Categorically he states, "God desires that we may live in good health."[29] He taught that healing is not only in the atonement, but that the Holy Spirit has been given to the church by Jesus Christ to bring healing to the nations.

> The Holy Spirit, the other Comforter who dwells among us and continues Jesus' work, enables us to understand and receive forgiveness because of Jesus' work on Calvary. As an evidence that we have been forgiven, He heals us. Through the Holy Spirit we have the grace of salvation with healing as its sign.[30]

Cho points out that there is a basic principle regarding healing: where there is strong faith, there will be more healing. He does not guarantee that all will be healed, but that the Christian who desires healing has the responsibility to cultivate a life of prayer and belief.[31]

The American Assemblies of God has from its beginnings held a strong conviction that divine healing is an essential component of the gospel message.

As we observe the ministry of both Jesus and the apostles, it is evident that divine healing was not something peripheral. It was an

---

[28] *Solving Life's Problems* (Plainfield, NJ: Logos International, 1980), 27.

[29] *Salvation, Health, and Prosperity*, 115.

[30] *Salvation, Health, and Prosperity*, 141.

[31] *Salvation, Health, and Prosperity*, 144-56.

important witness to Jesus, as the revelation of the Father, as the promised Messiah, and as the Savior from sin (see John 10:37, 38).[32]

The position paper does acknowledge that, in spite of the strong affirmation about the privilege of all believers to enjoy the blessing of divine healing, there remain mysteries.

In humility we recognize that we do not understand all that pertains to divine healing. We still see through a glass darkly. We do not understand why some are healed and others are not any more than we understand why God permitted James to be martyred and Peter delivered. Scripture makes it clear, however, that our part is to preach the Word and expect the signs to follow.[33]

The American Assemblies of God position paper on divine healing resonates closely with the teaching of Cho, except for the reservation made in the concluding paragraph that acknowledges the mystery pertaining to the fact that not all for whom prayer is offered are, in fact, healed. I do not think that Cho would teach anything contrary to this, although this qualification does not appear to be explicitly stated.

5. Conclusion

Pastor Yonggi Cho is a preacher with a strong message. He rose from poverty and obscurity to a position of enormous influence around the world. His preaching over the years has been directed to people whom he felt needed to hear a positive message of hope for a brighter future. The great response of the Korean people to his preaching discloses in a dramatic fashion that his message, indeed, was heard. He has been a key leader during the years in Korean history in which a devastated nation rose from the ashes to become a major power, not only in the world of international economics, but in the role of Christian statesmanship and missions. In my paper I have sought to demonstrate that Pastor

---

[32]"Divine Healing: An Integral Part of the Gospel," 45.

[33]"Divine Healing: An Integral Part of the Gospel," 54.

Cho's preaching is best seen in the light of the social situation in which he ministered. He indeed had an important message of spiritual and social transformation at a critical time in Korean national history.

KOREAN PENTECOSTAL SPIRITUALITY AS MANIFESTED IN THE TESTIMONIES OF BELIEVERS OF THE YOIDO FULL GOSPEL CHURCH

Myung Soo Park

One of the most widely used words during the last decade of the twentieth century was spirituality. This is evidence of human effort to find an escape route from the limitations and constraints of material civilization.

This study will analyze the spirituality of the Korean Pentecostal movement. To date, much research on the Korean Pentecostal movement has been published. However, many have limited their research to David Yonggi Cho's life and sermons. Of course, no one can deny his importance. Aside from Cho, it is difficult, if not impossible, to explain the Korean Pentecostal movement. Nevertheless, there is something more that we need to explore to understand the Korean Pentecostal movement: the spiritual experiences of ordinary Pentecostal believers.

Until now, Pentecostalism in Korea has been researched by studying different leaders in the movement. We now need to learn the effect these pastors and their messages have had on their congregations and on individual believers.

I think Cho understands market characteristics (i.e., suppliers/pastors and consumers/church-members) better than most religious leaders in Korea. He says that a church growth leader should be able to identify the needs of other people and meet them accordingly.[1] What is important to Cho is not the

---

[1]Institute for Church Growth, *Charis and Charisma*, eds. Sung-hoon Myuung and Young-gi Hong (in Korean; Seoul: Institute for Church Growth, 2003), 66.

systematic practice of a religious creed or doctrine but the effort to help poor, sick, struggling believers regain hope and courage. To meet this need, he speaks of divine healing, positive thinking and the power of faith in the Living God.

If so, how have Cho's messages been received by ordinary believers? Has his message given people hope and courage as he intended? In order to answer these questions, we have to examine the testimonies of ordinary believers, who listened to and have been led by Cho.

1. A New Dimension in the Study of the Pentecostal Movement: Testimonial Study

Testimonies hold special importance in the Pentecostal movement.[2] In the early days of the Pentecostal movement, a testimony was treated as an important highlight in a service. There are several reasons for this.

Firstly, the Pentecostal movement emphasizes religious experience. Neither conservatism, which stresses the absolute sovereignty of the word of God, nor progressivism, which understands a religion as ethics, treats a testimony equitably. Both conservatism and progressivism devalue testimony as a private religious experience. However, the Pentecostal movement regards true religion by one's experience and magnifies it by testimony.

Secondly, a testimony is narrative. Pentecostalism is a mass movement. Typically, a mass movement expresses itself through narrative rather than logic. A narrative can represent a vivid illustration of human life that logic can not portray. A testimony is a religious narrative about one's self. Through narrative, the Pentecostal movement developed. However, the theology of the Pentecostal movement is less developed.

Testimony has not been fully developed as an important resource for Christian religious study. That is because of the misconception that a testimony is a private matter rather than a

[2]Grant Wacker, *Heaven Below: Early Pentecostalism and American Culture* (Cambridge, MA: Harvard University Press, 2001), 3.

formal resource for theology. This is the objection raised by both conservatism and progressivism. However, Evangelical theology recognizes this issue and understands the testimony from a new perspective. In Evangelicalism, a testimony does not replace the revelation in the Bible but confirms it. In other words, a spiritual experience should not transcend the authority of the Bible, but it reflects the content of the Bible in contemporary life in its meaning. On this point, John Wesley understood such religious experience as an important source in Christian theology.[3]

Recently, theologians have begun to study this topic; among them, Nathan Hatch. Hatch of Notre Dame University opened a new chapter in the study of the history of nineteenth century churches by analyzing the religious experiences of ordinary believers.[4] Since then, many scholars of church history have accepted the religious testimonies and biographies of the public as important sources in their studies. This has opened a new horizon in the study of church history. This research method has contributed greatly in understanding the early history of American Methodist churches.[5] Recently it also influenced the study of the Pentecostal movement. Grant Wacker examined numerous religious experiences of Pentecostal believers and made a great contribution in understanding the early Pentecostal movement.[6]

When we study the faith of Pentecost, it is important to study its leaders. According to the assertion of Max Weber, a famous German sociologist, all great religions were created and propagated by charismatic leaders whose movements were systematized and indoctrinated. Weber asserted that a religious movement could not continue without going through this process.

---

[3]Rex D. Matthews, "'Religion and Reason Joined': A Study in the Theology of John Wesley" (Th.D. diss, Harvard Divinity School, 1986).

[4]Nathan O. Hatch, *The Democratization of American Christianity* (New Haven: Yale University Press, 1997).

[5]Nathan O Hatch and John H. Wigger, eds., *Methodism and Shaping of American Culture* (Nashville: Kingswood Books, 2001).

[6]Grant Wacker, *Heaven Below: Early Pentecostalism and American Culture* (Cambridge, MA: Harvard University Press, 2001).

However, the mentality and spirit of such charismatic leaders is better seen through the religious experiences of their congregational members than through systems, creeds, or doctrines. Thus, whether a religion can grow or not depends on whether its religious experience is dynamic and working. The validity of this approach is based on William James' *Variety of Religious Experience*. He claims that the true nature of all religions can be found in its religious experience. Any creed, doctrine, or system is secondary.[7]

In this regard, it is meaningful to study David Yonggi Cho, the founder of the world's largest church. We can find many testimonies through publications of the Pentecostal movement. An exemplar Pentecostal magazine in Korea is *Shinanggye* [World of Faith]. It is a monthly magazine spreading the Pentecostal faith through literary mission. Cho established a society of literary evangelism in December 1966 and published the first issue of *Shinanggye* in February 1967. Through this magazine, the Full Gospel has spread throughout Korean churches. *Shinanggye* currently has the highest circulation of all Christian magazines, and stories of overcoming poverty and miraculous healings have widely disseminated throughout Korea.[8]

The author examines Pentecostal spirituality and the leadership of David Yonggi Cho based on the testimonies published in *Shinanggye* in the later half of the 1970s. The testimonies published in *Shinanggye* use real names and detailed addresses of those blessed. Although the majority of the testimonies were from members of the Yoido Full Gospel Church (YFGC), some were from members of other churches. Included is a variety of socially well recognized people as well as ordinary people.

---

[7]William James, *Variety of Religious Experience* (Cambridge, MA: Harvard University Press, 1985).

[8]*Forty Year History of Yoido Full Gospel Church* (in Korean, Seoul: Shinanggye, 1998), 124.

2. The Starting Point of Pentecostal Spirituality: The Last Hope for Solving Problems of Life

What kinds of people join YFGC? How does Cho lead non-believers to Christian faith? This is an important starting point in understanding Cho's ministry.

The central motive for registering in the church, as shown through the testimonies of *Shinanggye,* is to seek faith to overcome obstacles in life. This is very different from a traditional view that faith is part of social life and a means to maintain social status. In Europe and the United States, as Christianity came into the social mainstream, one motive for faith was to join conventional society. According to Herberg, an American religious sociologist, going to a church in America meant that one was joining mainstream society.[9] However, believers of YFGC join with the strong purpose of overcoming life's problems. To Cho, Christian faith is not a means of fellowship, but is primarily God's answer to life's problems.

This motive is also distinguished from those who think of the life of faith as a means of social reform. Korean Christianity was the forerunner of introducing Korea to western culture. In the early twentieth century, when Korea was undergoing a cultural and political upheaval, an escape was sought from oppression through the church. During the Japanese colonization, the church was also on the front lines of the independence movement and a place to teach Korean to many illiterate people. After the liberation in 1945, the church was also a place to distribute relief supplies after the wars. While many may have attended churches in the past for various reasons as noted above, Cho has always emphasized the powerful God.

One testimony recounts the story of a brother of Seon-Won Song who suffered from an unidentified mental illness. He took medicines and sought help from a shamanist woman without relief. Doctors told him he needed brain surgery. The cost was too high, and the success of the operation was not guaranteed. At this

---

[9]William Herberg, *Protestant, Catholic, Jew: An Essay in American Religious Sociology* (Garden City, NY: Doubleday, 1960), n.p.

time, a district pastor of YFGC spread the message of the power of the gospel. Their mother came to the church as her last resort. "Now let's leave our last hope in the hands of God." A work of God began to be manifested in this family. And the brother was healed.[10] We find many testimonies in the *Shinanggye* of those who came to YFGC as a last recourse "to leave our last hope to God."

A traditional church does not offer clear solutions to people who are at the end of their rope. They may view circumstances as fate. In other words, they offer consolation through giving up. However, this kind of answer is very passive. People want more positive and active answers. Thus, those who attended traditional churches left their long-time place of faith and came to YFGC or other Pentecostal (in Korea popularly called "Full Gospel") churches.

Myung-ja Lee was born into a non-Christian home but attended Sunday school from a young age. However, she gave up living with faith as she grew up and began to suffer from all kinds of numerous diseases in the lung, stomach, heart and brain. She spent ten years of her life suffering from these diseases. Then, Lee started to listen to the sermons of Cho through a broadcast and came to YFGC, not by invitation, but after listening to the program. As soon as she attended the worship service, she gained peace and bowed to the cross. Then she had a firm conviction that her diseases would be healed if Cho placed his hands on her suffering body. Soon after, Cho did this and she was set free from disease.[11] We can see how Lee, who had a traditional faith, believed that she had found an answer to her problem through Cho's sermon. I believe this has been the main reason many believers leave their churches and come to a Full Gospel church.

---

[10] Seon-won Song, "On This Glorious, Joyful Day," *Shinanggye* (October, 1975), 86-87. All the testimonies published in this monthly magazine are in Korean. Instead of the conventional transliteration of the Korean titles, their English equivalents are given throughout this study.

[11] Myung-Ja Lee, "The Lord Who Recreated My Life," *Shinanggye* (January, 1976), 84-87.

Another reason some begin to attend a Full Gospel church is boredom with routine church services. Young-ui Kim became a Christian as a child and is a medical doctor licensed in the United States. To Kim, the lively faith of Cho and Pentecostal believers was a challenge; their lives were full of vitality, but his life was not. "I am a Christian also, yet why can't I live fully as they do?" This thought caused him to come to YFGC where he received the baptism in the Holy Spirit. This experience fundamentally changed his life of faith.[12] Many people, who have not found dynamic faith in a traditional church, have transferred to a Full Gospel church.

In fact, the Full Gospel is a challenge to nominal Christianity. Faith is just a formality and a system to many nominal Christians. However, this kind of faith is not dynamic. Suddenly, they begin to be skeptical about their religion and desire to clarify what they believe. The Full Gospel challenges them to greater dimensions of faith and introduces them to a faith in God that is practical, relevant, and life transforming even for ordinary people with ordinary problems.

3. Pentecostal Spiritual Training: "Cry out"

To Pentecostal believers, a spiritual life is not an end in itself. Cho teaches the necessity of spiritual warfare in order to solve human problems. The believers of a Full Gospel church continue to make a diligent, spiritual effort in order to solve their problems. Cho also teaches that the problems of life are not limited to things that can be seen. At the bottom of all problems, there lies a spiritual problem. One may need spiritual warfare in order to solve such problems.

This often requires all-night prayer, fasting, and hands-on prayer. Si-sook Chung of Chicago Full Gospel Church testifies to the following. "I have desperately relied on God's answer, praying all night, receiving hands-on prayer. After a week, while praying,

---

[12]Young-ui Kim, "The Living God," *Shinanggye* (January, 1976), 24-25.

the Holy Spirit was moved, granting me a fire baptism and the gift of speaking in tongues. Halleluiah!"[13] This process forms the spirit of Pentecostal faith.

One of the prominent characteristics of Full Gospel prayer is known as "crying out prayer." It begins by calling the Lord three times, "Oh, Lord, Lord, Lord." The biblical basis for this practice is found in Jeremiah 33:3: "Call to me and I will answer you" (NIV). Believing this verse, Full Gospel believers cry out to the Lord in unison. This prayer is not simply to talk to the Lord but desperately to hang on to God. As Jacob wrestled with the angel of God, this prayer wrestles with God. In fact, the churches in Korea have practiced "crying out" prayer since the 1907 great revival.[14] However, it is presently known as the Full Gospel style.

Laying on of hands by ministers takes a special position in Full Gospel faith. Experiences in the Holy Spirit often happen through this practice.

The husband of Ji-sook Chung of Chicago attended church regularly, but his faith was not firmly rooted. Jashil Choi, the mother in law of David Yonggi Cho, was leading a revival meeting in Chicago, and Chung asked Choi to lay hands on her husband in prayer. He received the fullness of the Holy Spirit and began to speak in tongues.[15]

These phenomena are often manifested in YFGC. David Yonggi Cho is regarded as an extraordinary minister with unusual gifts of the Holy Spirit, and receiving a hands-on prayer by him is considered a special privilege. A majority of Full Gospel believers share this belief.

Myung-ja Lee was growing in Christian faith, but she gave up. She became very ill and began to seek faith again in a Full Gospel

---

[13]Si-sook Chung, "Come, Come, Come to Me," *Shinanggye* (December, 1975), 90.

[14]Myung Soo Park, "Syungkyul Undonggwa Chogi Hankuk Kyohoeui Daebuheung" [Holiness Movement and the Great Revival of Early Korean Churches], *Christianity and History in Korea* 14 (2001), 47-77 (57).

[15]Si-sook Chung, "Come, Come, Come to Me, 2," *Shinanggye* (January, 1976), 83.

church. One month after she attended YFGC, she desired to receive special hands-on prayer by Cho. She thought, "I wish to have spiritual counseling and hands-on prayer from Cho," and with this clear goal, firm faith that a special prayer by Cho would solve her problem began to bud in her heart.[16] She later received hands-on prayer and a demon which caused sickness in her for ten years, was driven out.

The Full Gospel faith stresses the importance of all night prayer, as do all other Korean churches. It is not known exactly when the all night prayer started in Korean churches. However, there were often all night prayer meetings during revival movements in the early part of the twentieth century. A majority of revival meetings were held in the evenings, and after the worship service, cry-out prayer continued. When the believers were moved and filled with the Holy Spirit, these meetings continued into an all night prayer. However, the Korean churches held all night prayer regularly on Friday nights after the liberation from Japan.

Another special kind of prayer found in Full Gospel churches is fasting. Fasting prayer was especially emphasized by Jashil Choi and widely put into practice. Choi established a fasting prayer mountain in Osanni, where she trained believers for the Christian life and their illnesses were healed through fasting prayer. Pentecostals go to the Osanni Prayer Mountain when they are faced with difficult problems. There, they fast, cry out in prayer, and receive hands-on prayer from pastors. Then, they experience the wonderful grace of God. Choi believed and preached that over-eating causes most sickness. Thus, the practice of fasting can deal with the cause of the sickness. Speaking in tongues is also experienced in many cases along with divine healing.[17]

Central in the spiritual life of Full Gospel believers is prayer. This characteristic is distinguished clearly when compared with

---

[16] Lee, "The Lord Who Recreated My Life," 86.

[17] Jashil Choi, *Kumshik Gidoui Neungnyuk* [The Power of a Fasting Prayer] (Seoul: Seoul Books, 1977).

the practices of the Catholic Church or other traditional Protestant churches. The center of their spirituality is the sacrament and the word of God respectively. If the sacraments and the word of God are regarded as indirect approaches in one's relationship with God, prayer is a more direct approach. Prayer is conversation with God. Full Gospel believers talk to and receive God's answers through prayer.

In addition, prayer is a kind of spiritual warfare. Believers fight the schemes of Satan through prayer and fasting. When In-seong Kim received the Christian faith, his father was hitting his daughter severely. People said it was because the god of Jesus came into this family. The ancestral gods of this family were infuriated and afflicted many hardships. Kim confronted the demons of drunkenness and debauchery with prayer in tongues, fasting prayer, and all night prayer to drive them out. However, the situation did not improve. On the contrary, the hardships of the family worsened. Kim thought, "This is the last stand of the demons." To Pentecostal believers, prayer is neither a kind of meditation nor cultivation of the character. It is a desperate warfare with demons. If one does not understand this perspective, he/she can not fully understand the spirituality of the believers of the Full Gospel church.[18]

The reason that Christians can win in spiritual warfare is because the God of Christianity created the heavens and the earth while the other gods are demigods. Bok-hee Lim, who believed in shamanism and strongly denied the Christian faith, finally gave up the life of the shaman because Christians gathered around her neighborhood to pray. She said later, "Because it was a confrontation between a demigod and the almighty God, the demigod could do nothing but to be defeated in a groggy state without even having a real fight." Soon, Lim collected all the clothes and equipment that she used for her practice and burned

---

[18]In-seong Kim, "It Be as You Believe," *Shinanggye* (March, 1976), 88-89.

them all. This amounted to five carloads. Then, she destroyed the little temple for her god of shamanism in her backyard.[19]

The most important thing to remember in spiritual warfare is not only faith in the almighty God as the master of the heavens and the earth. The most important thing in spiritual warfare is the power found in the name of Jesus Christ. The Bible says God gave all sovereign authority to Jesus, which He promised to give to His disciples. When David Yonggi Cho prays for divine healing, he teaches one to say, "You, filthy Satan, I command you in the *name of Jesus of Nazareth*, be driven out from the saint."

The power of the name of Jesus is the strongest weapon in spiritual warfare. Nak-hyung Kim, who is a dentist and elder of YFGC, says that he can see when the power of bad spirits is harassing a patient during an operation. Then, he commands, "Filthy demons, come out in the name of the Lord Jesus."[20] In many cases, the patient regains faith, and the operation is finished successfully.

Pentecostals understand the life of faith as a sort of spiritual warfare. The Traditional belief of Koreans is that the ancestral gods of many generations would be infuriated if they converted and began worshipping the One God. Thus, having Christian faith has been risky. Pentecostals are trained to prepare for this process of converting a non-believer. They are told to tell the new converts, "There will be an attack from Satan. Do not be afraid of the attack, but stand strong and confront it. Never give up or be defeated."

Pentecostalism transforms believers into spiritual warriors. To them prayer is the most powerful weapon. The power of bad spirits is defeated through the power of the Holy Spirit. Cho leads believers of YFGC through rigorous prayer training.

---

[19]Bok-hee Lim, "Burning the Last Cloth of Shamanism," *Shinanggye* (February, 1978), 100.

[20]Nak-hyung Kim, "Faithfulness with All the Heart, Life, and Will," *Shinanggye* (July, 1976), 62.

4. The Turning Point in the Spiritual Life of the Full Gospel: The Baptism by the Holy Spirit

The essence of Pentecostal spirituality is found through the baptism in the Holy Spirit. The Pentecostal movement does not regard Christian faith as a simple transcendental faith rather as something that they can touch, feel, and experience. Experiential faith is emphasized. Cho teaches his members that there is a second grace of God called the baptism in the Holy Spirit, and he requests that they pray for it. In other words, a clear objective for Pentecostal believers that cannot be found in other believers is the baptism of the Holy Spirit.

This is the very point that distinguishes a Full Gospel church from a traditional church. Being part of a Full Gospel church is not an end in itself, but only a beginning. Cho continuously preaches about the Holy Spirit, and each parish pastor leads in this direction. Additionally, they teach that being armed spiritually through the baptism of the Holy Spirit, they will overcome hardships. All these elements make Pentecostal believers aggressive and strong.

This spiritual experience may come as an inexplicable warm feeling. Eui-ja Eom, the director of a marriage counseling center in Seoul, describes the feeling—"a light that has not been seen in this world shines and gives the feeling of being uplifted in the air." In many cases, the baptism by the Holy Spirit is manifested by a concrete and specific spiritual experience. Jin-hwa Kim says that "a hot fire of the Holy Spirit touched me" while in desperate prayer. This has been reported as a common experience of the baptism in the Holy Spirit.[21] Thus, the baptism of the Holy Spirit is often described as a "fire" baptism.

Often, the baptism in the Holy Spirit is manifested as light. A famous Korean musician, Myung-so Jeong was attending a revival meeting in the United States. The preacher prophesied that a person in this congregation would receive a great grace of God. After the meeting was over, she tried to fall asleep. Around 2 a.m.,

[21] Jin-hwa Kim, "God Who Cured My Sterility," *Shinanggye* (December, 1975), 83.

"a white light and a red light began to shine on me strongly. The brightness was something that I could not handle," she said, and she arose quickly.[22] Joy is also a frequent manifestation of the Holy Spirit's presence. Jeong continues, "An indescribable joy sprang up. It was a kind of drunken feeling." She expressed her great joy by singing hymns. After experiencing the grace of the Holy Spirit, hymns continuously came. Alone, she started singing, "Jesus is All the World to Me" over and over. "In many cases, after receiving the grace of God, a favorite hymn is found, and the hymn is sung repeatedly."[23]

In the Pentecostal movement, the baptism by the Holy Spirit is accompanied by speaking in tongues. If the warm, hearty, indescribable joy is the inner evidence, speaking in tongues is a more objective evidence. Jeong, after experiencing the grace of the Holy Spirit, testifies that "a strange voice comes out of my mouth." While awakened from sleep, "strange words come out of my mouth, and I am talking with God through such words."[24]

Byung-hyuk Chun was on his way home from an all night prayer meeting on the twentieth day of attending the church. Then, he experienced "a feeling of my heart swollen with joy and floating in the air. Out of so much joy and thanks, I prayed to God. Then, I started speaking in tongues and cried uncontrollably."[25] Speaking in tongues is a specific evidence of believers who have received the baptism by the Holy Spirit.

Pentecostals believe that speaking in tongues is not only clear evidence of the living God but also specific evidence that God loves them. A notorious punk, Young-seok Jeon, managed to commit all the sins in the world. Nevertheless, he was led by his Christian wife to YFGC and attended all church meetings with zeal. "The Lord gave me the baptism by the Holy Spirit as the sign

---

[22]Myung-so Jeong, "God, You Are the Living God," *Shinanggye* (August, 1976), 32.

[23]Jeong, "God, You Are the Living God," 32.

[24]Jeong, "God, You Are the Living God," 32.

[25]Byung-hyuk Chun, "Powerful God," *Shinanggye* (February, 1976), 93.

of His love for me."[26] Jeon was shunned by the society. However, with the baptism by the Holy Spirit, he began to have a firm conviction that he was a child of the absolute sovereign God. This conviction served as the turning point in his life.

Speaking in tongues, however, has also been the subject of mockery. Rev. Jashil Choi was criticized by fellow students even in the Pentecostal Bible college to stop speaking in tongues. Out of disappointment, she stopped praying in tongues for a while. However, her heart was saddened. She thought that being ashamed of a spiritual gift was to be ashamed of God. From that point on, she began to pray in tongues again courageously and loudly. Then, her heart was refreshed and the sadness in her heart disappeared.[27]

5. The Life of Being Filled with the Holy Spirit: New Heart, New Action and Powerful Work

The Full Gospel Church teaches believers to continue being filled with the Holy Spirit *after* receiving Spirit baptism. Hearts are changed, behaviors are changed, and convictions are strengthened when people have been filled with the Holy Spirit.

First, fullness is manifested by an absolute repentance for sins. This is a typical characteristic of the modern revival movement. Many people repent wholeheartedly despite the fact that sermons of the Full Gospel church often do not emphasize the law of God. In many cases, they do not receive the Holy Spirit after repenting, but the work of repentance is revealed when they receive the Holy Spirit.

Chang-yeon Won was advised to go to a theological seminary by David Yonggi Cho and was agonizing over this issue. He prayed earnestly. Within 30 seconds after the prayer, he felt his heart and body suddenly warm, and joy and hope filled him. He

---

[26]Young-seok Jeon, "The Joy of Working for Others," *Shinanggye* (December, 1976), 91.

[27]Jashil Choi, *Nanun Hallelujah Azummayutda* [I Was Mrs. Halleluiah] (Seoul: Seoul Book Center, 1978), 139-40.

started to weep, and felt as if his world turned upside down. At this point, all his sins were vividly revealed to him. He even saw himself stealing peaches in the backyard gardens of his neighbor. He then started to repent of his sins one by one. Before this, he had been cursing life in general, but now that he was filled with the Holy Spirit,[28] he was filled with thanksgiving. Won repented of all of his sins only after receiving the grace of the Holy Spirit.

This forceful work of the Holy Spirit was revealed to Il Kim. He started to attend a Full Gospel church at the advice of his friends while suffering from a dreadful disease. Kim did not know anything about Christianity nor the concept of sins that he had committed. He received the grace of God the first time he went to the church. "The day of receiving the grace, the day that the Lord showed his love for me was my attendance at Full Gospel Central Church. After hearing the pastor's sermon and the communion service, a strange thing happened to me. Tears were pouring, and the place of pain was wrapped in strange warmth. I felt that Jesus was pardoning my sins. Since this day, I could taste the peace and joy of my mind that I have never felt before."[29]

Young-seok Jeon was a former gangster. However, since he received grace, his heart was changed as well as his behavior. "My life was transforming day by day. Liquors, tobaccos, bad temper, doubts, negative thinking, etc. began to leave its place in my life. . . . The former gangster, Jeon was crucified on the Cross as well, and the changed Jeon resurrected and emerged out of the tomb that confined the gangster. . . . People, who used to know me, began to pay attention to me. . . . Then, I definitely testified, 'There was no one in this world to save and change me, but Jesus changed me completely.'"[30]

One of the most specific changes in the lives of Korean Christians is that they quit smoking and drinking. The Full Gospel

---

[28]Chang-yeon Won, "The Grace of Making One, Who Was Bound to Die, Live Again," *Shinanggye* (October, 1976), 82.

[29]Il Kim, "Amazing Love," *Shinanggye* (October, 1976), 86.

[30]Young-seok Jeon, "The Joy of Working for Others," *Shinanggye* (December, 1976), 91-92.

church continues this tradition with other Korean churches. The father of In-seong Kim exhibited a very bad temper when drunk. He would beat and harass his family members who were converted Christians. He targeted Kim, who was diligent and faith-filled. Kim embarked on all night prayer, fasting prayer, and prayer in tongues eagerly. Then, one day, her father lost his job and was led to church by his daughter. However, he could not give up his drinking habit. While he was praying and fasting at the Osanni prayer hall, he quit drinking and smoking in five days. His bad temper while intoxicated was over, and he now began to live a new life.[31]

Many believers testify that unreasonable fears began to disappear after receiving grace. Traditionally, Korean women have obeyed their husband and mother-in-law. Nevertheless, many wives who have experienced the grace of the Holy Spirit are persecuted at home. The mother-in-law oppresses the daughter-in-law saying that a hardship is happening in their home because of her faith. The husband threatens to divorce his wife, who does not listen to him anymore. Nevertheless, believers who have experienced the grace of the Holy Spirit do not yield to these persecutions.

The testimony of Hee-jeong Kim is a case in point. She testifies, "a power or a force to pull and push sprang up in me."[32] With this power, faith is declared and persecution is overcome. One of the characteristics of Pentecostalism is power manifested through faith. This is not only power for the mission of spreading the gospel but also power to overcome the obstacles in life.

---

[31] In-seong Kim, "Let It Be as You Believe," *Shinanggye* (March, 1976), 88-89.

[32] Hee-jeong Kim, "A Faith Budding by a Recorded Tape," *Shinanggye* (March, 1977), 84-85.

6. Problem Solving: Divine Healing, Blessing and New Christian Life

As people's problems are overcome by the power of the Holy Spirit, they begin to ponder the meaning of life. The fivefold gospel and threefold blessing messages of David Yonggi Cho suggest specific answers to these intrinsic life issues.

Hardly anyone questions that one characteristic of the Full Gospel church is divine healing. It is the most important aspect of the ministry of David Yonggi Cho and has contributed to the phenomenal growth of Yoido Full Gospel Church. Most of the testimonies printed in *Shinanggye* are of healing experiences. To the believers of the Full Gospel church, sickness is not just a physical concern. They believe that the body belongs to a deeper dimension. Thus, they believe healing of sickness is possible with help from the supernatural world.

Many believers of Full Gospel churches consider that sickness is a punishment from God for disobedience. They presume that God punishes them with sickness if they are not living the life of faith. In many cases, after coming to church for a while, some begin to wander about again, and soon after they neglect keeping the Lord's day holy and giving the tithe. Thus, some believe that it was part of the healing process to help them realize their mistake and to return to God.

Jae-yeol Kim was a fervent believer in a Full Gospel church. However, her husband did not have faith and suffered from sickness. Moreover, he could not stand his wife's life of faith. She started fasting prayer to avoid persecution. Several days later, during the early morning prayer, all her sins from her childhood were shown to her like a movie clip. She realized that she was the root of the problems. She desperately repented. After fasting prayer, she returned home to find that her husband was healed.[33] This illustrates that the repentance of the wife was very much related to the healing of the husband.

---

[33]Jae-yeol Kim, "Answer to a Prayer," *Shinanggye* (October, 1976), 88.

Pentecostal believers claim that they experience divine healing during Cho's healing prayer. David Yonggi Cho names several specific diseases during the healing prayer after his sermon, and then proclaims divine healing in the name of Jesus. Many are healed at this time.

Myung-hwan Kim's right eye was so weak that he could not see clearly. During an evening worship service of Yoido Full Gospel Church, David Yonggi Cho proclaimed, "the person with a weakening right eye, stand up at this time. You are healed tonight." Immediately, he stood up and thanked the Lord. He was healed. Several months later, he decided to have an eye examination to see if this improved vision was for real or just a temporary illusion. His eyesight had been restored and he could see even very small letters clearly.[34]

Healing is related to fasting prayer in many cases. Many come to the fasting prayer hall to seek healing as a last resort. Kwan-ock Kim had suffered from bronchial asthma for a long time. He went up to the Osanni fasting prayer hall at the suggestion of friends. After a week, he felt a twitching in his stomach and ran to the rest room. As soon as he sat on the stool, a fistful lump of feces was excreted, and he spotted a lump of worms (probably parasites) in the bloody stool. After this incident, he was cured of the asthma and other miscellaneous diseases.[35]

When we analyze divine healing, most people relate it to the experience of the Holy Spirit. The work of divine healing is revealed when a person experiences the fiery Holy Spirit, atones for his/her sins, and has a firm conviction of becoming a child of God. Some people are critical saying that healings of the Full Gospel church only cure disease and do not produce changes in lifestyle. Nevertheless, when we read the testimonies we see that these are only superficial criticisms.

---

[34]Young-hwan Kim, "The Best Ophthalmologist," *Shinanggye* (April, 1976), 95.

[35]Kwan-ock Kim, "Healing by a Fasting Prayer," *Shinanggye* (November, 1975), 87-89.

Nak-Hyung Kim, a dentist and elder of a Full Gospel church, testified of his experience. He had to take a leave of absence his junior year in dental school due to tuberculosis. At this time, he was invited to a tent church meeting of Seodae-moon Full Gospel Church where he witnessed a miracle healing. He prayed that the same miracle would happen to him. "Without a single doubt, I implored God to heal me just like the person in front me. Then, the heaven opened and came into my body to operate on me. In a split second, my tuberculosis was completely cured. The fire of the Holy Spirit came into me like a flood." Along with this healing experience, he continued to experience the grace of God, forgiveness, peace and joy.[36] In the testimony of Kim, we can see that the grace of divine healing does not end with the healing.

David Yonggi Cho always stresses the blessings of the soul, material prosperity, and health. Material blessing is central in his ministry. Traditional churches avoid this blessing; however, Cho takes it very positively. He believes that a good God will give good things to His children.

Cho teaches that giving the tithe is like sowing a seed of blessing. It is called the law of sowing. Just as a seed needs to be sown to reap fruit, the tithe has to be offered to receive material blessing. Korean Christians believe that the blessing is received through tithing. Ahn, Jeong-Soon heard Cho's teaching that the tithe is the stock seed for blessing, and she determined to offer the tithe faithfully. Consequently, she and her family received abundant material blessing.[37]

Pentecostals believe that tithing keeps the home in blessing. Seong-hye Park was well off financially, however, she did not give her whole tithe. She grudgingly thought the tithe was a waste. Whenever she withheld her tithe, her family suffered from disease, accidents, and miscellaneous incidents. She decided to give the tithe. After that, she and her family were protected from hardships and their blessings increased day by day. Thus, she believes the

[36] Nak-hyung Kim, "Loyalty with All the Heart, Life and Will," *Shinanggye* (July, 1976), 60-61.

[37] Jeong-soon Ahn, "Condition for a Marriage that Required a Conversion" *Shinanggye* (January, 1977), 106.

tithe is the forbidden fruit of modern society. As Adam and Eve ate the forbidden fruit and were expelled from the Garden of Eden, someone who does *not* give a wholesome tithe drifts away from the blessed garden.[38]

Diligence is as important as tithing and keeping Sundays holy. Harvey Cox published an analysis of David Yonggi Cho's sermon emphasizing diligence. In his opinion, this teaching has contributed greatly in helping Korean Christians attain a middle class lifestyle.[39] If Korean Minjoong theology stressed liberation from poverty through changes in social structure, the Pentecostal movement encouraged the poor to strive for the middle class by living diligently. On this point, it can be said that the Pentecostal movement contributed to the modernization of Korean society.

Sook Hwang's business hit bottom and was on the verge of bankruptcy. Then, she listened to David Yonggi Cho. Cho always preached, "If you want blessing, sow the seeds of faith." She then decided to give generously as he taught. He also spoke of the principle of sowing and reaping. That is, one has to work hard. Hwang then made every effort in her business and in her life of faith and she endeavored to teach others. Hwang succeeded once more in her business. She has traveled around the world and come to the conclusion that Korea is the best country to live in for her.[40]

Numerous testimonies printed in *Shinanggye* tell of those who have fallen into despair and regained the courage to start over. Instead of poverty they gain material blessings and often move into the middle class. In this regard, the evaluation of Harvey Cox seems to be justified and appropriate.

As much as material blessing is important, the blessing of the home is also important. If the home is not peaceful, one cannot speak of blessing. Kim, So-Ja was severely beaten by her husband

---

[38]Seong-hye Park, "Tithe is the Second Forbidden Fruit," *Shinanggye* (June, 1978), 91.

[39]Harvey Cox, *Fire from Heaven: The Rise of Pentecostal Spirituality and the Reshaping of Religion in the Twentieth-First Century* (Reading, MA: Addison-Wesley, 1995), 234-37.

[40]Sook Hwang, "Sow the Seeds of Faith," *Shinanggye* (December, 1976), 88-89.

because of her Christian faith. She planned to pray at the Osanni fasting prayer hall for ten days. On the seventh day, her husband appeared in a dream. But, the news she heard from home was that her husband was becoming even more violent. Then, on the ninth day of her fast, her husband came to the prayer hall with their daughter and promised her that they would live the Christian faith together. He became a faithful saint of the church.[41]

Traditionally, Korean churches have told wives to obey their husbands and convert their husbands with faith and patience. However, in the majority of cases, this advice ends in failure. However, Full Gospel faith understands this kind of confrontation is spiritual warfare. They advise one to confront the issue courageously with faith. Here, the confrontation is not physical but spiritual through prayer. It seeks deliverance from darkness through a change of heart.

7. Analysis: The Characteristics of Korean Pentecostal Spirituality

We have examined the spirituality of believers in Full Gospel churches through their testimonies as recorded in *Shinanggye*. They reveal the typical spiritual life of Pentecostal believers. Most begin their spiritual journey in a desperate environment. This can be sickness, business failure, or discord in the family. They strive to solve their life problems with their whole hearts. Typically, they seek the Lord through many forms of prayer, including all night prayer, fasting, prayer in tongues, and cry-out prayer.

During this process the baptism in the Holy Spirit, (the distinguishing substance of the Pentecostal movement), often was poured out upon them. A fiery hot feeling and speaking in tongues accompanied this. Many also experienced divine healing at the same time as receiving the baptism in the Holy Spirit. Through this, many began to have a firm conviction that God now recognized them. This religious experience continued also in their daily lives. That is, many quit drinking and smoking, began to

---

[41]So-ja Kim, "Upon the Answering of God," *Shinanggye* (March, 1976), 86-87.

keep Sundays holy, offered the tithe, and worked diligently. Through these processes and experiences as well as the teachings on blessing of Cho, believers in Full Gospel churches grow in faith. They are convinced that they are children of God, and become deeply involved in the faith community through Full Gospel/Pentecostal churches.

Next, is an evaluation of several characteristics of Pentecostal spirituality visible in the ministry of David Yonggi Cho and the Full Gospel churches in Korea.

Firstly, is the aspect of primitive religion. Many religious scholars have understood the appearance of the Pentecostal movement as a resurrection of primitive religion. Harvey Cox, a religious scholar of Harvard Divinity School, has said that speaking in tongues is a primitive language and that a miracle represents primitive piety. In fact, primitive religion has been regarded as superstitious in existing society. However, it is captivating the minds of the common people. Primitive religion deals with the problems of sickness and disaster more specifically than modern religion. David Yonggi Cho deals with the basic needs and problems of people which existing traditional religions have neglected.

Some scholars classify religions as either formal or informal.[42] Formal religion emphasizes ethical and social responsibility as well as theological theories. Informal religion is passed down as folk religion. Dream interpretation, astrology, miraculous healing, belief in angels, etc. are examples.

However, human religious desires are often not satisfied with a formal type of religion. Thus, even people who belong to a traditional religion seek some informal elements. Currently, formal religions are losing a foothold while informal religions are gaining ground.[43] David Yonggi Cho has accepted the informal elements of a religion and made the Christian faith more approachable for the masses.

---

[42] Meredith B. McGuire, *Religion: The Social Context* (Belmont: Wadsworth Publishing, 1997), ch. 4; Roof, *Spiritual Marketplace*, 37-38.

[43] Roof, *Spiritual Marketplace*, 38.

Secondly, Pentecostal faith is a spirituality for the masses. It is different from the traditional monastic life which seeks self-actualization or enlightened sanctification through the silence of lengthy meditation. However, the spirit of a Full Gospel church is manifested in crying-out prayer, often seemingly "shouting prayer." The public would rather cry out to express something that is deep inside than to think about and train themselves through meditation. Cho has developed spirituality for the masses through fasting prayer, all night prayer, and prayer in tongues.

Heribert Muehlen, a German leader and theologian of the Catholic Charismatic Renewal movement, thinks that the popular spirituality of the New Testament was somehow transformed into the elite spirituality of the monastery in the Middle Ages. This eventually led to the institutionalization of the Catholic Church.

In contrast, he goes on to say that the Pentecostal movement returned the church to the masses and that this is an appropriate expression of spirituality in contemporary times. Muehlen adds that one way the Catholic Church can meet modern needs is to follow the example of the Pentecostal movement.[44] David Yonggi Cho is an excellent religious leader for the masses in modern society.

Thirdly, the spirituality found in the Full Gospel church is private in that it focuses on problem solving. As we can see in the testimonies, most believers of a Full Gospel church come to the church with private, individual problems. Their faith is matured during the process of overcoming numerous problems such as sickness, poverty, disaster and family issues. David Yonggi Cho takes these concerns seriously and deals with them directly. Recently, Full Gospel churches have begun to speak out to/for society, but they have traditionally held a strong orientation toward the individual.

Religious sociologists identified one element of modern religion as privatization. Religion no longer serves to function in public matters and is now limited to private matters. This is distinctly seen in the United States, where church and state are

[44] H. Muehlen, *Reform of Christian Faith: Charisma, Gift, Reform*, trans. Jung-won Kim in Korean (Seoul: St. Paul Publishing, 1980).

clearly divided. So, religion is evaluated not in the context of finding meaning in a public forum but in the context of how it satisfies the needs of religious consumers, the members of the church.[45] From this perspective, the fact that Full Gospel churches have focused on the problems of individuals is an indication of good understanding of the their role in modern society.

Fourthly, Pentecostal believers find meaning and a sense of belonging through the experience of the Holy Spirit. Many people, regarded as "losers" in life, receive the firm conviction that they are children of God after receiving the baptism in the Holy Spirit. Believers of Full Gospel churches care for their members through organizational zones. Spiritual assistance is provided through prayer and sharing rather than by financial aid alone. Through this process, a strong fellowship among the believers emerges. This sense of belonging serves as an oasis for lonely people during urbanization.

Wade Clark Roof, a religious sociologist of the University of California, Santa Barbara, asserts that the most important duty of a religion in modern society is to provide personal meaning for one's existence and a sense of social belonging.[46] Robert Wuthnow, a religious sociologist at Princeton University, agrees with Roof, likening its purpose to that of a support group. In modern society where everything is specialized and done by a division of labor, people feel like lost children without a sense of belonging. Religion supports them and instills a sense of belonging.[47] Full Gospel churches are serving this purpose in their congregations.

Fifthly, David Yonggi Cho relies on the supernatural and emphasizes the transcendental works of God. Many people have lost all their resources and worldly hope before they come to a church as their last resort. They earnestly desire a miracle of God.

---

[45]Peter Berger, *Religion and Society*, trans. Yang-gu Lee in Korean (Seoul: Jongno Books, 1981).

[46]Roof, *Spiritual Marketplace*, 77

[47]Robert Wuthnow, *Sharing the Journey: Support Groups and America's New Quest for Community* (Princeton, NJ: Free Press, 1994).

In this regard, a miracle is the essence of Pentecostal spirituality. It is evidence that testifies of the living of God. Doubts vanish.

John Locke, a British experiential philosopher of the eighteenth century, said that in order for Christianity to remain vital in a modern society, a miracle needs to be manifested to prove that their religion (God) is alive. According to Locke, during the era of close relationships between church and state, the nation supported the religion for its survival. However, when support from national governments has officially ceased, support from believers is essential. Therefore, a miracle is imperative to prove that their religion is alive. In fact, the most revived churches of modern society are those where the supernatural miracles of God have been manifested. The transcendental spirituality of David Yonggi Cho is needed today.

Finally, in understanding Pentecostal spirituality, some misconceptions of the Pentecostal movement need to be addressed. Being filled with the Holy Spirit is a holistic experience that changes the mind, heart, and life of a believer. Most of the accounts that have been investigated testify to a change in lifestyle, which accompanied the charismatic experience.

However, this point has been neglected in the past. In my opinion, Pentecostal activists may have over emphasized the aspect of charismatic manifestations. Manifestations are outward, physical, objective phenomenon of the experience of the baptism in the Holy Spirit. We also see inner evidence of peace and joy overflowing in the lives of the testifiers. Pentecostal theology should stress this point more intently in the future.

Historically, the Pentecostal movement originated from (came out of) the Holiness movement of the nineteenth century. They both believed the work of the Holy Spirit results in a change in the heart. Pentecostals claimed that the physical, objective evidence is speaking in tongues. Thus, if the Pentecostal movement is to remain faithful to its historical conception, it must emphasize the inner manifestations of a change of heart as well as the objective charismatic manifestations of speaking in tongues and healing.

THE MISSIOLOGICAL CHALLENGE OF DAVID YONGGI CHO'S THEOLOGY[1]

Hwa Yung

1. Introduction

The story of Dr. David Yonggi Cho and the Yoido Full Gospel Church (YFGC) is well-known throughout the world. Cho comes from the Evangelical and Pentecostal tradition.[2] His theological teachings and ministerial practices are many faceted. The concern of this paper is to focus on the implications of Cho's theology for Christian mission today.

The primary task, therefore, is not to examine Cho's teachings as a whole, but to critique those aspects of his theology that are relevant to mission in the twenty-first century. This paper will therefore begin by laying down what is deemed to be an appropriate set of criteria for a theology that would enhance mission. It will then go on to examine to what extent Cho's theology fulfills these criteria. Suggestions will also be offered as to how a more careful reformulation of his teachings would increase the missiological impact of his theology.

---

[1]An earlier version of the paper was presented in the First Young San International Theological Symposium, 26-27 Sept 2002, Hansei University, Seoul.

[2]The church belongs to the Assembly of God denomination.

2. What Constitutes a Missiological Theology?

In order to examine the missiological implications of Cho's theology, we need first to look at what mission is and why Christian theology properly conceived must be missiological and pastoral in orientation.

What is mission? In the twentieth century there have been intense debates on this question. At one time, conservatives emphasized primarily evangelism and church growth, and liberals or radicals social concerns and political action. But it is increasingly recognized that mission is holistic. It involves both the vertical dimension which concerns our need to be reconciled to God, as well as the horizontal dimension which deals with reconciliation between human beings. Further, mission is the proclamation of the kingdom of God and the lordship of Christ over all of life. It involves calling individuals to repentance and faith in him, deliverance for those in bondage to demonic powers and diseases, and bringing Christ's love to the weak, needy, broken-hearted and hungry, as well as God's righteousness and justice to a world wherein suffering and oppression is rife. Thus mission involves evangelism, healing and deliverance ministries, social concerns and political action for justice in a broken world.[3]

In what follows, we will examine this understanding of mission in greater detail. But before doing so, I would like to draw

---

[3]What is stated here is representative of an increasing number of evangelicals in their thinking concerning the mission of the church. See e.g., John R. W. Stott, *Christian Mission in the Modern World* (London: Falcon Books, 1975); C. Rene Padilla, *Mission between the Times: Essay on the Kingdom* (Grand Rapids, MI: Eerdmans, 1985); Ronald J. Sider, *One-Sided Christianity? Uniting the Church to Heal a Lost and Broken World* (Grand Rapids, MI: Zondervan, 1993); Vinay Samuel and Chris Sugden, eds., *Mission as Transformation: A Theology of the Whole Gospel* (Oxford: Regnum, 2000); A. Scott Moreau, *et. al.*, *Deliver Us from Evil: An Uneasy Frontier in Christian Mission* (Monrovia, CA: MARC, 2002).

attention to the nature of theology, which is, that it must be fundamentally rooted in mission and pastoral practice.

2.1 Theology as Missiological and Pastoral

One of the unfortunate aspects of theology today is that much theological writing has degenerated into an academic exercise, often unrelated to the life and mission of the church. In part, this is due to the influence of Enlightenment thinking in the western intellectual tradition. Under the Kantian paradigm, building upon Greek idealism, "pure" or "theoretical" reason took priority over "practical" reason. This helps accentuate the shift from theology as "practical" to theology as "speculative." Thus much of western systematic theology today is quite unrelated to the mission and pastoral concerns of the church.[4] But, properly understood, this is not what theology should be. Rather, at its best, theology has always been rooted in the mission and pastoral ministry of the church.

This emphasis is clearly seen in the New Testament records. Every book therein was written in response to some evangelistic or pastoral need of the church. As George Peters puts it, "the Bible is not a book about theology as such, but rather, a record of theology in mission—God in action on behalf of the salvation of mankind."[5] Or, as David J. Bosch argues, the New Testament books were not written by the equivalent of modern-day scholars writing at leisure. Rather they were written "in the context of an 'emergency situation,' of a church which, because of its missionary encounter with the world, was forced to theologize."[6]

---

[4]See discussion in David J. Bosch, *Transforming Mission: Paradigm Shifts in Theology of Mission* (Maryknoll, NY: Orbis, 1991), 420-51; Randy L. Maddox, "John Wesley—Practical Theologian?" *Wesley Theological Journal* 23 (1988), 122-147.

[5]George W. Peters, *A Biblical Theology of Missions* (Chicago, IL: Moody, 1972), 9.

[6]Bosch, *Transforming Mission*, 16.

The same thing can be said of theology in the early church. Reflecting on the writings of many of the church fathers, Jaroslav Pelikan asserts that "when the church confessed what it believed and taught, it did so in answer to attacks from within and from without the Christian movement."[7] In other words, the Patristic fathers wrote out of the dual concerns, on the one hand, of dealing with heresies and other pastoral problems within the Christian community, and on the other, of defending the church from external attacks by pagans as well as commending the gospel to them.

We may go on to point out that this emphasis of rooting theology in mission and sound pastoral practice has also characterized the church during the most vibrant periods of its history, including the Reformation and the eighteenth century Evangelical revivals.[8] It is therefore not an exaggeration for Martin Kahler to assert that mission is "the mother of theology."[9]

2.2 What Is the Measure of a Missiological Theology?

If theology must be missiological how do we assess whether the works of a particular writer is indeed so? The test of such a theology would be whether it empowers and enhances the church in its life and mission. If that is so, then it must fulfill at least three criteria. The first is that it should help the church to be effective in its evangelism and pastoral ministry. Second, it should empower the church to act effectively in social transformation. And third, it must take culture seriously. Briefly, I will give my reasons for each of these.[10]

---

[7]Jaroslav Pelikan, *The Christian Tradition: A History of the Development of Doctrine. The Emergence of the Catholic Tradition (100-600)* (Chicago and London: University of Chicago Press, 1971), 11.

[8]Cf. Maddox, "John Wesley," 122-47.

[9]Cited in Bosch, *Transforming Mission*, 16. I have also argued this point at length in Yung Hwa, *Mangoes or Bananas? The Quest for an Authentic Asian Christian Theology* (Oxford: Regnum, 1997), 18-26.

[10]For a much more detail treatment, see Hwa, *Mangoes or Bananas?* 61-145.

Except for those Christians who accept more radical interpretations of the faith, little needs to be said about the importance of evangelism. Until the advent of liberal theology in the modern period, it has always been taken seriously by the church—even if at times Christians have approached it in a spirit that is very different from that of Christ. It involves the verbal proclamation of the gospel, and the calling of men and women to repentance and salvation in Christ. Often, it also involves power encounters through prophecy, healing, exorcism or some other supernatural acts. Converts must then be discipled, nurtured to maturity in Christ and brought into communities of faith through proper and effective pastoral care. This is what church growth is all about. The more liberal and radical segments of the church today continue to reject this as relevant to mission. But that does not change the fact that this is rooted in the ministry and teachings of Jesus Christ and the apostles in the New Testament. Therefore, the first criterion of a missiological theology is that it should enhance the work of evangelism and pastoral oversight.

The gospel however is not only about personal salvation in a mere spiritual sense. It is also about Christ coming to redeem the whole world. Salvation therefore is personal, social, global and cosmic. As noted earlier, for much of the twentieth century, Evangelicals forgot Christ's command to love our neighbor, and failed to recognize his concern for the poor and needy, and for social righteousness and justice in the world. But there has been an abundance of studies in recent years by Evangelicals to point us back in the right direction.[11] The Lausanne Covenant sums this corrective up succinctly in its paragraph on "Christian Social Responsibility:"

> Although reconciliation with man is not reconciliation with God, nor is political liberation salvation, nevertheless we affirm that evangelism and socio-political involvement are both part of our Christian duty. For both are necessary expressions of our

[11]E.g., Sider, *One-Sided Christianity?* especially 49-77.

> doctrines of God and man, our love for our neighbor and our obedience to Jesus Christ.[12]

Thus, if a theology is missiological, it must also empower the church in the task of social transformation.

The third criterion for a missiological theology is whether it takes the culture of the recipient of the gospel message seriously. This has emerged as one of the key issues in modern missiological discussions. Increasingly, it has been recognized that western missions in the last two centuries have often been ethnocentric, with too much emphasis given to the supposed superiority of western culture and ignoring the integrity of other cultures. This resulted in the gospel often being given in an alien manner to those in the non-western world, thus causing unnecessary cultural offense. Chinese intellectuals in the early part of the last century used to mock Christians with the saying, "One more Christian, one less Chinese!"

One of the key elements of the gospel is the doctrine of incarnation. Jesus Christ, though fully God in himself, took on human flesh within a particular human culture, at a specific point in space-time history, so as to bring the gospel to us in a way that we can understand. Without the incarnation there would have been no gospel. In the same way the gospel must be incarnated in every culture and historical context to which God sends us. As Andrew Walls has argued, all of us want the church to be "a place to feel at home." The implication of the incarnation is, "Whenever He (Christ) is taken by men in any time and place He takes that nationality, that society, that 'culture,' and sanctifies all that is capable of sanctification by His presence."[13] He calls this the indigenizing principle. This is what makes the gospel communicable and also much more easily acceptable!

---

[12] Para. 5 on "Christian Social Responsibility" in the Lausanne Covenant, International Congress on World Evangelization, Lausanne, Switzerland, July 1974.

[13] Andrew F. Walls, "The Gospel as the Prisoner and Liberator of Culture," *Missionalia* 10:3 (1982), 93-105 (97-98).

In other words, unless the gospel is incarnated into a particular culture, it will never effectively penetrate the people of that culture. But the principle goes even further than that. It is when a person becomes a Christian without losing touch with his or her own culture that the individual is thereby in turn empowered to proclaim the gospel in a manner that speaks with power to one's own culture and people. Thus, taking culture seriously is indispensable to effective mission.[14]

This, of course, does not mean that the Christian accepts and baptizes everything within the culture of those to whom he or she brings the gospel. There will be some things that will need to be rejected outright, especially if they are clearly idolatrous and immoral. Others will need to be redeemed and transformed by the gospel. This brings us to the pilgrim principle, of which Andrews Walls also speaks. It reminds the Christian that "he has no abiding city and warns him that to be faithful to Christ will put him out of step with his society; for that society never existed, in East or West, ancient time or modern, which could absorb the word of Christ painlessly into its system."[15] Thus the Christian message, which must be intentionally incarnational, should also at the same time be counter-cultural when necessary. Taking culture seriously in theologizing requires us to hold both principles in proper tension always. Any truly missiological theology must do the same.

Having outlined the three criteria for a missiological theology, I would like now to look at the missiological implications of Cho's theology. I will begin with the evangelistic and pastoral dimensions of his theology.

---

[14]I have argued this at length in Hwa Yung, *Kingdom Identity and Christian Mission* (Singapore: Discipleship Training Centre, 2000).

[15]Walls, "The Gospel as the Prisoner and Liberator of Culture," 99.

3. The Evangelistic and Pastoral Dimension

Cho's theology is clearly very strong in this area. The fact that he is the pastor of one of the largest churches in the world should itself be adequate proof of this. However, for the purpose of drawing out clearly the implications of his theology, I will look in turn at his emphasis on evangelism and church growth, his pastoral methods and the emphasis on "signs and wonders."

3.1 Evangelism and Church Growth

Evangelism and church growth is fundamental to Cho's understanding of mission. In a paper titled "The Secret behind the World's Biggest Church," he states that his "ultimate purpose…is winning souls" and that his prayer is "that churches all around the world may grow so that they can glorify God through their ministries."[16] Much of his thinking on this subject is enunciated in his book, *More Than Numbers*, wherein he "shares the secret of church growth."[17] In this, he distinctly differs from those, like the *Minjung* theologians, who espouse a radical political version of Christianity which denies a proper place to evangelism and church growth in the mission of the church.

This commitment to evangelism and church growth is not only seen in his teachings, but also in the ministry and programs of the YFGC. Before starting the current church he had pioneered at least two other large churches. His present church has also planted many other churches in Korea and elsewhere. For the purpose of disseminating principles of church growth throughout the world, Church Growth International was set up in 1976.[18] Furthermore,

---

[16]"The Secret behind the World's Biggest Church," in *Azusa Street and Beyond: Pentecostal Missions and Church Growth in the Twentieth Century*, ed. L. Grant McClung (South Plainfield, NJ: Bridge Publishing, 1986), 99-104 (104).

[17]*More than Numbers* (Waco, TX: Word Books, 1984).

[18]Cho and Harold Hostetler, *Successful Home Cell Groups* (Seoul: Seoul Logos, 1981/1997), 97-105.

the latest count shows the church supporting 579 cross-cultural missionaries working in churches spread over 57 countries throughout the world.[19]

There are some key elements in his church-planting method. To begin with, prayer is central. His response to the question, "How have we maintained such unusual growth in our local church?" is "The real answer is prayer."[20] This includes private prayer, regular and extended group sessions at the YFGC, such as the Friday night prayer meetings, and also fasting. Also, members and groups are encouraged to spend extended time at the prayer mountain near the North Korean border.[21] The second is his emphasis on the power of the Holy Spirit in working signs and wonders. More will be said about this below. The third is the extensive use of home cell groups for evangelism and pastoral nurture. He writes: "'Do you think it is important to save souls?' If the answer to that question is yes, then the cell system is for you."[22] The fourth is his strong emphasis on developing lay-leadership.[23]

But Cho is also concerned that his ideas do not degenerate into a mere set of techniques for church growth. "Church growth is more than a series of ideas and principles which will, when put into practice, automatically make your church grow

---

[19]As stated in the video clip, "Through Hardship to Glory—Yoido Full Gospel Church, Sr. Pastor Dr. David Yonggi Cho," distributed in September 2002.

[20]*More than Numbers*, 99.

[21]*More than Numbers*, 99-108; cf. also Philip D. Douglass, "Yonggi Cho and the Korean Pentecostal Movement: Some Theological Reflections," *Presbyterion* 17:1 (1991), 16-34 (20).

[22]*More than Numbers*, 46.

[23]Cho with John W. Hurston, "Ministry through Home Cell Units," in *Korean Church Growth Explosion*, eds. Bong Rin Ro and Martin L. Nelson (Seoul: Word of Life Press; Taichung: ATA, 1983), 270-89; *More than Numbers*, 31-38; "The Secret behind the World's Biggest Church," 103.

numerically."[24] One needs to grasp the underlying theology and philosophy, and not just the surface principles and practices. In particular, church growth has a lot to do with the heart of the leader because that is where it all begins. This is clearly a corrective to what has been called by some as "managerial missiology," which perceives church growth primarily in terms of the result of applying certain techniques properly.

3.2 Pastoral Structures for Growth and Nurture: Cell-Groups and Lay Training

For a church to grow, evangelism in itself is not enough. Proper and effective structures must be emplaced to nurture new converts. As already noted, the heart of Cho's method here is the use of cell groups.[25] These are crucial to evangelism because that is where non-Christians can be brought into the life of the church through the non-threatening setting of home or work-place. It is where the discipling process takes place through the personal ministry of praying for one another and the study of the Bible.[26] It is also the place for the developing of Christian community in the midst of the increasing anonymity of modern life.[27] To enable the groups to gel quickly and effectively, Cho prefers homogenous groups with people coming from similar backgrounds to heterogeneous ones.[28]

The YFGC is made up of tens of thousands of cell groups. Obviously, for that to be possible the laity must be entrusted with

---

[24] *More than Numbers*, 11.

[25] For details see Cho & Hostetler, *Successful Home Cell Groups*; Cho & Hurston, "Ministry through Home Cell Units"; *More than Numbers*, 39-54.

[26] Out of the one hour for the meeting, 45 minutes is set aside for Bible study and praying for individual needs. See for example, *The Homecell Group Study Guide*, vol. 1 (Seoul: Seoul Logos, 1990/1997).

[27] Cho & Hostetler, *Successful Home Cell Groups*, 49-56; *More than Numbers*, 49.

[28] *More than Numbers*, 42-45.

leadership. Thus, each group is led by a trained lay person who is in turn supervised by a more senior leader. Women are also included in leadership in spite of the inherited conservatism of traditional Korean culture where leadership has always been in the hands of men.[29] By giving serious attention to the development and use of lay leadership, he shows the seriousness with which he takes the New Testament understanding of "body life" in the church, and turns it into an effective program of pastoral oversight.

Here again, Cho's theology is soundly missiological. Twentieth century ecclesiological discussion has drawn repeated attention to "God's frozen people," referring to the laity who has been denied a meaningful role in the mission and ministry of the church. This has been one of the key reasons why many traditional churches have not grown. Cho's approach not only takes the priesthood of all believers seriously, and thereby releases an abundance of energy for effective ministry. It also provides the only practical manner in which large churches can be pastored effectively with the needs of individuals met in the context of a caring community of believers. Further, Cho admits that one of the key motivations behind his use of cell groups is the Communist threat.[30] In the event of a repeat of the Korean War, pastors can be removed and church buildings destroyed. But as the experience of the house churches in neighboring China so eloquently testifies, the church can remain vital through the cell groups.

Perhaps it would be appropriate to add a peculiarly Methodist observation at this point. In the eighteenth century revival in England, the two great leaders were John Wesley and George Whitefield. All contemporary records indicated that, of the two, Whitefield was the more powerful evangelist. But strange as it seems, it is Wesley's work that has survived and thrived through the years in the worldwide Methodist movement, whereas the Calvinistic Methodist Church linked with Whitefield is today a small denomination restricted largely to Britain. Yet the reason is

---

[29] *More than Numbers*, 43-44; Cho & Hostetler, *Successful Home Cell Groups*, 23-29.

[30] *More than Numbers*, 40-41.

not hard to find. It lies in the genius of Wesley's pastoral structures. All his converts were channeled into "classes" of about ten to twelve each. Here each member was nurtured to maturity and usefulness in ministry. More mature ones were channeled into "bands" where standards were even more demanding. And out of the class and band leaders came the lay preachers of early Methodism who went on to become the leaders of the next generation. From these emerged the worldwide Methodist movement. The unfortunate thing was that about a hundred years after the revival first began, Methodists in both Britain and in America began losing interest in the class and band meetings. This was one key reason for the loss of spiritual vitality in Methodism. This observation clearly points to Cho's wisdom in making cell groups an essential part of the pastoral structures in his church.[31]

3.3 The Place of Signs and Wonders

We now turn to Cho's emphasis on divine healing through prayer which he links inseparably with church growth. To him, the lack of emphasis given to the miraculous is often a cover up for the powerlessness of the church. This is grievous to the Spirit. "Signs, wonders and the power of the Holy Spirit are essential for successful preaching of the gospel."[32] In his ministry, he repeatedly finds that people turn to faith in the Christ when healing takes place.

---

[31] For an introduction to this aspect of Methodism, see Snyder, Howard A. Snyder, *The Radical Wesley and Patterns of Church Renewal* (Downers Grove, IL: IVP, 1980). It should be noted that it is not certain that Cho's cells approach the level of rigor, commitment and mutual accountability required in Wesley's classes and bands.

[32] *Salvation, Health and Prosperity: Our Threefold Blessings in Christ* (Altamonte Springs, FL: Creation House, 1987), 143; cf. also *More than Numbers*, 87. It should be noted however that there is relatively little discussion on deliverance ministry of the demonized in Cho's writings. It would be surprising if this is not common phenomenon within Korean Pentecostalism.

For Cho, healing is closely linked to the cross. In line with Pentecostal atonement teaching, Christ's death not only brought us spiritual salvation but also physical healing.[33] At the same time, unlike some Pentecostal and charismatic teachers who insist that all can be healed provided the necessary conditions are met, he is careful to point out that sometimes it may not be God's will to heal.[34]

Here again, Cho's teaching and practice is consistent with what is clearly seen in the growth of the church throughout the world today. Wherever the church is growing rapidly, be it among Pentecostals in Latin American, African Independent Churches in Africa, or house churches in China, invariably we see the manifestation of signs and wonders through the work of the Holy Spirit. It is, therefore, evident that this emphasis, together with his teaching on evangelism, cell groups and lay leadership all contribute significantly to the growth of the church. In other words, measured by its evangelistic impact and pastoral efficacy, Cho's theology cannot be faulted. In this area, his ideas and practices carry profound missiological implications for the global church.

4. The Social Transformation Dimension

We come now to the second criterion for a missiological theology, which is the extent to which it empowers the church to address the social problems and political challenges in its context. We will look at this aspect of Cho's theology under three sub-headings: the social outreach programs of the Yoido Church, the sociological dynamics of Pentecostalism and Cho's teaching on the "treble blessings."

---

[33] *Salvation, Health and Prosperity*,121, *The Homecell Group Study Guide*, vol. 1, 225-28; *How Can I Be Healed?* (Seoul: Seoul Logos, 1999), 35-37, 62-63.

[34] *Fourth Dimension*, 3rd ed. (Seoul: Seoul Logos, 1996), 108-13; *How Can I Be Healed?* 135-140.

4.1 The Social Outreach Programs of Yoido Church

The YFGC has a very strong social welfare ministry. It includes caring for the elderly, vocational training for underprivileged, financing hundreds of open-heart surgeries for children, outreach to youth and various other forms of welfare ministry.[35] Two particularly impressive social outreach programs are the Elim Welfare Town and the Good People World Family. The former provides vocational and spiritual training for unemployed youth, housing for senior citizens, and care for socially depressed neighborhoods. The latter is concerned with global social outreach to developing countries.

At the same time, however, Cho has not been noted for his advocacy of active sociopolitical participation. For example, during the difficult years of military dictatorship in the sixties through to the early eighties in South Korea, he kept away from all anti-government protests. One observer, Sung-Hoon Myung, however, comments that since 1987 the leadership of Cho's church has begun to pay increasing attention to sociopolitical needs and challenges of Korea.[36] One significant initiative in this direction is the *Kukmin Daily* which represents a serious attempt to influence Korean society through a national newspaper. In sum, Cho's theology is clearly much stronger on social concerns than on sociopolitical involvement.

4.2 The Sociological Dynamics of Pentecostalism

To some observers, the above analysis of Cho appears to confirm the common perception of Pentecostalism as "the haven of the masses," as a socially escapist religion in the midst of injustice and oppression. However, some recent studies have

---

[35] Daniel J. Adams, "The Life and Ministry of Cho Yonggi: A Theological Inquiry," *Chinese Theological Journal* 3:1 (1988), 31-57 (38-39).

[36] Sung-Hoon Myung, "Spiritual Dimensions of Church Growth as Applied in the Yoido Full Gospel Church" (Ph.D. Dissertation, Fuller Theological Seminary, Pasadena, CA, 1990), 258-60.

indicated that such a characterization of Pentecostalism is too simplistic and in need of revision. For example, Donald Dayton, on the basis of an analysis of the Pentecostal history in the North American context, has suggested that one can make a strong case for the power of Pentecostal and charismatic experience as a form of empowering and conscientization that both sustains in the face of oppression and enables resistance and movement toward change—and affects inner transformation that may have long range social significance.[37]

Dayton's study has found support from a number of other scholars. In a recent study on Latin American Pentecostalism, the sociologist, David Martin, has suggested that the evidence shows clearly that Pentecostalism, though existing at the margins of society, can through its inner spiritual dynamics bring about social transformation within that society. He argues that "poor and marginal people could initiate a revision of consciousness amounting to a cultural revolution."[38] Pentecostals may be morally conservative, "but sociologically, they are one of the forward factors of radical social change."[39] In sum, Pentecostalism contains within itself powerful elements for the conscientization of the poor and oppressed.

Radical *Minjung* theologians can rightly claim that they have been in the forefront of advocacy for social transformation, especially during the difficult years of military dictatorship, when theological conservatives have generally ignored the wider sociopolitical issues. But this claim must be balanced by another perspective on South Korean realities. This is found, for example, in Seyoon Kim's comment on *Minjung* theology *vis-a-vis* Cho's Pentecostalism. He pointedly asks:

---

[37] Donald W. Dayton, "Pentecostal/Charismatic Renewal and Social Change: A Western Perspective," *Transformation* 5:4 (1988), 7-13 (13).

[38] David Martin, *Forbidden Revolutions: Pentecostalism in Latin America, Catholicism in Eastern Europe* (London: SPCK, 1996), 66.

[39] Martin, *Forbidden Revolutions*, 60.

> If it is in fact the case that some of the *minjung* draw consolation, encouragement, and strength from the charismatic fellowship of the Choongang Assembly of God Church . . . and in some cases manage to escape from sickness and poverty and to climb up the social ladder with the help of the ministry of the church, what right does . . . any . . . *minjung* theologian have to tell them that they are mistaken or duped and stand in need of the proper guidance of the *minjung* theologians? And if others of the *minjung* find that their faith in Jesus Christ as presented in the classic confessions of the Christian church gives them strength to escape the poverty and oppression—as often happens—what right does a *minjung* theologian have to tell them that they have been duped by a theology of the ruling class and must be taught the doctrine of self-redemption through socio-political struggle?[40]

In light of this, our perception of the sociopolitical significance of Cho's theology would need careful reappraisal. It would be correct to say that Cho needs to develop in his theology a deeper grasp of the sociopolitical implications of the gospel. In this, he shares the same weakness of much of Evangelical and Pentecostal thinking of the twentieth century. At the same time, it could well be that over the long-term, his Pentecostalism may have a far stronger impact on social transformation in Korea than *Minjung* theology. For, apart from the evidences adduced from studies on Pentecostalism above, there are other evidences and arguments which convincingly show that evangelism and pastoral nurture of Christian converts into strong counter-cultural communities are not antithetical, but complementary, to more pro-active approaches to the process of social change.[41]

---

[40]Seyoon Kim, "Is '*Minjung* Theology' a Christian Theology?" *Calvin Theological Journal* 22:2 (1987), 251-74 (262-63); the Yoido Church used to be called the Choongang Assembly of God.

[41]Stephen C. Mott, *Biblical Ethics and Social Change* (New York: Oxford University Press, 1982), 107-208 argues that the "paths to justice" include evangelism, the church living as counter-cultural community, strategic non-cooperation and political action.

4.3 The Treble Blessings Teaching

But before leaving this section we need to look at one more aspect of Cho's teaching, the "treble blessings" that we have in Christ. For Cho, the Christian message is one of hope. He defines this hope in terms of 3 John 2, translated in English as, "I wish above all things that thou mayest prosper and be in health, even as thy soul prospereth."[42] He interprets this to mean that salvation is holistic: it includes the salvation of the soul, the healing of the body and material blessings from God—a "triple salvation." We have already looked at the first two blessings and have suggested that his teachings on these are fully consistent with the Bible. But it is that third aspect of this that have given rise to problems for others because it seems to be no more than a Korean version of the American gospel of prosperity or "health and wealth gospel" preached by those belonging to the Faith movement within North American Pentecostalism.[43]

What does Cho actually teach on material blessings? It would be best to let him speak for himself. He argues that the Bible teaches that God intends it that we through Christ's "poverty might be rich" (2 Cor 8:9). He further states that,

> If we do not receive the "riches" as stated in scripture, we make the poverty of Jesus of no effect. We have an important responsibility: to receive the prosperous life…which He made possible for us by living in poverty. If we live a life of poverty without a special reason, as described earlier, we are insulting Jesus. Here the legitimate reasons could be that we volunteer to become poor by giving all we have to the work of God, or that under a great persecution we become poor to give glory to God. Other than these reasons, if we do not enjoy the prosperity provided for us by Jesus Christ, but we live in poverty, we bring

---

[42]"The Secret behind the World's Biggest Church," 102-103; *Salvation, Health and Prosperity*, 11-12. The scripture quotation here is from KJV.

[43]Cf. B. Barron, "Faith Movement (Word Movement)," *Dictionary of Christianity in America*, eds. Daniel G. Reid, et al. (Downers Grove, IL: IVP, 1990), 426-27.

> shame to the name of Christ who became poor so that we might become rich . . . Make up your mind that you will do your best to prosper, and God will help you. This is the way to glorify Christ scripturally.[44]

Is this then another version of the American prosperity gospel? To answer this, we need to note the following.

First, the historical context of the genesis of Cho's teaching is of crucial importance in understanding his teaching. Unlike middle-class Americans pursuing the "American dream," the people among whom Cho was ministering in the Korea of the 1950s were trying to scrape out a living amidst the chaos of the aftermath of the Korean War. Cho's struggle was that he appeared to be preaching merely a God of future salvation in heaven while his congregation lived in destitution and grinding poverty in the present! And in his despair he prayed: "Where is the God of the present? With what can I give hope and new life to these people who are in despair, starved and poorly clothed?"[45] It was out of this struggle that his teaching emerged. Cho has insisted that his is a contextual theology arising out of widespread poverty and gross human need.[46]

Elsewhere he has tried to clarify his teaching on the issue. In an interview with the magazine, *Charisma & Christian Life*, in 1988 he argues that American Charismatics tend to equate prosperity with money, which is undoubtedly problematic. They therefore need to redefine their understanding. He argues that,

> . . . in the Orient we have a different idea. Prosperity means successfully fulfilling the goal. . . . One must not connect prosperity with financial success, because in many cases, having prosperity means losing all. For example, in order to have a

---

[44]*Salvation, Health and Prosperity*, 68.

[45]*Salvation, Health and Prosperity*, 11.

[46]In small group discussion on 27 Aug 2002, Seoul, at which the author was present.

> prosperous church, I gave up my time, my home, my salary—everything . . . yet I prospered tremendously in church growth.[47]

Second, prosperity is equated with success in fulfilling the goal that God sets before us in whatever sphere of life—whether spiritual, material, academic, social and political—and whereby God is glorified. His teaching on material blessing must, therefore, be understood within this wider definition of prosperity with which he works.

Third, insofar as his teaching touches on material blessings, even there he lays down some very clear safeguards. He insists that motivation must be right, and that it is God that we seek and not "money, fame and prestige." As a corollary of putting God first, tithing must be practiced.[48] Elsewhere, he argues that those who have received the threefold blessings of Christ should live in true Christian freedom—in particular, freedom from covetousness.[49] Finally, given the changed circumstances of South Korea today from that of the 1950s and 60s, he has suggested that we should now place greater emphasis on sacrifice than blessing.[50]

What then are we to make of his teaching on "treble blessings"? Given the above clarifications, it would be unfair to accuse Cho of teaching a Korean version of the American gospel of prosperity. Indeed he has suggested that his own teaching is a "gospel of need," in contrast to the gospel of prosperity which is a "gospel of greed."[51] However, Cho may have unwisely opened himself to that accusation by basing his teaching on 3 John 2, which is the same verse that American prosperity gospel teachers use. Quite apart from the questionable exegesis of the verse used by these teachers, it may be wiser if Cho builds his argument on

---

[47]Stephen Strang, "Cho's Problems with Prosperity," *Charisma & Christian Life* (March, 1988), 69-71 (69). Cf. also his definition of success in *Salvation, Health and Prosperity*, 97-98.

[48]*Solving Life's Problems* (Seoul: Seoul Logos, 1980), 30-41.

[49]*Salvation, Health and Prosperity*, 158-59.

[50]In small group discussion; see footnote 46.

[51]In small group discussion; see footnote 46.

other clear teachings in the Bible on God's desire to bless his people. He would then be able to place his teaching on a sounder exegetical basis with the necessary refinements, and at the same time, not allow it to be associated with wrong teaching that he rejects. Perhaps Myung, a Korean scholar who has carefully examined Cho's theology, sums up the matter well. He suggests that there is a danger that Cho's theology is not as strong on sanctification as it could be, and that a much stronger emphasis on sacrifice and self-denial is necessary if it is to avoid ending up as "another typical health and wealth gospel contributing to self-centered dreams."[52]

Yet having stated all these, we must return to our fundamental question: What are the missiological implications of Cho's teaching on material blessings? I believe that it is far more important than previously thought to be. Evangelicals in the main have rightly rejected the American gospel of prosperity as sub-Christian. But not many have developed a robust and sound biblical doctrine of God's desire to bless in its place. After all, the Bible is replete with God's promises on this from the Old Testament teaching on shalom to the New Testament's "Seek first his Kingdom and his righteousness, and all these things shall be given to you as well" (Mat 6:33, NIV). And if the God of the Christian faith cannot be called upon to "Give us this day our daily bread," then surely he does not deserve our worship and adoration at all.

If this is right, then the missiological implications are immense. As we have argued, the gospel is not merely about spiritual salvation when we die. It is also about the coming of the kingdom of God and the lordship of Christ over all of life. One of the most pressing needs facing us is that of hunger and poverty in the world today. Economic globalization has further aggravated these problems. This is true in much of Asia and Africa today. Further, missiologists have often noted that there is still today a large overlap between the areas of the world where people are poor materially and where the gospel has not yet been preached.

---

[52]Myung, "Spiritual Dimensions of Church Growth," 258.

Even in Africa, where large parts have become at least nominally Christian, poverty still reigns. For example, the latest UNCTAD report shows that of the twenty-four poorest countries in Africa, almost nine out of ten people live on less than $2 per day (on a purchasing power parity basis) and two-thirds survive on less than $1 per day.[53] Within the context of such widespread poverty, what gospel or good news does the church have for the suffering world? Many economists have given up on Africa as a basket case. But the Christian missionary, armed with the gospel and the good news of God's intention to bless, does not need to follow suit! For the gospel remains "the power of God unto salvation to all who believe" (Rom 1:16), even in the material and economic realm.

But to facilitate this process and to make the gospel of God's blessing one that is truly liberating for those living in the bondage of poverty, there is a real urgency to restate it more carefully to prevent it from leading us into false teaching. Part of this task includes endeavoring to bring together all the relevant elements—personal conversion, revival in churches and nations, God's desire to bless, moral and cultural values and economic growth—into an integrated understanding of the relationship between the gospel and sociopolitical transformation. I believe that this constitutes a fundamental missiological and theological challenge to all of us. Properly carried out, this will help the church to release the saving power of the gospel of Christ to bring about a powerful transformation in many situations of extreme poverty in the world today.[54]

---

[53]"Poverty in Africa," *The Economist* (July 13, 2002), 90.

[54]I am not suggesting any simplistic approach to developmental economics here. The Korean church was able to build on Korean cultural values which in many ways helped to bring about the economic miracle that Korea experienced. I am simply saying that there is also a very important place for the spiritual dimension to be taken seriously, not least in its ability to bring about the inculcation of values like hard work, discipline, thrift, supportive family ties, and so forth, all of which contribute towards the "social lift" often observed in periods of revivals in church history. For this task to be done effectively, it will require a most serious effort in Christian social ethical rethinking.

In summary, as we have already noted, in line with much of twentieth century Evangelical theology, Cho's theology needs to develop a stronger grasp of the sociopolitical dimension of the gospel of Christ. At the same time, aspects of his theology have some very important missiological implications with respect to the gospel's power to effect social change.

5. The Cultural Dimension

We come now to the third criterion for a missiological theology: whether it takes culture seriously. Cho's writings do not say a lot in this area, but enough for us to see that he does take it with real seriousness.

First, he consciously seeks to develop Christian traditions which would help Korean converts to remain rooted to their own indigenous culture. In his book, *More Than Numbers*, he writes:

> We evangelical Korean Christians have developed our own traditions. This is very important because it makes it possible for us to be Christian without being less Korean. In the past, missionaries not only brought their religion but also their culture to the countries they evangelized. So it became apparent that the new converts lost much of their natural heritage. I believe that this produced an unnecessary hindrance to the acceptance of the gospel of Jesus Christ, which is for all people.[55]

One cannot get a more explicit statement than that for the purpose of affirming the importance of culture in the development of our Christian teachings and practices.

Secondly, we have earlier noted the same emphasis in his teaching on prosperity. He insists on a distinctively oriental understanding of this, which he argues is different from the western or American.

Thirdly, we see this also in his emphasis on healing which is such an important component of his teaching. Western Evangelical

---

[55] *More than Numbers*, 9.

theology in the last century had little place for healing, except within some Pentecostal and later charismatic circles. The influence of the Enlightenment and the development of modern science prevented many Christians from taking the miraculous seriously. However, it is not just forms of western Pentecostalism and charismatic Christianity that have reemphasized the place of healing in the life of the church. Indigenous churches in the non-western world have always taken it seriously. This is true of the African Independent Churches, the house churches in China, Asian Christian leaders like John Sung of China or Petrus Octavianus of the Indonesian revival, and so forth. Thus, the strong emphasis on healing cannot be attributed merely to the Pentecostal tradition from which Cho comes. It is also a direct response on his part to the felt needs of the Korean people who need to see the reality and power of God.

One interesting point relates to the criticism by some that Cho is guilty of "shamanizing" Christianity. This accusation focuses especially on his healing and exorcism ministries.[56] I believe the criticism is misplaced. It appears that the proper understanding of Cho on this point is to see his healing and exorcism ministries as illustrative of his efforts to contextualize the gospel in order to address the felt needs of a people. As Cho sees it, he is consciously seeking "to show the miraculous power of God *to those who still believed in shamanism*."[57] One critic states, "The only difference is that a shaman performs his wonders in the name of spirits while Rev. Cho exorcises evil spirits and heals in the name of Jesus."[58] But this only goes to reinforces Cho's defense of his own view, which is that the power that he exercises is not shamanistic power but that of the Holy Spirit. What Cho does is to provide what missiologists call a "functional substitute" in the

---

[56]E.g., Boo-woong Yoo, "Response to Korean Shamanism by the Pentecostal Church," *International Review of Mission* 75/297 (1986), 70-74.

[57]"The Secret behind the World's Biggest Church," 100. Italics are mine.

[58]Yoo, "Response to Korean Shamanism," 74.

context of Korean culture, which demonstrates his seriousness in contextualizing the gospel!

Fourthly, this does not mean that Cho follows Korean culture slavishly. Where the need arises, he is prepared to be counter-cultural as well. This is seen in his acceptance of women leadership in the church. He recognizes clearly that Korean culture "decisively puts women in a subordinate role throughout society."[59] Yet when convinced of the theological rightness and practical wisdom of the decision, he was prepared to risk misunderstanding from his fellow male leaders in the church to seek their agreement to implement it.

All these do not prove that Cho's work has always been carried out in the most culturally sensitive manner. It may be that his church, like much of the Asian church, needs to be much more intentional about indigenizing the gospel in Asian soil. But it does point clearly to the fact that he takes culture seriously, and that insofar as it is possible, he does not wish to give any cultural offense that may hinder the mission of Christ in the world today. And that is something that all involved in mission should affirm.

6. Conclusion

In the above we have attempted to look at aspects of Cho's theology from a missiological perspective, and note that there are some very important lessons that we can learn if we are serious about the work of Christian mission in the world today. This is particular true of his concern for evangelism and cross-cultural missions, the use of cell groups for pastoral nurture, the healing and deliverance ministry, the social concerns of the YFGC in caring for human welfare, the sociological dynamics of Pentecostalism, his teaching that God is concerned to bless us materially, and his stated concern to take culture seriously so that one can be Christian without losing one's Korean identity.

Given the significance of the various aspects of his thought, the challenge would be for him and his colleagues to refine them

---

[59]Cho & Hostetler, *Successful Home Cell Groups*, 24.

further in order to make them truly missiologically empowering for the church. In conclusion, I will restrict myself to one example to illustrate what is meant. Cho's theology of blessing was first formulated in the 1950s when most Koreans were poor and destitute. Given the fact that the socioeconomic situation has changed completely, with Korea soon to join the ranks of the developed nations, the theology of blessing needs much more careful restating today. Otherwise, it will end up essentially encouraging Korean Christians to go after the American dream, or its Korean equivalent, and end up leading covetous and materialistic lives where God is increasingly pushed aside. When that happens—and there are clear signs that it has begun in various parts of the Korean church[60]—it will only lead the church into serious spiritual decline.

[60]Cf. Young-gi Hong, "Nominalism in Korean Protestantism," *Transformation* 16:4 (1999), 135-41.

INDEX

THE PNEUMATOLOGY OF PAUL YONGGI CHO[1]

Simon K.H. Chan

Going through the many writings of Yonggi Cho, one is left without a doubt that the doctrine of the Holy Spirit plays a very vital role in his understanding of the Christian life and mission. Cho refers repeatedly to the Holy Spirit throughout his writings.[2] But his theology of the Spirit (in the sense of reflecting on the Spirit and expressing these reflections in a coherent framework) is largely implicit rather than explicit. My aim in this paper is to highlight some broad features of his teachings concerning the Holy Spirit, make explicit certain pneumatological motifs and offer a critique.

1. A Classical Pentecostal Pneumatology

Cho's teaching on the Holy Spirit adheres very closely to the classical Pentecostal position. He believes in speaking in tongues as the "initial evidence" of baptism in the Holy Spirit and that it is an experience distinct from the new birth.[3] He sees the Christian life as progressing towards a deeper faith as one is filled with the

---

[1]An earlier version of the paper was presented at the Second Youngsan International Theological Symposium, Hansei University, Goonpo, Korea in May 2003.

[2]For a book that brings all these teachings together see *The Holy Spirit, My Senior Partner* (Altamonte Springs: Creation House, 1989).

[3]The Holy Spirit, My Senior Partner, 97-117.

Holy Spirit. Through the Spirit one receives "revelational knowledge" in contrast to "sense knowledge." Through earnest prayer one receives the gifts of the Spirit, but one needs also to have constant filling with the Spirit in order to mature in faith.[4] For Cho, this traditional Pentecostal understanding is not just a "tenet of faith" but a reality that he takes seriously. It is translated into an on-going practice, what he calls revival 365 days a year.[5] It finds expression within a key institution in Cho's church: the cell group system. Cho insists that every cell leader must be "filled with the Spirit" in this unambiguous, traditional Pentecostal way.[6]

> Dependence upon the Holy Spirit is essential if a person is to lead the members of his cell group. In our church that means the leader must be baptized in the Holy Spirit, with the evidence of speaking in tongues. Then we are assured of a person who can lead others to Christ and who can pray powerfully for the people's needs. This is particularly essential in praying for physical and spiritual healing.[7]

I would describe Cho as an "unreconstructed" Pentecostal as far as his doctrine of Spirit-baptism is concerned. I intend the term to be taken as a compliment, for I regard the traditional understanding as a strength rather than a liability. Much of Cho's teachings are set within a basic framework of Evangelical and Pentecostal orthodoxy. This gives many of his teachings a solid grounding in the larger Christian tradition.

Cho may be unwittingly traditional in other ways too. His Bible Study for New Christians shows that much of what Cho considers basic to new Christians is also widely shared by other Christians. I find it interesting that included in his "basics" for new Christians are the Lord's Prayer and the Ten Commandments, two

---

[4]*Born to Be Blessed* (Seoul: Seoul Logos, 1993), 12-14.

[5]*Successful Home Cell Groups* (Seoul: Seoul Logos, 1997), v-vi.

[6]Successful Home Cell Groups, 111, 112.

[7]Successful Home Cell Groups, 112.

of the three components found in traditional catechisms.[8] The Lord's Prayer occupies a special place in Cho's teaching on prayer.[9]

Some of Cho's teachings regarding the Spirit which have come under attack by some Evangelicals may have much deeper roots in the Christian tradition than his Evangelical critics realize. E.g., the controversial idea of "visualization" seems to have its counterpart in the medieval idea that what we see intensely would be impressed upon the soul and transform it. In Ignatius Loyola's meditations, extensive images of gospel scenes are vividly visualized. Using "composition of place" as Ignatius calls it, one places oneself in the very scene that one creates imaginatively and in the process one becomes deeply affected by it. The final outcome is a transformed soul who is now in a position to be led by God's Spirit to make a major decision. Similar techniques are also found in Puritan devotional manuals in the seventeenth century. The Puritan Isaac Ambrose describes what happens when the Christian "looks" intensely at Jesus:

> God receives none to contemplate his face but he transforms them into his own likeness by the irradiation of his light, and Christ hath none that dive into these depths of his glorious and blessed incarnation but they carry along with them sweet impressions of an abiding and transforming nature.[10]

Cho's understanding of the spiritual progress of the Christian owes much to earlier holiness and Keswick teachings. This is seen especially in his exposition of the first of the Three-Fold Blessing: the prosperity of the soul. Human nature is understood in

[8]E.g., *The Catechism of the Catholic Church* (Mahwah, NJ: Paulist, 1994). n.p.

[9] See his *Praying with Jesus* (Altamonte Springs, FL: Creation House, 1987), n.p.

[10]Looking Unto Jesus (1658), 350.

trichotomous terms reminiscent of Watchman Nee.[11] Advance in the Christian life involves the progressive conquest of the "soulish" life by the Holy Spirit through hardships, trials, etc. until the Christian is totally surrendered to the Lord.[12] Cho also insists that being baptized in the Holy Spirit is not enough; believers must also be led by the Spirit continually and have "continuous fellowship with God as the Holy Spirit leads them."[13] The fivefold gospel which includes Spirit-baptism must be applied to daily living as the threefold blessing which includes continuous filling with the Spirit.[14]

There are a number of other promising ideas that are left largely undeveloped. For example, Cho recognizes not only different "kinds" of prayer but degrees of prayer, which reflect older strands of Christian spirituality. "Unison prayer together with others is more beneficial to young believers because one can hear what he is praying for and at the same time the sound of others praying together encourage him to pray fervently or learn to pray fervently at the same time." "However, only those who have had disciplined prayer lives for years are able to pray quietly or silently."[15] Another example: when Cho refers to the Holy Spirit as the one who spans the ages by making present the great events of the past,[16] there is much potential for such an understanding to be further developed, as can be seen in the pneumatology of

---

[11]As seen in Nee's popular study of theological anthropology, *The Spiritual Man*, vols. 12-14 of *The Collected Works of Watchman Nee* (Anaheim, CA: Living Stream Ministry, 1992).

[12]*Salvation, Healing and Prosperity: Our Threefold Blessings in Christ* (Altamonte Spring: Creation House, 1987), ch. 2. The book was first published in Korean in 1977.

[13]Born to Be Blessed, 119-120.

[14]*Born to Be Blessed*, 119-120, cf. 123-24.

[15]Born to be Blessed, 19.

[16]*Praying with Jesus* (Altamonte Springs, FL: Creation House, 1987), 18.

Eastern Orthodoxy.[17] I would like to suggest that if Cho's pneumatology were to become an adequate basis for his other teachings and practices, these pneumatological motifs need to be systematically elaborated.

2. A Practical Pneumatology

I suppose Cho's response would be that of a practitioner rather than a theologian of the Pentecostal faith. He is more concerned with implementing what he believes to be true rather than reflecting on the truth and drawing out its larger ramifications. This brings me to my next point. I would characterize Cho's pneumatology as a practical pneumatology.

I have just noted above that Cho insists that all his cell group leaders be filled with the Spirit in the classical Pentecostal sense. Quite clearly Cho's pneumatology suffuses his organization and cell group system. The nature of the cell meetings includes "ministry to one another" and "making it clear to everyone that the Holy Spirit works in those meetings just as He does in the church services."[18] Pneumatology is a practical, working reality and not just a doctrine.

This practical pneumatology is translated into a way of life that includes extraordinary and unpredictable features. Cho's books are peppered with extraordinary but real-life stories. For example, when Cho affirms that the Spirit gives power and boldness, righteousness, peace and joy, all these are not just a matter of talk but are actual experiences. There is always a real-life story to confirm the teaching. The stories are not just of ordinary boldness, righteousness, etc., but boldness of an extraordinary kind.

---

[17]On this, see my article "Mother Church: Toward a Pentecostal Ecclesiology," *Pneuma: Journal of the Society for Pentecostal Studies* 22:2 (Fall 2000), 177-208.

[18]Successful Home Cell Groups, 114.

The story of Pastor Kim, an associate of Cho, who fell asleep in the snow and was kept warm through the night by a mountain tiger sleeping on top of him, confirms not any ordinary boldness but a distinctively Pentecostal boldness which can only be attributed to the work of the Holy Spirit.

The moving story of a politician, Miss Park, who made her peace with God after being caught by a North Korean soldier, and her prayer for her executioner as she was led out to be shot that brought the soldier to his knees—this is not about ordinary peace and joy. It is a peace "that passeth all understanding" and a joy that borders on recklessness and defiance, something that is wrought unmistakably by the Spirit of God in the human heart.[19]

I am inclined to think that the attractiveness of Cho's pneumatology owes much to his demonstrating that larger-than-life experiences can happen to any Christian through the powerful working of the Holy Spirit. The very size of his church itself is one such evidence.

3. The Person of the Spirit in the Trinity

When practical pneumatology plays such a critical role in so many aspects of the Christian life and ministry, it is understandable that the Holy Spirit should become the subject of Cho's special attention. This is one of the great strengths of Cho's pneumatology, especially when the person of the Holy Spirit is understood within the framework of a classical Pentecostal theology, as noted above.

But there is one aspect of his emphasis with which one must take issue. Cho considers the Holy Spirit as the "senior partner" in God's business of winning souls.[20] But if the Holy Spirit is to function effectively as the senior partner, the Christian must learn to cultivate intimate "fellowship with the Spirit." By this he means

---

[19]A Call in the Night, 92-98.

[20]*The Fourth Dimension*, vol. 2, *More Secrets for a Successful Faith Life* (Plainfield, NJ: Bridge Publishing, 1983), 11-14.

that Christians need to have an intimate relationship with the person of the Spirit.

> He's a person—but a person who lives inside me. To live with a person means to have fellowship with that person. It means recognition of each other. It means intimate fellowship and communication.[21]

Cho seems to think that fellowship with the Holy Spirit is much like fellowship with the Father and with the Son (1 John 1:3).[22]

> . . . when we read the Bible, it not only commands us to have fellowship with the Father and with His Son, Jesus Christ, it also commands us to have fellowship, or *communion* with the Holy Spirit (2 Cor 13:14).[23]

Thus he would encourage direct address to the Spirit just as one would address the Father and the Son:

> Nowadays I always force myself to recognize the Holy Spirit, to welcome the Holy Spirit and to worship the Holy Spirit, because He is a person. . . . Dear Holy Spirit, I welcome you, I recognize you and I love you. I depend upon you. . . . Dear Holy Spirit, now I'm starting. Let's go. Supply all the knowledge and wisdom and discernment, and I'm going to give it out to the people. . . . Dear Holy Spirit, we did a wonderful job together, didn't we? Praise God![24]

---

[21]Successful Home Cell Groups, 120.

[22]Successful Home Cell Groups, Ibid., 121.

[23]*Successful Home Cell Groups*, Ibid., 124. See also *The Holy Spirit, My Senior Partner* (Altamonte Springs: Creation House, 1989), 17-19.

[24] *Successful Home Cell Groups*, Ibid., 124. Cf. *The Fourth Dimension*, vol. 2, 9-11. Here, Cho speaks of "fellowship with the Holy Spirit" as a new thing God revealed to him in 1964.

Cho seems to think of the triune God as simply three coordinates with whom we sustain an intimate relationship. Just as we pray to the Father and to the Son, we should also pray to the Spirit. But is this the way Scripture understands the place of the Spirit in the Christian life?

There is no question that the scripture links *koinonia* specifically to the ministry of the Holy Spirit, but I have serious difficulty seeing the link in the way Cho does. It is almost certain that the Pauline benediction in 2 Cor 13:14 does not speak of communion with the Spirit but communion of the Spirit. Whether we take "of the Spirit" as a subjective genetive or objective genetive, the phrase cannot possibly be construed in the way Cho construes it. Most commentators favor the subjective genetive; that is to say, it is the Spirit who creates the fellowship of believers. The subjective genetive would be consistent with the two preceding phrases: grace of Jesus Christ and love of God.[25] If it is understood as an objective genetive it has the meaning of the Holy Spirit as "the object in which Christian people share."[26] In brief, the Holy Spirit is not the one with whom we fellowship, but the one who creates or makes possible the fellowship of believers (subjective genetive) or the one in whom all believers have fellowship (objective genetive). The objective genetive is the obvious construction of 1 Cor 12:13: "we were all made to drink of one Spirit" (NASV). The idea here is that all Christians share the same Spirit. They are in fellowship with one another because of the one Spirit they all receive.[27] In either case, the relevant texts say nothing about our personal fellowship with the Holy Spirit. In fact, there is not one instance in the New Testament where believers are said to have direct fellowship with the Spirit.

---

[25] See commentaries by F. F. Bruce, *Second Corinthians*, New Century Bible Commentary (Grand Rapids: Eerdmans, 1971), in loc.; Jan Lambrecht, SJ, *Second Corinthians* (Collegeville, MN: Liturgical, 1999), in loc.

[26] Colin Kruse, *Second Corinthians*, Tyndale series (Leicester: IVP, 1971), 224.

[27] See Gordon Fee, *First Corinthians*, New International Commentary of the New Testament (Grand Rapids: Eerdmans, 1987) in loc.

Certainly we need to recognize the Holy Spirit as a person, but to do so is to recognize his distinctive role in the triune relationship. While the scripture is clear about directly addressing our prayer to God the Father and to the Son, there is no instance of prayer directed to the Spirit. Historically, there are few instances of prayer to the Spirit.[28] This is because in the triune relationship, the Holy Spirit, as Yves Congar puts it in his magisterial study on the Holy Spirit, is always the one who points us to the Father and the Son. The Spirit is the person "without a personal face."[29] The Spirit's role as the third person in the divine economy of salvation is not to draw attention to himself, but to point us to the Son. The Spirit is glorified precisely when Christ is glorified.

Again, when Cho refers to speaking in tongues as speaking the language of the Spirit, he sees it as the language of personal communication and intimacy with the Holy Spirit.[30] But is this the way the scripture understands glossolalia? Glossolalia, as I have argued in my book *Pentecostal Theology and the Christian Spiritual Tradition*, is indeed the language of intimacy. But intimacy with whom? The intimacy is not with the Spirit, but with God the Father to whom we speak by the indwelling Spirit "with unutterable groanings" (cf. Rom 8:26). It is the Spirit who creates the intimacy between the believers and God the Father. The Spirit, as Augustine tells us, is the bond of love between the Father and the Son. He is also the bond of love between the children of God and their heavenly Father. The Spirit is the one who dwells within us to enable us to address God as "Abba, Father" (Rom 8:15).

---

[28]The classic study of Josef A. Jungmann, *The Place of Christ in Liturgical Prayers*, trans. A. Peeler (London: Geoffrey Chapman, 1965, 1989), 221 shows that prayers to the Holy Spirit "attained significance only in Armenia (221). They are rarely found elsewhere, such as in the Byzantine liturgies from the seventeenth century (84). They are found most frequently in prayers addressed to the Holy Trinity, and are motivated by the concern to protect the equality of the Spirit with the Father and the Son (220-21).

[29]Ives Congar, *I Believe in the Holy Spirit*, III (New York: Seabury, 1983), 5.

[30]Successful Home Cell Groups, 132.

Unless we recognize the distinctive role of the Spirit in relation to the Father and the Son as revealed in the scripture, there is a danger of giving to the Spirit an independent status and to divorce the work of the Spirit from the Father and the Son. The result, as the history of the church has shown, can be an unbridled enthusiasm that places a special premium on extraordinary phenomenon and supernaturalistic manifestations. It is a short way to making special manifestations of the Spirit an independent object of interest. I am not saying that Cho is guilty of this. On other occasions Cho's understanding of the Spirit comes closer to the truth, as when he rightly understands the Spirit as the one who brings to us the love of God and the grace of Jesus Christ, or when he says, "God wants us to have intimate fellowship with Him through the Holy Spirit."[31] Unfortunately such understandings are not developed in his discussion on the Holy Spirit.

The problem of Cho's pneumatology is that it suffers from a lack of precision, with the result that the personal work of the Spirit is misconstrued. Cho's point seems to be that because the Holy Spirit is a person, therefore, we ought to have the same relationship with him as we have with the Father and the Son.[32] This is to misunderstand the trinitarian relationship as revealed in the scripture. The problem with Cho's construal of the Spirit will become apparent when we examine his teaching of the "threefold blessing." A more nuanced pneumatology could have been derived by attending more closely to the language of the scripture and to the historic teachings of the Church.

4. The Fivefold Gospel and Threefold Blessing

The fivefold gospel with a threefold blessing is a central motif in Cho's preaching, but it is also the most controversial. Its centrality can be seen in the fact that Cho regards the threefold blessing as an intrinsic part of the "full gospel." As he puts it, the

---

[31]Successful Home Cell Groups, 132.

[32]*Born to Be Blessed* (Seoul: Seoul Logos, 1993), 14.

"truths of these threefold blessings of Christ are the foundation stones which formed my faith" and "the philosophical basis for my preaching of the gospel."[33] Cho finds support for the threefold blessing in the Abrahamic promise. God's blessing of Abraham and the giving of that blessing to the gentiles is taken to mean that all Christians should receive the threefold blessing of salvation, health and wealth. But the *locus classicus* is 3 John 2: "Beloved, I wish above all things that thou mayest prosper and be in health, even as thy soul prospereth" (KJV).

I think Cho is basically correct to see God's blessing as not purely "spiritual." There is much dualism underlying a "spiritualized" conception of the Christian life in much of Christian history that needs to be corrected. Salvation in the fullest sense includes the renewal of the physical realm. I think Cho is also right to see in the redemptive work of Jesus the reversal of the curse of original sin, and that God's original blessing to Adam was not purely "spiritual" but had very much an earthly dimension. The relationship between the threefold blessing and the "full gospel" is well summed up in his book *A Bible Study for New Christians*:

> There are seven aspects of Full Gospel Faith. The doctrinal conversion of the message of the seven aspects of Full Gospel faith is now called the Fivefold Gospel. The applicational conversion is called the Threefold Blessing. As Christians, we can confirm through the Threefold Blessing the fruit of Christ's redemption, the Fivefold Gospel.[34]

I think Cho is again right in seeing pneumatology as undergirding the threefold blessing.[35] Cho believes that the Holy Spirit gives to believers "dreams and visions" to enable them to experience the blessing of Abraham in the threefold manner.

---

[33]Salvation, Health and Prosperity, 5.

[34]*A Bible Study for New Christians* (Seoul: Seoul Logos, 1997), 47.

[35]In the second volume of *The Fourth Dimension*, Cho begins his discussion with a chapter on the Holy Spirit, thus showing the centrality of pneumatology in the development of the threefold blessing.

> Visions and glorious dreams are a part of our Christian walk. The Holy Spirit places them in our hearts to encourage us in our faith. All of a man's activity is unfolded through his dreams. . . . Yes, the fundamental power to overcome hardships comes from having a dream in the heart. . . . You can be strong when you have a dream for a better tomorrow.... My prayer...is that you will have more abundantly according to the three-fold blessings of salvation and the five-fold message of the gospel.[36]

The way by which the Spirit brings forth the threefold blessing is more fully elaborated in *The Fourth Dimension*. Cho believes that there is a spiritual realm, the "fourth dimension," that controls the physical, three-dimensional world. It is a realm in which three distinct spirits can be identified: the Holy Spirit, the devil and the human spirit.[37]

> The spirit is the fourth dimension. Every human being is a spiritual being as well as a physical being. They have the fourth dimension as well as the third dimension in their hearts. . . . So men, by exploring their spiritual sphere of the fourth dimension through the development of concentrated visions and dreams in their imaginations, can brood over and incubate the third dimension, influencing and changing it.[38]

But this ability to control the physical through the spiritual dimension can be done either through the evil spirit or the Holy Spirit. Cho believes that it is the former that accounts for the miracles in non-Christian religions and philosophies.[39] We, the Christians, however, "can link our spirit's fourth dimension to the fourth dimension of the Holy Father—the Creator of the universe—we can have all the more dominion over

---

[36]Born to Be Blessed, 125-26.

[37]The Fourth Dimension: The Key to Putting Your Faith to Work for a Successful Life (Plainfield, NJ: Logos, 1979).

[38]Fourth Dimension, 39-40.

[39]Fourth Dimension, 40.

circumstances."[40] The Holy Spirit does this by giving to us dreams and visions, and through "visualizing" them we could "incubate our future" and "hatch the results."[41] Cho is quick to point out that this is not a simple process, but requires us to speak the *rhema*-word which "releases Christ."[42] *Rhema* is a word from God: "a specific word to a specific person in a specific situation."[43] *Rhema* comes from "waiting upon the Lord."[44] Cho goes to great lengths to specify the conditions under which God's *rhema* is received: the will needs to be surrendered to God; desires must be sanctified and "screened" by the written word of God; one must wait for God's signal to move and be spiritually sensitive to God's timing.[45] One detects a robust asceticism which is characteristic of many traditional forms of spirituality. This is another commendable feature of Cho's teaching that is often forgotten by many modern charismatics looking for quick success in ministry.

Cho's threefold blessing—more precisely, the health and wealth components of it—is perhaps the least traditional aspect of an otherwise very traditional Pentecostal orthodoxy. One can understand why it has received considerable attention from both critics as well as sympathizers. The latter would often point out that Cho's prosperity teaching should be understood in the context of poverty in Korea rather than in terms of the North American context where it has tended to be wedded to a consumerist culture.[46] But it could be argued that if Cho's teaching on the

---

[40]Fourth Dimension, 41.

[41]Fourth Dimension, 44

[42]Fourth Dimension, 81.

[43]Fourth Dimension, 91.

[44]Fourth Dimension, 97-100.

[45]Fourth Dimension, 106-113.

[46]Papers presented in the first Youngsan International Theological Symposium in Hansei University, Goonpo, Korea in Sept 2002, under the theme, "Dr. Yonggi Cho's Theology: A Theological Paradigm for the 21st Century." See especially the articles by Allan Anderson (34-35) and Hwa Yung (98-100). The revised versions of these studies are now published in this issue of the journal.

subject is contextual, so also is Kenneth Hagin's. What makes the contextualization of Cho's message right and the other wrong? What are the criteria by which we justify Cho's teaching on prosperity and question Kenneth Hagin's? Does the situation of poverty alone justify such a teaching? Are we to assume that there are no other options? These questions highlight the need for criteria other than sociological ones if Cho's threefold blessing is to be properly evaluated.

If we look into the history of the church we will see that the issue of poverty was also very real. The kind of prosperity that we know of today was quite unknown in the ancient world and for much of human history. Why is it that the church in the past did not come up with the "prosperity" answer that seems to come so naturally to a number of modern Christians? We cannot rule out the fact that it is only in the modern world of mass production and distribution of goods that the prosperity teaching as it is understood today is made plausible. In other words, it is essentially a modern response to a modern situation and would not have been possible in the past. I am not saying that just because it is modern it is wrong; all I am saying is that we need at least to consider the wisdom of the ancient church and recognize other possible responses. One option in the past was the voluntary acceptance of poverty as a way of life. It is of interest to note that the acceptance of poverty was taught precisely in the context of mass poverty, whereas today, it is offered (quite rightly) as an antidote to a consumerist culture.[47]

Another possible response has come from the Calvinist doctrine of vocation. According to Calvin, every person is given a calling by God and one must faithfully exercise oneself in his or her calling.[48] Calvin makes no distinction between what we now call "full time" calling into the ministry and "secular" vocation. He recognizes the difference of callings, but insists that one is as much a divine calling as the other. There is no bifurcation of life

---

[47]E.g., Richard Foster, *The Freedom of Simplicity* (London: SPCK, 1981).

[48]Institutes of the Christian Religion 3.10.6.

into "sacred" and "secular." It is this concept of calling that produced in the subsequent century what Max Weber calls the puritan work ethic which over time generated wealth.[49] But it must also be noted that the focus of the doctrine of vocation is not on wealth but on the need to be faithful to the divine calling. The fact that in time one becomes wealthy as a result of being diligent in the exercise of one's calling is quite incidental. "Blessing" is never the focus of attention; it is only a by-product. Cho's teaching, however, sometimes gives the impression of a fixation on "blessings" especially when blessings are seen as part and parcel of the "full gospel." The problem is not the threefold blessing per se, as noted earlier, but the way it is understood in relation to the doctrine of the Spirit.

In other words, besides learning from history, the threefold blessing needs to be evaluated according to theological criteria, or more specifically, the pneumatological criterion. Theologically, the real problem with the threefold blessing is that it is set within an inadequate conception of salvation-history. This misconception of salvation-history is in turn due to a failure to understand the proper role of the Holy Spirit in the economy of salvation. What is needed is a more nuanced doctrine of the Spirit that steers between the extremes of an under-realized and an over-realized eschatology. In the Scripture, the Spirit is the "foretaste" of the new creation. What we have now is a "downpayment" not the fullness of the reality. We need to maintain the tension between the "already" and "not yet" if we are to maintain the threefold blessing biblically and with integrity.[50] In fact, this tension is implicit in the fivefold gospel. The fourth component of the fivefold gospel (namely "blessing") must be seen in relation to the fifth component: the return of Christ and the fullness of the new creation. The presence of the Spirit now, is a reminder of the

---

[49]Max Weber, *The Protestant Ethic and the Spirit of Capitalism*, trans. Talcott Partsons (New York: Charles Scribner's, 1958), especially 98-128.

[50]Cho acknowledges the present and future aspects of the kingdom of God, but in practice the accent falls almost exclusively on the present. See *More Than Numbers* (Waco, TX: Word, 1984), 77-80.

absent Christ.[51] The basic mistake of Cho's theology of the threefold blessing is that he sees it as confirming the fivefold gospel. What should be said is that the threefold blessing partially confirms the fivefold gospel. They are a foretaste of a reality that will only be fully realized at the second coming of Christ. This is what it means when the scripture refers to the Spirit as a "pledge" or "deposit" that guarantees the full inheritance which is still future (2 Cor 1:22; 5:5; Eph 1:14). The fivefold gospel, therefore, cannot be simply resolved into the threefold blessing without distinguishing between present and future fulfillments. There is a dimension of the gospel, namely, the return of Christ and the full redemption of the body that lies in the future. The physical dimension of the divine blessing in this present age is given provisionally. If the provisional nature of divine blessing is recognized it would make a difference to the way it is applied. Take, for instance, the matter of prosperity. Although Cho acknowledges that there are "special reasons" for poverty, including the legitimacy of voluntary poverty, these are only given passing mention. Cho seems to think that if there is legitimate poverty in the Christian life, it is meant either to be temporary in order to test one's faith or for a very small number of people who are given an exceptional calling, such as the Apostle Paul.[52] For all practical purposes, the positive reality is the only reality that matters; the negative reality is banished to the fringe of the Christian life, applicable only to a few exceptional cases. The "not yet" is virtually swallowed up by the "already." This is not a faithful representation of biblical eschatology.

The failure to take biblical eschatology seriously is seen again in the way Cho answers the question: why are not all healed? The reasons Cho gives are: 1) People do not wait on the Lord for the *rhema* to be given; 2) They are not right with God; 3) They must wait for God's time; and 4) Sometimes God does not deliver us in

---

[51]For a fuller account of this, see Douglas Farrow, Ascension and Ecclesia: On the Significance of the Doctrine of the Ascension for Ecclesiology and Christian Cosmology (Edinburgh: T. & T. Clark, 1999).

[52]See Salvation, Health and Prosperity, 55-56, 68.

order to accomplish a greater good, such as the salvation of others.[53] Nowhere does Cho anticipate the possibility that God's *rhema*—his specific word in a specific situation—to a sick person may be: "Son/daughter, I am going to take you home in this illness." (This was the case with Hezekiah's illness in Isaiah 38.) The whole emphasis is on "thinking positively, thinking in terms of miracles and developing an orientation to success" as the conditions for receiving a *rhema*-word from God.[54] How does such an emphasis square with the acknowledgment that healing is according to God's sovereign will?[55] Does God's *rhema* have no room for any results other than positive ones? While Cho in theory allows for God's *rhema* to be decisive, in reality it is our own positive thinking that determines how God's *rhema* will come to us. Properly understood, the *rhema* teaching could become a powerful means of opening up the Christian to a life described by Joyce Hugget as "listening to God" in life's specific situations.[56] This is how we can expect relationship with the personal, triune God to be; it is not just a matter of going by general principles and rules. The problem is not with Cho's teaching on *rhema* as such, but *rhema* wedded to an over-realized eschatology.

Another feature of the threefold blessing is that it tends to be applied selectively. For example, the environmental blessing that offsets the environmental curse is understood exclusively in social and psychological terms; the ecological dimension is conspicuously missing. Speaking of the removal of the environmental curse he says, "we are removed from the curse of poverty; we are made rich."[57] In place of the "thorns of hatred, anxiety, unrest, fear, and failure . . . our hearts will overflow with

---

[53]Fourth Dimension, 100-104.

[54]Fourth Dimension, 151.

[55]Fourth Dimension, 101.

[56]Joyce Hugget, *Listening to God* (London: Hodder and Stoughton, 1986), 28-31. A similar idea can be found in the seventeenth century spiritual writer Jean-Pierre de Caussade, *The Sacrament of the Present Moment*, trans. Kitty Muggerridge (New York: HarperCollins, 1989).

[57]Bible Study, 63.

the ever flowing river of peace."[58] This is clearly a selective understanding of environmental blessing. In Genesis the curse clearly covered the physical environment. Obviously, real thorns and thistles are not yet removed from the earth, although in recent years some "Third Wavers" are claiming that this is happening in certain parts of Latin America: the healing of the land is alleged to be taking place. But even if there is real healing of the physical earth as there is real healing of the physical body, such healings are at best "foretastes."

Much damage has been done when "divine healing" ministries highlight only the "already" but choose to remain silent about the "not yet." Furthermore, when physical healing becomes the most prominent feature in the divine healing ministry, it will only raise false expectations and unresolved tensions. Pastorally, how are we to help people who come expecting healing but are not physically healed? Is there no place for a *rhema* from the Lord like Isaiah's word to Hezekiah: "This is what the Lord says: Put your house in order, because you are going to die; you will not recover"? It is of interest to note that Hezekiah miraculously recovered after he prayed. But the consequences were grave. He became proud and callous (Isa 39, see especially v. 8) and during that fifteen years of his extended life he sired Manasseh, one of the most wicked kings of Judah. When the starting-point of one's theology is an over-realized eschatology, the question why all are not healed becomes an intractable problem. It is then rationalized away, sidestepped, soft-pedaled or ignored. Any responsible answer to this question must begin with a pneumatology that takes full cognizance of the provisional nature of the present age—the age of the Spirit between Pentecost and the *Parousia*.

---

[58]Bible Study, 64.

5. An Evaluation

A congregation that continues to grow for the last forty years to become the largest in the world needs some explaining, even if one does not believe that size is proof of soundness. One way to account for the continuing dynamism of the Yoido Full Gospel Church is in terms of Bruce Reed's "oscillation theory."[59] Dynamic religions go through a pattern of oscillating between what Reed calls "intra-dependence" and "extra-dependence." Intra-dependence is a phase in which believers are engaged in institutional religion with a sense of self-assurance, while extra-dependence refers to the sense of dependence on something outside of oneself for sustenance. The oscillation between the two is what he calls "process," while the attempt to give meaning to or "institutionalize" the process is what he calls "movement." There is a "symbiotic" relationship between "process" and "movement:" "Movement gives form to process; process gives life to movement." Movement serves as "container" to what is "contained," that is the "process."[60] What we see in Cho's approach to "church growth" is to keep this oscillation pattern on-going with the emphasis on continuous revival ("revival is 365 days") and a cell-group structure in which this revival finds meaningful expression.

But what sort of pneumatology is implied in Cho's attempt to maintain the 365-day-a-year revival? Surprisingly, it is the classical Pentecostal belief in baptism in the Spirit as a subsequent work of the Spirit distinct from the work of conversion, and evidenced by speaking in tongues, followed by continuous fellowship with the Spirit. The Spirit provides the dynamic for the implementation of his distinctive *ordo salutis* (that is, the fivefold

---

[59]I am indebted to David Reed for the application of the oscillation theory in another context. See his "From Movement to Institution: A Case Study of Charismatic Renewal in the Anglican Church of Canada" (Summary of the Proceedings of the Forty-Fifth Annual Conference of the American Theological Library Association, June 1991), 173-94.

[60]Bruce D. Reed, The Dynamics of Religion: Process and Movement in Christian Churches (London: Darton, Longman and Todd, 1978), 121.

gospel and threefold blessing). Cho faithfully keeps to this position, even though this classical Pentecostal belief is being questioned everywhere.[61] Cho maintains the classical position and insists on its being faithfully implemented especially among his key people: the cell group leaders. Cho's stance has demonstrated the practical viability of the classical Pentecostal belief, even though that belief may not have been adequately expressed in the classical Pentecostal statements of faith or convincingly explained by traditional advocates.[62] I consider the stance Cho takes as the greatest strength of his practical pneumatology.

On the other hand, there is a danger that a practical pneumatology could easily become a pragmatic pneumatology when it is not properly developed under the strict control of the scripture and the scrutiny of the larger church. This danger comes through quite clearly in Cho's many writings. There is a tendency to encourage the cultivation of certain virtues with the aim of gaining practical results. Some of them are:

1) Humility and obedience will bring blessings.[63]
2) When we have "special faith" we are "bound to" experience miracles.[64]

---

[61] While most Protestant Charismatics have rejected the classical Pentecostal distinctive, nonetheless most of them seem to have glossolalia as a central experience—some kind of "initial evidence" experience. See Henry I. Lederle, "Initial Evidence and the Charismatic Movement: An Ecumenical Appraisal," in *Initial Evidence: Historical and Biblical Perspectives on the Pentecostal Doctrine of Spirit Baptism*, ed. Gary G. McGee (Peabody, MA: Hendrickson Press, 1991), 131-41 (132). Studies on Charismatics in different contexts seem to confirm this observation. See *We Believe In the Holy Spirit: A Report by the Doctrine Commission of the General Synod of the Church of England* (London: Church House Publishing, 1993), 26, 27 and Reed, "From Movement to Institution," 187, cf. 191.

[62] In my book *Pentecostal Theology and the Christian Spiritual Tradition* (Sheffield: Sheffield Academic Press, 2000) I have argued that the classical Pentecostal position in fact makes good sense in the light of the larger Christian spiritual tradition.

[63] Born to Be Blessed, 23-33.

3) Perseverance in faith and prayer, speaking affirmatively rather than negatively, forgiveness of each other will bring God's miracles into one's life.[65]
4) We need to wait upon the Lord for his *rhema* in order to have real success.[66]

This is not to deny that humility, perseverance, etc. will bring blessings. After all, the Bible does tell us that God will exalt those who humble themselves. The problem is that unless we consciously make the effort to distinguish between the aim and the result of an action, the two can very easily be confused. We are to be humble, not in order to be blessed, but because this is what we are meant to be: followers of the One who humbled himself and became obedient unto death. Blessing is a result but not what we aim at.[67]

The main weakness in Cho's pneumatology lies precisely at the point where he introduces his own distinctive teachings into the "full gospel," namely, the "blessing" in the fivefold gospel. It is a moot point whether Cho's peculiar teaching on the person Holy Spirit in relation to the Trinity (see III above) is the cause or result of his peculiar teaching of the threefold blessing. What is certain is that when pneumatology hangs loose from the doctrine of the Trinity, the Spirit begins to take a life of his own instead of being seen in relation to the triune economy of salvation.

The Spirit is God's distinctive gift to the church between the ascension and the *parousia*. This is the period of redemptive history characterized by what Farrow calls "the ascension/*parousia* differential" in which the Spirit takes the place of the absent Christ.[68] It is the "interim" between Christ's bodily

---

[64]Born to Be Blessed, 38.

[65]Born to Be Blessed, 41-46.

[66]The Fourth Dimension, 97-100.

[67]A similar tendency can be seen in Benny Hinn: one fasts and prays in order to get "the anointing." See his *The Anointing* (Nashville: Thomas Nelson, 1992).

[68]*Ascension and Ecclesia*, 46. It should be noted that Farrow's concern lies elsewhere: he is more concerned with showing the

departure and bodily return. The chief characteristic of this age is that the Spirit brings the past and the future together in the present; it is an age in which the church, especially in the eucharistic celebration, engages in *anamesis* and *epiclesis*, i.e., in remembering what Christ had done and in anticipating the fuller reality at the *parousia* through the Spirit. In short, in these acts the Spirit holds the "already" of Christ's redemptive work and the "not yet" of Christ's return in a healthy tension in the present age. The problem begins when the tension is resolved in favor of either the "not yet" or the "already." Too much emphasis on the "not yet" produces an under-realized eschatology; the Spirit's work is collapsed into the work of the Son, making it indistinguishable from Christ's. Too much emphasis on the "already" produces an over-realized eschatology. The mission of the Spirit then becomes separated from the mission of the Son.

The problem in Cho's pneumatology, as I have pointed out, is that the tension is resolved in favor of an over-realized eschatology. The Spirit's person and work become an object of special attention. This is encapsulated in his designation of the Holy Spirit as "my senior partner." Cho sees mission as essentially a partnership between the Christian and the Holy Spirit as the senior partner. This means that one follows the "dreams and visions" of the Spirit. "If you want to work with the Holy Spirit you must speak His language, the language of visions and dreams." [69] The issue is not the process of dreaming and visualizing, but what is being dreamed and visualized: it is the unlimited possibilities contained in the gospel of the threefold blessing of salvation, health and wealth. Cho's fivefold gospel and

---

difference between salvation-history and world-history and to rebut a common tendency in modern theology of making the Spirit's work in the world and in the church indistinguishable. In other words, while modern theology seeks to dissolve the 'spatial' differential between the church and world, Cho's pneumatology (and this is also generally true of the "signs and wonder" movement), by contrast, seeks to dissolve the temporal differential between the "now" and the "then."

[69] *A Call in the Night*, Sermon series 1 (Seoul: Seoul Logos, 1983, 2002), 83.

threefold blessing will continue to generate controversy and suspicion unless the eschatological tension is restored; and it can be restored only if his pneumatology is re-rooted in trinitarian theology and sound biblical eschatology.

Cho, however, consciously eschews theological categories and opts for the language of the practitioner of the faith. One could argue that this is the only way to communicate to the "populace" effectively—which is true. But however popular we make our presentation, if we value truth, a measure of conceptual precision is needed to undergird our practical teaching. This is what I find lacking in Cho's teachings. This lack of conceptual precision has two serious consequences.

First, some of Cho's teachings are easily misunderstood because they are not well integrated into the broader framework of his own teaching. Many of Cho's critics miss the mark because they fail to take this fact into account. As a result, Cho has been accused of false teachings that he may not have intended to teach. Dave Hunt and T. A. McMahon, for example, see Cho's visualization technique as a case of shamanism.[70] But Cho has explicitly distinguished between those who are linked to the Holy Spirit and those who are linked to the devil in the "fourth dimension," and this must surely provide a context for understanding his visualization technique.

Cho also recognizes a third possibility, namely, the capacity of the human spirit to operate in the fourth dimension apart from either the Holy Spirit or evil spirits (the "unconscious").[71] While I do not think that visualization as such can be equated with shamanism in light of the larger context of the Christian spiritual tradition, it does not mean that there is no danger either. If there is a case for the charge of shamanism it is not in the technique of visualization *per se*, but in the control that one is tempted to exercise over the objects visualized. In Cho's case, the temptation

---

[70]Dave Hunt and T. A. McMahon, *The Seduction of Christianity* (Eugene, Oregon: Christian Life Publications, 1986). The authors simply lump together all forms of "visualization" techniques as dabbling in the territory of the devil (112-31).

[71]The Fourth Dimension, 41-43.

to control is perhaps much greater, especially when the objects are invariably concerned with "blessings." There needs to be adequate safeguards when one delves into the spiritual realm, whether Christian or non-Christian. Without an adequate conceptual framework to make these safeguards explicit—here we can learn much from men like Ignatius Loyola and Jonathan Edwards to "discern the spirits"—the possibility of abuse of power will always be present and the charge of shamanism will not easily go away.

Perhaps a more pertinent example is when Cho says that *rhema* "releases Jesus" or use some such terms that seem to suggest the human ability to control God. This could easily be misconstrued as quasi-magical and another piece of evidence of shamanistic influence. But Cho also tells us that *rhema* comes to those who are sensitized to the Holy Spirit through long waiting upon God. What he is saying, then, is not very different from the Desert Fathers, who believe that through close communion with God, one may be given a special prophetic word suitable for a specific occasion.[72] Again, what I find lacking is an explicit theology that links *rhema* to a holistic spirituality that safeguards the use of *rhema*.

Another consequence of theological imprecision is that some seeking to replicate his success might easily turn his teachings into "formulas for success" without considering the larger spiritual context in which these teachings are set. The *rhema*-word is a good example of a practice that can be easily abused (e.g., the Kansas City prophets). There is no assurance that the controls that keep Cho's practical pneumatology from becoming purely pragmatic (such as his own personal integrity) will function effectively with those who try to replicate his strategy for success. This is why it is necessary for those controls to be consciously built in as part of a coherent theology. E.g., a proper theology of the threefold blessing must include, among other things, some warning of possible abuse (especially in the light of the human

[72]Kallistos Ware, "The Spiritual Father in Orthodox Christianity," in *Spiritual Direction: Contemporary Readings*, ed. Kevin G. Culligan, O.C.D. (Locus Valley, NY: Living Flame Press, 1983), 21-23.

propensity to love things above God), and the recognition of the place of poverty and sickness as part of a holistic spirituality within the context of a sound, biblical eschatology.

5. Conclusion

When I began the study of Cho's pneumatology, I must confess to having strong reservations about it. My previous view of Cho had been formed more by what I had read about him than what I had read by him. But after going through many of his writings, my earlier reservations have been considerably reduced, but not entirely removed. I am hopeful that a strong underlying spirituality, expressed in terms of the classical Pentecostal doctrine of Spirit-baptism, continuous in-filling of the Spirit, and a rigorous spiritual discipline,[73] could serve as a safeguard against abuses, but it needs to be made explicit and brought directly to bear on his threefold blessing. But I still have my remaining reservations. They have to do with a pneumatology that is so loosely conceived that it threatens to overwhelm the orthodox trinitarian doctrine, and an eschatology that tends to swallow up the future. I am also confident that within Cho's overall scheme of things the threat can be overcome and the tendency corrected, but unless they are actually overcome and corrected my reservations will remain.

[73]I have not discussed this third element at length as it is not directly pertinent to this paper.

THE QUESTION OF GOOD AND EVIL IN FULL GOSPEL FAITH: A STUDY OF THE THEOLOGICAL FOUNDATION FOR THE THREEFOLD BLESSING OF YONGGI CHO

Sam-hwan Kim

1. Introduction

According to Augustine, God is the supreme good and all good emanates from him.[1] It implies that the very source of good is found in God. God is as he is ("I am who I am": *Ego sum qui sum*, Ex 3:14). He is the ultimate existence, the Supreme Being, whose existence is unalterable as there is no possibility of any other existence, for he is the same always. God is good (Ps 106:1). As such, good is Being itself. Also, it is certain that all creation which are created by the good God are good as the source of their creation is good. All things (*res*) or substance (*substantia*) are good as long as they are created by God. Despite such fact, humankind experience bad things, falling victim to hardship, disease, sin and other evil. Why is it that humans must face sin, condemnation, hardship, disease and evil? Where did they come from? What is the source of their creation?

The solutions to these problems are related to David Yonggi Cho's "Threefold Blessing" (TFB) which provides physical health and general well-being, even as the spirit is made well. The TFB seeks fundamentally and essentially to remove evil from one's life. The elimination of the evil of sin from one's spirit leads to the

---

[1]Omne autem bonum, aut Deus, aut ex Deo est; Augustinus, De vera religione, 18, 35.

salvation and well-being of the spirit, or a spiritual blessing. The elimination of the evil of hardship leads to well-being of one's life on earth—the blessing of well-being. The elimination of the evil of disease leads to the salvation and well-being of the physical body—the blessing of health. In order to remove such evil in the theological realm, it is necessary to understand the metaphysical nature of evil and its ontological significance. Also, with the elimination of evil necessary for the TFB, the question of the TFB is fundamentally related to the question of theodicy, and not to general anthropological value. It necessitates the study of the TFB from the dimension of theodicy, concerning good and evil, rather than from an anthropological viewpoint. Only when viewed in this way, can the TFB, as related to the elimination of evil, be rightly addressed.

2. The Exact Nature of Evil and Its Origin

In order to understand the fundamental nature and origin of evil, all discussions must consider God as the Creator of all the universe. The Creator of all things, the very source of all existence, is the good God. God is self-existing and is ever unchanging (James 1:17). He is the supreme and absolute good; He is the Supreme Being, perfect in nature and unsusceptible to any change. God is undoubtedly the supreme and perfect being. But the existence of the created being is not self-existing. Therefore, it is of lesser good than that of God, while God's being is self-existing and unchanging, so, it is absolutely good.

According to Augustine, all created beings are *not really existent, but they exist.*[2] In other words, the existence of all creation is not perfect good, however, as the perfect God has created them, they do possess a degree of good more or less. Simply put, all existing things imply a certain measure of good. Denying such good in all created things implies, as could be seen in the case of the Manichaeism, a fifth-century heresy that

---

[2]Augustinus, *Confessiones*, 7, 11.

regarded all the physical reality as evil, the real being of evil, and it leads to the rejection of the monism of the good, and to the conclusion of dualism of good and evil.

With the understanding that very existence implies good, evil is the antithesis of existence, which would be nothingness.[3] In God who is self-existing and unchanging, such evil cannot be found. However, the possibility of evil can be found in all created things as they were created *out of nothingness* (*ex nihilo*) and they are not un-changing. The traditional Christian doctrine supports that God created out of nothingness (*creatio ex nihilo*); the nothingness here is characteristically different from the *nonbeing* (*meon*) which was argued by Plato. He believed that prior to coming into existence, there is a state of *possible* being where the exact nature of the being has not yet been decided but exists in a state of readiness to take form. The nothingness (*nihil*) here is an absolute nothingness which denies even the possibility of being.[4] It, therefore, can be categorized as the negative nothingness (*nihili negativum*), from which nothing can be made (*ex nihilo nihil fit*), and different from its antithesis, positive nothingness (*nihili positivum*). It was only by God that the world was created out of this negative nothingness, and the phrase "*ex nihilo nihil fit*" can be used to reveal the absolute creative power of God.

All creation has been created by God, and, therefore can share in the *being*. But also, as the creation has come from nothingness, it can also share in the nothingness. This very possibility of being able to share in the nothingness has made it possible for all creation to share in evil. The fact that all creation is susceptible to *change* toward the lesser good also implies that it participates in evil. As the degradation away from the absolute being proceeds, there would be an increase in nothingness rather than being, and that increase implies more evil. In the end, the effort to share in being is considered good, while the effort to share in nothingness is considered evil. All that have been created share in the being and therefore cannot be absolutely evil. The existence of creation

---

[3]Augustinus, *Confessiones*, 7, 12.

[4]Augustinus, *De immortalitate animae*, 12, 19.

itself is good. In the same way, the fruit of the Tree of the Knowledge of Good and Evil which was planted in Eden is good.

However, when a person's heart longs more for the existence of the things in this world rather than for the existence of God the Creator, it means that his or her heart longs for the lesser perfection, the lesser good. It would imply a degradation from the perfect to the lesser perfect, and therefore, it would be an act of evil. The human physical body, also created by God, is good. But, if a person who has the physical body has a greater love for the body than love for the supreme being of God, it would be an act of evil. While one should love oneself and the creation of God, that love must not take precedence over the love for God. For loving the creation more means having love for that which is a less perfect being, and a degradation toward the nothingness brings about evil upon oneself. Holding God not as the object of our genuine love but for an ulterior motive for personal benefit, and seeking God for a certain answer or response rather than seeking God himself as one should do reflects the folly of placing God below the answer which comes from God. Such foolishness is the seed of evil. God is not a being that we can manipulate according to our motives; he is the one we should look upon with love. Such love toward God (*frui*) must be toward only God and none other, as there can only be one master (Luke 9:62). While we can manipulate the things of the creation, we cannot manipulate God; we must look upon God with love and not upon the creation. Looking upon God with love allows one to share in the perfect existence and brings forth the genuine blessing; it is the greatest good that the created being can share in.[5]

Evil is not a *substance*. Evil refers to a state of non-existence or a state of existence which digresses toward the less perfect state of existence. Evil is non-existence or the lack of existence. As the notion of good can be substituted for the state of existence, evil is the lack of good (*privatio boni*) or the degradation of good toward the lesser good.

---

[5]Augustinus, *De vera religione*, 44, 82.

3. The Good of God and the Possibility of Being Evil

There is simply no possibility for nothingness to intrude upon the perfect existence of God, for God is self-existent and is unchanging, which implies perfection. The creation retains that possibility toward nothingness as it was created out of nothingness. Accordingly, the goodness of God is that which does not even contain the possibility of evil, while the goodness of the creation, although it may not exist as an actual evil, has potential toward evil. As such, the goodness of the creation that retains the potential for evil is an imperfect goodness. The goodness of the created being cannot reach the perfect good. However, through love for God and inclination toward Him, it can reach a level of perfection within itself.

4. Cho's TFB and the "God Is Good" Theology

The fundamental assertion of Cho's TFB has to do with *well-being*. As stated in 3 John 2, the TFB seeks the well-being of the spirit which also leads to the well-being of the physical body and of general circumstance (in all things). Well-being implies wellness, and this *wellness* is the practical aspect of good. Good without wellness is meaningless. God who is good also provides wellness. On the other hand, when circumstances go wrong, it means they are going *bad*, and this is the practical aspect of evil. As the good of God does not include even the possibility of evil, God cannot be the source of things going wrong, bad or evil.

The grace of God does not destroy the pursuit of people for the anthropological good. If God's grace were to destroy or oppose the pursuit of the good, it would mean that the ontological source and value system for humans were not in line with God. However, because of his love for his creation, the humankind, God helps them to transcend their limited longing for good and set their eyes upon the goodness of God, thereby bringing about perfection of the good of humankind. The grace of God does not destroy nature, but perfects it. It is important to note that the grace of God does not disregard the human aspiration of the wellness, the practical aspect of the anthropological good, asserted by Cho's TFB. Rather, the grace of God perfects human aspiration for wellness. All discourses on the TFB retain a *theological* significance, only through the argument upon such perfection, in relation to the question of good and evil.

5. Concerning the Spiritual Well-being

5.1 What Is the Evil of Sin?

Just as evil is the lack of good, as sin is another form of evil; so, sin cannot exist as its own. Then, how can sin be defined and what is it a lack of? Just as the lack of good is evil, sin is the lack of love. The state of lacking in love can be put in two categories, lack of love for God and lack of love for humans. The lack of love for God can be seen, on the first level, in the rebellious act of Adam and Eve (as love for God leads to obedience, John 15:10-12; 1 John 5:3), on the second, fearing God (as there is no fear in love, 1 John 4:18) and hiding (Gen 3:10).

The first level reveals the active sin of disobeying God's command and the second level reveals that the state of being in sin transforms one's existence to fear. In the second case, as stated by Paul Ricoeur, it is related to the state of contamination (*souillure*), the ontological evidence of the fallen humanity, punished for original sin.[6] Both cases of sin clearly reveal that the evil of sin resulted from the lack of love for God. Sin arising out of the lack of love for humans can be clearly seen in the first sin of murder committed by Cain and by his answer to God who searched for Abel, "Am I my brother's keeper?" (Gen 4:9). We see here the active sin of murder due to hatred, and the passive sin of irresponsibility, both revealing a lack of love for humans.

Adam's sin committed against God and Cain's sin of murder both include active and passive aspects, but the active part came

---

[6]Paul Ricoeur, Finitude et Culpabilité II: La Symbolique du Mal (Paris: Aubier, 1960).

first. In the first case, the command from God was not one which required Adam "to do something," but "*not* to do something." Where the command which requires one "to do" would lead to a passive sin of inaction, the command which requires one "not to do" leads to an active sin of "doing" against God's command. Another active sin can be seen in the case of Satan whose fall resulted from a purposeful sin (Isa 14:13-14). Can such an active sin also be considered to be the *lack* of love? It would be easy enough to make the assumption that, while the lack of love could be related to the passive sin of *not-doing* or avoidance of responsibility or lack of care, the active sin is to be related to some form of *purposeful doing* by hatred. This assumption leads us not to regard Adam's and Cain's active sins as that which are rightly addressed by the *lack* of love. However, the problem would be resolved when the fundamental nature of love is clarified, and illustrates also the nature of active hatred as lack of love as below.

Love unifies certain contradictory properties. For the realization of love, there must be first a need to establish a certain difference and distance between two parties, as a reciprocal relationship should be requested. Love is not possible without relationship, and relationship is not possible without distance and differentiation between two parties. At the same time difference and distance is overcome by the uniting power of love. It is the same in the case of the Trinity. Being time-transcendent, to realize love, there first is a need for differentiation and distance, and afterward, differentiation and distance are overcome by the power of unification through love. According to St. Thomas concerning the Trinity, the distance for relationships among the three persons is as real as the three persons.[7] It implies that the unity of three persons represents a contradictory unification. When differentiation and distance are not overcome by the power of unification of love, hatred becomes manifest.

Hatred is a state of imperfection, of *lack* of love and of having been unable to make unification through love. Hatred cannot exist as a real substance in its own. For hatred to come into existence, a

---

[7]Thomas Aquinas, *Summa Theologiae*, vol. 7, 39, 1.

certain relationship with the other party has to be established, namely, one of differentiation and distance. Hatred aims toward annihilation of the other party at the same time, so, hatred tries to destroy the very relationship needed for hatred itself. Without the other party, hatred cannot exist. That is the reason why hatred cannot exist as a real substance in its own. However love is the state of union by the power of unification, even as differentiation and distance exist between the two parties. Here union should not be mistaken for fusion, where the two become one and indistinguishable. As hatred aims toward the annihilation of the other, it is not able to exist as a substance, but it exists only as a lack of love, that is, lack of the will to unite. So, although hatred is an active will, it does not mean that it is able to exist of its own as a substance. This active will of revolt against the contradictory unification, as lack of love, lies behind the sin of Adam and Eve, and Cain.

God who is self-existing is not only good; he is also love (1 John 4:8). In the end, there exists a relationship among being, good and love. Evil is a lack of being, good, and love. The evil of sin is lack of love.

5.2 The Elimination of the Evil of Sin from the Spirit

As discussed above, the evil of sin committed by those who disobey God has to do with the lack of love. If so, the well-being of the spirit means eliminating this lack of love. What does it mean to eliminate the lack of love from the spirit?

As the evil of sin cannot exist as a substance, it will not be removed as if it were an object: it can only be removed by being filled with the good of love. It is similar to the relationship between light and darkness: darkness exists only as a lack of light. Darkness itself cannot be removed as if it were an object, but only by being filled with light. The Bible also commands, “Overcome evil with good” (Rom 12:21). Christ came to this world not to convict the world of sin, but to save the world through himself (John 3:17). Cho’s theology of TFB stresses the forgiving grace of God through love rather than judgment. This attitude comes from the comprehension of the fundamental nature of sin and evil as discussed above. Full Gospel faith does not condemn sinners who are in despair of nothingness, which lies at the heart of evil, but through the power of the Holy Spirit, offers them the love of Christ through salvation.

It is also evil to move from a greater being to a lesser being, to increase nothingness. To reveal this kind of evil one needs an ability to distinguish the states of *being* as a lesser or a greater. Convicting a person, whose spirit is already mired in evil by revealing his evilness is another nothingness. It means another evil. Convicting a person who is seeking to commit a sin by moving from a greater being to a lesser being, brings about good, as it can only be possible through the good of knowledge to distinguish the states of being, and as it prevents spirit from seeking such degradation. Prophets in the Bible who brought the message of judgment did not increase another evil, but brought about a change in direction to the good, to salvation. The message of TFB seeks such good. It takes pity upon the sinners and gives them the message of the gospel of forgiveness and salvation. However, by convicting the persons who are going to commit sins, they are prevented from falling into evil, thus seeking good. By doing so, it may be possible to remove the evil of sin and to bring about the well-being of the spirit.

To have love for that which is good in nature is also good in itself. However, having a greater love for the creation, which is a lesser good than God, the perfect good, would be increasing the nothingness and therefore be an act of evil. By the same reasoning, it would also be sin to love equally the creation and God. In order to remove such evil from the spirit, the degree of love must be in accordance to the order of being. Having a lesser degree of love for that which has a higher order of being would be an act of evil, as much as having greater love for that which has a lesser order of being. In order to remove such evil from the spirit, one needs to have a degree of love in accordance with the order of being. As an example, in the case of love for God, it should be our complete devotional love. However, loving oneself with such love would be an act of evil. Loving one's physical body more than one's spirit would be also an act of evil. Removing the evil of sin from the spirit thus means realizing that there are different orders of being for which different levels of love should be held.

6. Concerning the Physical and Circumstantial Well-being

Blessing, from an anthropological viewpoint, is what humans naturally yearn for universally, and that which the grace of God does not negate, but makes complete. Should the grace of God oppose or negate such natural human yearning, theology and anthropology would forever run parallel; God would forever be the transcendental being who does not associate with humanity. It would also lead to a deviation of the very meaning and purpose of the ministry of salvation of Christ who is both God and man; it would lead to the collapse of the very *raison d'être* of Christianity. The TFB reveals more aptly than any other theologies the human, universal yearning of humanity, the holistic well-being of the spirit, the body and the circumstance. The TFB regards the anthropological element which theology must not overlook as an essential issue in theology. However, what the depraved human nature seeks is also corrupt and depraved, and it cannot be considered as good until it must be made perfect itself through the grace of sovereign God. Only then, the TFB can fundamentally acquire the theological essence.

For the removal of the evils of disease and hardship to acquire the theological essence of blessing of physical health and circumstantial well-being, the elimination of the evil should not be the elimination of various phenomena of disease and curses, but the very ontological removal of the disease and the curse themselves. The essence of disease itself is the source of all ills; the essence of the curse itself is the source of all curses. The very essence of the disease and the curse is the *nothingness* itself, evil. Removal of the very essence of evil is only possible through the *being* of the good God. If evil is not eliminated, various diseases and curses can only be suppressed temporarily, but cannot be eliminated permanently or fundamentally. Should such evil not be eliminated, all the phenomena of good and evil, health and disease, blessing and curse cannot work for the ultimate good in God as stated in Romans 8:28.

The ontological removal of the disease itself leads to the permanent removal of disease (Rev 21:4). And that which manifests as strength and weakness (cf. 2 Cor 12:7) can be brought together for the ultimate good. The ontological removal of the curse itself leads to the permanent removal of the curse, and that which manifests as well-being, or as hardship can be brought together for the ultimate good.

The ontological removal of the evil could be described by symbols. Symbol and allegory differ in the fact that the former reach the ontological depth of things, while the latter does not. During Jesus' ministry on the earth, he used various methods of healing such as exorcism (Luke 11:14), laying on of hands in prayer (Mark 6:5), verbal command (Mark 7:34) or forgiving of sin (Mark 1:5). While the methods he used do not imply any symbolism, Jesus' injury as he was whipped in Pilate's courtyard does symbolize the nature of the source of disease. His injury symbolizes the pains of disease: it symbolizes the ontological depth of the pain of the disease itself. Christ was injured in order to heal us (Isa 53:5). Such healing is the ontological redemption of disease itself. Rather than healing each and every manifestation of illness and disease, it was the elimination of the disease itself. In the same vein, the crown of thorns is also symbolic (Gen 3:17-19). Wearing the crown of thorns and being nailed to the cross, Jesus took upon himself the curse of humanity (Deut 21:23); by doing so he has redeemed us from the curse of the law as written in Deuteronomy chapter 28. This curse of the law hung over humankind who rebelled against God, and the curse was redeemed (Deut 21:23; Gal 3:13-14). The curse which Jesus removed on the cross is the curse itself as symbolized by the *thorn*, the very source of all the curses imposed to the first couple. Through redemption, various aspects of all curses have been fundamentally dealt with. By the very elimination of the curse itself, there was a holistic solution of great importance. Because the various phenomena of unhappiness could be connected to the ulterior good of happiness, the question is that all come together to result in the ultimate good (Rom 8:28). The faith of the TFB should realize such importance, and by longing for the ontological and holistic solution, it becomes complete.

7. Conclusion

The FGB of Cho and the Full Gospel faith begins with the question of evil that humanity faces in their existential life. Full Gospel faith sincerely asks and seeks the answer to the anthropological question more than any other faiths do. Examination and understanding of Cho and the life he has lived leads to the realization that the TFB did not arise from coincidence. There are ultimate questions such as "Who am I and where is my life headed?" They concern our life, unhappiness, and the evil discovered therein led him to the discovery of the goodness of God and the TFB of the Full Gospel faith. In the end, the foundation of the development of the TFB is the goodness of God. However, God's goodness is not what man considers good. It is necessary to understand the evil that mankind experiences in an Augustinian light. Only when the understanding of evil is further developed on an ontological level, can the understanding of the goodness of God be reached. Only an ontological understanding of the TFB can serve as the guidepost to the wholeness of the Full Gospel faith.

THE CONTEXTUAL PENTECOSTAL THEOLOGY OF DAVID YONGGI CHO[1]

Allan Anderson

1. Introduction

The work of Dr David (Paul) Yonggi Cho and the Yoido Full Gospel Church (YFGC) is known all over the world. Why this single congregation has been more effective in reaching Korean people than most others (if not all others) have been is due to several factors, of which the work of the Holy Spirit in this church is surely the most significant. In this article, I analyze how the context of Korea has affected the appeal of the message of Yonggi Cho, depending mostly on the eighteen books written by Cho (in English) in my possession, two visits to Korea, and working with Korean graduate students over eight years. Although Cho's books are devotional and inspirational rather than theological, I concentrate on those writings that deal with Cho's own context of Korea and attempt to draw out how his implicit theology may be regarded as "contextual." He writes mainly about his understanding of the Bible and his own experiences as a pastor, but sometimes refers to the context in which these experiences and understanding were developed. His books abound with biblical illustrations and teaching, but he develops his theology in a

---

[1]This is a revised version of a paper presented at the Youngsan International Theological Symposium, Hansei University, Goonpo, Korea in September 2002 and published as "The Contribution of David Yonggi Cho to a Contextual Theology in Korea," *Journal of Pentecostal Theology* 12:1 (October 2003), 87-107.

particular context. It is important that Pentecostals in different parts of the world realize the important role of the "freedom in the Spirit" to formulate, often unconsciously, a theology that has meaning for people in different life situations, and Cho's theology is a leading example of this. This contextual pneumatology is one of the most important features of Pentecostalism and is often overlooked.

In my research and work among Pentecostals in southern Africa I have found that theology is more than written, academic theology; it is also to be found in the preaching, rituals and practices of churches that have contextualized Christianity in such a way as to make it really meaningful to ordinary people. This "enacted theology" or "theology in practice" is found in Pentecostalism all over the world,[2] and Cho's theology will be evaluated from this perspective. One of the main reasons for the phenomenal growth of Pentecostalism has been its remarkable ability to adapt itself to different cultural and social contexts and give authentically contextualized expressions to Christianity. Pentecostalism is inherently adaptable to contextualization: the vibrancy, enthusiasm, spontaneity and spirituality for which Pentecostals are so well known and their willingness to address problems of sickness, poverty, unemployment, loneliness, evil spirits and sorcery has directly contributed to this growth. We see these features in the ministry of David Yonggi Cho.

2. The Importance of Contextualization

Missiologists have promoted "indigenization" for a long time, and Pentecostal scholars like Melvin Hodges have written profoundly about an "indigenous church."[3] These terms have

[2]Allan Anderson, Zion and Pentecost: The Spirituality and Experience of Pentecostal and Zionist/ Apostolic Churches in South Africa (Pretoria: University of South Africa Press, 2000), 2; Allan Anderson, African Reformation: African Initiated Christianity in the Twentieth Century (Trenton, NJ & Asmara, Eritrea: Africa World Press, 2001), 217.

[3]Melvin L. Hodges, *The Indigenous Church* (Springfield, MO: Gospel Publishing House, 1953).

become somewhat anachronistic because they assume that the gospel message and Christian theology is the same in all cultures and contexts, and they tend to relate this "constant" Christian message to so-called "traditional" cultures. The idea of a self-supporting, self-governing and self-propagating church has been an important feature of many Pentecostal missions. "Contextualization," on the other hand, assumes that every theology is shaped by its particular context, and must be so to be relevant and meaningful. It relates the Christian message to all social contexts and cultures, especially including those undergoing rapid change. The ideas of "contextual theologies" were first formulated in the World Council of Churches in 1972.[4] In the West, particularly in North America where the evangelical/ ecumenical divide was most acute, these ideas were more difficult for evangelicals to accept, although many of them had used different words to describe the same ideas, some speaking of a "deeper indigenization" or words to that effect. The rise of particular contextual theologies like "liberation theology" in Latin America, "Black theology" among African Americans and South Africans, and "Minjung theology" in Korea increased evangelical concerns that this new trend in theology would lead to "syncretism" and a placing of the social context above God's revelation in the Bible. But gradually, evangelical scholars like Charles Kraft and David Hesselgrave began to give prominence to the importance of culture.[5] Kraft spoke of "the constant message in alternative forms," and of "dynamic-equivalence theologizing," and that "all theologizing is culture-bound interpretation and communication of God's revelation."[6]

All theologies are contextual theologies, but we should not confuse the essential and universal aspects of the Christian

---

[4]"Mission as Contextualization," in *Readings in World Mission*, ed. Norman Thomas (London: SPCK, 1995), 169-184 (175).

[5]Charles H. Kraft, *Christianity in Culture* (Maryknoll, NY: Orbis, 1979); David Hesselgrave, *Communicating Christ Cross-Culturally* (Grand Rapids: Zondervan, 1978).

[6]Kraft, Christianity in Culture, 257, 291.

message from the local, contextual ones.[7] Lesslie Newbigin writes that "every communication of the gospel is already culturally conditioned," but reminds us that the gospel "is not an empty form into which everyone is free to pour his or her own content," but that the content of the gospel is "Jesus Christ in the fullness of his ministry, death, and resurrection."[8] Evangelicals now more readily accept the importance of contextualization. Gilliland defines the goal of "contextualization" as "to enable, insofar as it is humanly possible, an understanding of what it means that Jesus Christ, the Word, is authentically experienced in each and every human situation."[9] He says that the Christian message must be proclaimed in the framework of the worldview of the particular people to whom it is addressed, it must emphasize those parts of the message that answer their particular questions and needs, and it must be expressed through the medium of their own cultural gifts. In assessing Cho's theology, these considerations are very important, as we cannot try to understand his ministry from a western perspective. Culture and worldview, of necessity, include religious beliefs; and in a discussion of a "contextual" theology we cannot avoid questions of religious pluralism, especially in a country like Korea. Cho's theology must be assessed from the perspective of the post Korean War context in which it was shaped.

Christianity in general and Pentecostalism in particular had taken on a distinctive form in Korea, quite different from that found in the West. Observers who have tried to emphasize the "North American" nature of Pentecostalism throughout the world or the "Americanization" of Christianity in Korea and elsewhere often miss this important fact. Creative innovations and the selective transformation of foreign symbols are constantly

---

[7]David J. Bosch, Transforming Mission: Paradigm Shifts in Theology of Mission (Maryknoll, NY: Orbis, 1991), 423.

[8]Lesslie Newbigin, *The Gospel in a Pluralist Society* (London: SPCK, 1989), 142, 152-53.

[9]Dean Gilliland, "Contextualization," in *Evangelical Dictionary of World Missions*, eds. A. Scott Moreau, Harold Netland, and Charles van Engen (Grand Rapids, MI: Baker, 2000), 225.

occurring and naturally, a synthesizing process takes place as a new form of Christianity like Pentecostalism interacts with older Korean religions like shamanism and Buddhism. For example, the prayer mountain movement in Korea is well known, and YFGC has its own prayer mountain near the border of North Korea. There are now hundreds of Christian prayer mountains all over South Korea. Mountains and hills as places of spiritual retreat and pilgrimage have been a characteristic of Korean religions for centuries. Beliefs in the mountain as the place to which God descends,[10] are not only part of Korean tradition but are also ideas fully at home in the Old Testament. Buddhist temples are usually built on mountainsides and Korean cemeteries are found on hills outside residential areas. Traditionally, the many mountains of Korea were believed to be places where good spirits lived, and both shamans and ordinary pilgrims would receive power from the particular spirit on each mountain. At the risk of oversimplification, the prayer mountain movement may be said to be a culturally relevant form of Christian practice that reflects the ancient spirituality of Korean people. Similarly, Korean people suffering from their accumulated grief or han seek healing and "blessings" from traditional shamans to alleviate their deep pain, such as in the years following the Korean War or more recently, during the IMF crisis. The fact that a prominent part of Cho's message is to proclaim that God brings "blessings" and healings is a contextual message for Korean people that is readily accepted. These are two examples of how Korean Christianity is contextualized by taking the good practices of ancient religions and transforming them with new Christian meanings.

3. Cho's Detractors

Yonggi Cho has been seriously criticized by various writers, especially those for whom the idea of contextualization is rejected

---

[10] Sung-hoon Myung, "Spiritual Dimension of Church Growth as Applied in Yoido Full Gospel Church" (Ph.D. dissertation, Fuller Theological Seminary, 1990), 156.

or unknown. Some of the earliest criticisms were indirect and from within the US Assemblies of God, where Gordon Fee criticized the "alien gospel" of the "cult of prosperity" in the official magazine The Pentecostal Evangel. In 1980, the General Presbytery of the Assemblies of God officially condemned the "positive confession" teaching increasing in the USA at that time through the work of Kenneth Hagin and others.[11] None of these documents mentioned Cho, but its criticisms were directed at the "wealth and health" movement in the USA. On the contrary, in the years 1967-2000, The Pentecostal Evangel published at least twenty-eight articles by or about Yonggi Cho.[12] Later, Assemblies of God college professor Terris Neuman published an article condemning the "Word-Faith" movement and directly linking Cho to it.[13] Criticisms also came from US evangelicals in 1985, when Dave Hunt and T. A. McMahon published *The Seduction of Christianity*, where Cho is accused of such fantastic charges as being part of "sorcery" and "occultism,"[14] of supporting "Eastern mysticism,"[15] of reviving the ancient art of shamanism,[16] and of promoting the teaching of "mind-science cults."[17] All this was based on a western misinterpretation of "visualization."[18] Hunt and McMahon suggest that Cho's teachings came from the prosperity

---

[11] Gordon D. Fee, "The 'Gospel' of Prosperity: An Alien Gospel," *The Pentecostal Evangel* (June 24 1979), 4-8; General Presbytery of the Assemblies of God, "The Believer and Positive Confession," *The Pentecostal Evangel* (November 16, 1980), 8-11, 18-20.

[12] Information gleaned from the website of the Flower Pentecostal Heritage Center (http://agheritage.org/research/periodicalsearch.cfm), checked: July 3, 2002.

[13] H. Terris Neuman, "Cultic Origins of Word-Faith Theology within the Charismatic Movement," *Pneuma: The Journal of the Society for Pentecostal Studies* 12:1 (Spring 1990), 32-55.

[14] Dave Hunt and T. A. McMahon, *The Seduction of Christianity: Spiritual Discernment in the Last Days* (Eugene, OR: Harvest House, 1985), 20, 33, 102, 143-145.

[15] Hunt & McMahon, Seduction of Christianity, 111.

[16] Hunt & McMahon, Seduction of Christianity, 123.

[17] Hunt & McMahon, Seduction of Christianity, 139.

[18] Hunt & McMahon, Seduction of Christianity, 113.

gospel in the USA, and back through Robert Schuller and Kenneth Hagin to the "positive thinking" of Norman Vincent Peale, Jungian psychology, Christian Science, Mormonism, and Scientology—all these declared to be evidence of a "New Age" conspiracy.[19] Other evangelical scholars like Da Silva and Daniel McConnell (who called this a "different gospel") repeated Hunt and Mahon's criticisms in different forms.[20] These allegations could be simply discounted if many evangelicals (including Presbyterians in Korea) had not taken it so seriously. Some of the presuppositions behind this "New Age" conspiracy theory and especially those of McConnell have been more recently exposed and refuted.[21] However, in keeping with most evangelicals, Cho expressly rejects Jungian psychology that leads to belief in the inherent goodness of humanity and the "humanistic theology" of Schleiermacher and other modern theologians,[22] ideas prevalent in the "positive thinking" school.

A second form of critique came from more "liberal" theologians and included such famous names as Walter Hollenweger and Harvey Cox. The first critical study of Cho was conducted by Minjung theologian Kwang-sun (David) Suh and published by the Christian Academy of Korea in 1981.[23] These scholars did not as much accuse Cho of false or "heretical"

---

[19]Hunt & McMahon, *Seduction of Christianity*, 24-25.

[20]Antonio Barbosa da Silva, "The 'Theology of Success' Movement: A Comment," *Themelios* 11:3 (April 1986), 91-92 (91); Daniel R. McConnell, *A Different Gospel: A Historical and Biblical Analysis of the Faith Movement* (Peabody, MA: Hendrickson, 1988).

[21]Dale H. Simmons, *E.W. Kenyon and the Postbellum Pursuit of Peace, Power, and Plenty* (Lanham, MD: Scarecrow, 1997); Geir Lie, "E.W. Kenyon: Cult Founder or Evangelical Minister?," *EPTA Bulletin* 16 (1996), 71-86; Geir Lie, "The Theology of E.W. Kenyon: Plain Heresy or within the Boundaries of Pentecostal-Charismatic 'Orthodoxy'?," *Pneuma: The Journal of the Society for Pentecostal Studies* 22:1 (Spring 2000), 85-114.

[22]*The Fourth Dimension*, vol. 2 (South Plainfield, NJ: Bridge Publishing, 1983), 52-53, 79.

[23]Myung Soo Park, "David Yonggi Cho and International Pentecostal Movements," *Journal of Pentecostal Theology* 12:1 (October 2003), 107-128 (109).

teaching as to suggest a positive link between Cho's theology and Korean shamanism. In this respect, these scholars might regard Cho as "contextual." An entire chapter of Hollenweger's 1997 book *Pentecostalism* is entitled "Korea: The Oral Shamanistic Culture in Pentecostal Transformation." [24] Hollenweger acknowledges that the chapter is "heavily based" on the writings of his former Ph.D. student at the University of Birmingham and Korean Presbyterian missionary in Kenya, Boo-woong Yoo. [25] Yoo's doctoral thesis was published in 1988 as *Korean Pentecostalism: Its History and Theology*, and is not about Pentecostalism in its present form, but is a reflection on earlier revival movements, the "Korean Pentecost" of 1907 and the mystical "pentecostal movement" of the 1930s. The only mention of YFGC and Cho is indirect in a quotation from Suh's critique.[26] It is incredible that this academic work on "Korean Pentecostalism" only once briefly mentions the YFGC, the most visible and influential representative of Pentecostalism in Korea, and it mainly devotes itself to a discussion of the relationship between the Korean revival movement in the Presbyterian and Methodist churches and Minjung theology. At the end of his work, Yoo also makes a short reference to the need for "a pentecostal exploration of Shamanism."[27] At the same time that Yoo was doing his research in Birmingham, Jae Bum Lee did a very different Ph.D. study at Fuller Theological Seminary in the USA. The first academic work by a Korean Pentecostal in the English language, Lee's thesis has set the pattern for many that followed, particularly his including the early twentieth century revival movement as "Pentecostal" and using revival leaders Sun-ju Kil, Ick-doo Kim and Yong-do Lee as paradigmatic of Korean

---

[24]Walter J. Hollenweger, *Pentecostalism: Origins and Developments Worldwide* (Peabody: Hendrickson, 1997), 99-105.

[25]Hollenweger, *Pentecostalism*, 99 n.1.

[26] Boo-woong Yoo, *Korean Pentecostalism: Its History and Theology* (Frankfurt am Main: Peter Lang, 1988), 206.

[27]Yoo, Korean Pentecostalism, 223.

Pentecostalism.[28] He draws attention to the fact that Korean revivalism has always been accompanied by what he calls "Pentecostal type experiences" including Spirit baptism, healing, miracles and exorcism.[29]

Several western writers suggest that Korean Pentecostals in general and YFGC in particular have succeeded because they have combined Christianity with shamanism. Yoo's doctoral supervisor, Walter Hollenweger, was probably the first to do so. A footnote declares that the "famous Korean Pentecostal pastor Paul Yonggi Cho…could be considered a Pentecostal Shaman par excellence."[30] He suggests that Korean Pentecostalism should be interpreted "with the categories of a Shamanistic culture" rather than from historical and theological categories imposed from outside.[31] Harvey Cox also takes up this theme in his *Fire from Heaven* in a chapter on Korean Pentecostalism (with particular reference to YFGC) entitled "Shamans and Entrepreneurs: Primal Spirituality on the Asian Rim."[32] He too acknowledges the thesis of Boo-woong Yoo in his bibliographical notes at the end.[33] In what is now a well known passage, Cox says that in his opinion the YFGC "involves a massive importation of shamanistic practice into a Christian ritual."[34] All of this is to support his overarching theory of Pentecostalism as "primal spirituality" that permeates his book. Cox assumes that religions succeed when they possess "two capabilities": first, to include and absorb the "old" religions (in this case, shamanism), and second, to prepare people for living in

---

[28]Jae Bum Lee, "Pentecostal Type Distinctives and Korean Protestant Church Growth" (Ph.D. dissertation, Fuller Theological Seminary, Pasadena, 1986), 180-86.

[29]Lee, "Pentecostal Type Distinctives," 169.

[30]Hollenweger, *Pentecostalism*, 100 n. 2.

[31]Hollenweger, *Pentecostalism*, 104.

[32]Harvey Cox, Fire from Heaven: The Rise of Pentecostal Spirituality and the Reshaping of Religion in the Twenty-First Century (London: Cassell, 1996), 213-41.

[33]Cox, Fire from Heaven, 328.

[34]Cox, Fire from Heaven, 226.

a rapidly changing world. He declares, "Both of these key ingredients are present in Korean Pentecostalism."[35]

Cho does not dispute Cox's second point, as he writes of the rapid changes in the world that are "not necessarily obstacles but opportunities." He says, "The church cannot be a victim of change; she must be a guiding light in the midst of change."[36] He sees his "cell group system" with its use of women leaders as one way of accomplishing this relevance in the midst of rapid social change.[37] But Cox's most controversial passage is probably the following: "One of the key reasons for Korean Pentecostalism's extraordinary growth is its unerring ability to absorb huge chunks of indigenous Korean shamanism and demon possession into its worship," of which the YFGC "is an especially vivid case in point."[38] This idea of a link between Korean Pentecostalism and shamanism has been assumed and perpetuated in western literature to such an extent that it is now almost taken for granted.[39] But the so-called "link" with shamanism should be assessed in quite a different way. As Myung Soo Park has pointed out, it is more appropriate to see Cho's reaction to shamanism and his teachings on healing and "threefold blessings" within the context of his contact with international Pentecostalism.[40] In other words, Korean Pentecostalism should be assessed not only from within the internal cultural and religious context of Korea, but also from the external influence of globalization.

---

[35]Cox, Fire from Heaven, 219.

[36]*More than Numbers* (Waco, TX: Word Books, 1984), 134.

[37]David Yonggi Cho with Harold Hostetler, *Successful Home Cell Groups* (Seoul: Seoul Logos, 1997), 54.

[38]Cox, Fire from Heaven, 222.

[39]David Martin, *Pentecostalism: The World Their Parish* (Oxford: Blackwell, 2002), 161; Mark R. Mullins, *Christianity Made in Japan: A Study of Indigenous Movements* (Honolulu: University of Hawaii Press, 1998), 175.

[40]Park, "David Yonggi Cho," 110.

4. Cho's Contextual Theology

Cho's theology may be presented as contextual from several perspectives. In his recent doctoral thesis in Birmingham, Chong Hee Jeong points out that Harvey Cox has overlooked two important elements in the appeal of Pentecostalism in Korea: "its emphasis on empowered contextual transformation through the Holy Spirit and the role of divine healing."[41] He writes of Korean Pentecostalism as having a "dynamic contextual theology" and of Cho's "contextual ministry."[42] Similarly, Hyeon-sung Bae has written of Cho's "Full Gospel theology" as an "indigenized form of Pentecostal theology in Korea."[43] We must consider to what extent Cho's Pentecostal message is a contextual theology that has adapted to and transformed its cultural and religious environment. Clearly, Cho himself has wanted to be seen as such, although he does not use the word "contextual":

> Being a Korean and having been saved out of the Buddhist religion, I have been able to appreciate the distinctive position of Christians who come from the Third World. . . . We evangelical Korean Christians have developed our own traditions. This is very important because it makes it possible for us to be Christian without being less Korean. In the past, missionaries not only brought their religion but also their culture to the countries they evangelized. So it became apparent that the new converts lost much of their natural heritage. I believe that this produced an unnecessary hindrance to the acceptance of the gospel of Jesus Christ.[44]

---

[41]Chong Hee Jeong, "The Formation and Development of Korean Pentecostalism from the Viewpoint of a Dynamic Contextual Theology" (Th.D. thesis, University of Birmingham, 2001), 201.

[42]Jeong, "Formation and Development," 196, 215.

[43]Hyeon-sung Bae, "Full Gospel Theology and a Korean Pentecostal Identity," in *Asian and Pentecostal: The Charismatic Face of Christianity in Asia*, eds. Allan Anderson and Edmong Tang (Oxford: Regnum, 2004 forthcoming).

[44]More than Numbers, 9.

Nevertheless, Cho does not advocate uncritical use of Korean cultural principles. This is especially apparent in his "revolutionary" use of women leaders. In spite of Korean culture being "male-oriented," Cho took these steps because "God showed me."[45] The success of Cho's Pentecostalism should not be attributed to a conscious syncretism, but should be seen as a response to the influence of the worldview of shamanism that permeates and underlies Korean society. Korean Pentecostalism and older Korean religions both acknowledge the world of spirits and respond to this, as Korean Pentecostal scholars have pointed out. Lee Jae Bum speaks of the "spiritual preparedness of the Korean people due to their animistic beliefs," which he identifies particularly as an awareness of supernatural power, sins and evil spirits, and the need for blessings and healing. What he calls the "Pentecostal distinctives" found in many churches in Korea, met the needs of shamanistic people.[46] Sung-hoon Myung speaks of shamanism as "one of the folk religious groups most responsive to the Gospel in Korea." He says that shamanists are "aware of supernatural power…[and they] use magic and worship in order to reach out to their gods… [They] are aware of their sins, and they have a fear of spirits." And significantly for this discussion, they also "want blessings and healings from their gods."[47] Shamanism provides a *praeparatio evangelica*, a fertile ground into which the Pentecostal "full gospel" is more easily planted. If Pentecostal pastors sometimes appear to be functioning as "shamans," it is simply because they are responding to the needs arising from a shamanistic world. Korean Pentecostal leaders, however, emphatically deny any mixture of shamanism and like Pentecostals all over the world, see shamanism as something evil to be rejected.[48] Similarly, the dominant conservative Protestant Christianity with its strict moral law finds fertile ground in peoples

[45]More than Numbers, 43; cf. Cho, Successful Home Cell, 23-29.

[46]Lee, "Pentecostal Type Distinctives," 298.

[47]Myung, "Spiritual Dimension," 235.

[48]Cf. Allan Anderson, "Pentecostalism in East Asia: Indigenous Oriental Christianity?" *Pneuma: The Journal for the Society for Pentecostal Studies* 22:1 (Spring 2000), 115-132.

whose cultures are heavily influenced by Confucianism—as is clearly the case with Korean and Chinese societies.[49] Cho refers to the Confucian background of Korea often in a favorable light, and usually points out that Confucianism is not a religion but an ethical system observed by Koreans.[50]

The writings of Cho demonstrate firstly that his "contextual theology" is born in the particular situation of Korean suffering; and secondly, they illustrate how Cho has advocated a "Pentecostal theology" that is standard classical Pentecostal theology throughout the world, influenced by Pentecostal healing evangelists like Oral Roberts and by his years of working with North American Pentecostals.[51] Cho is uncompromising and polemical with regard to the religious background of Korea: his former experience as a "devout Buddhist" could not help him nor solve his problems. He considered it foreign to the compassion of Christ, and he had known only what he calls "well-organized and sterile Buddhist philosophies and rituals," which were "theoretically very profound,"[52] but which he referred to as "heathenism"[53] and "doctrines of devils."[54] Zen Buddhism in particular is singled out for his critical treatment, and Cho compares and contrasts it with Holy Spirit "Fourth-Dimensional Christianity."[55] But at the same time, Cho's concept of the "fourth dimension" is linked to his knowledge of Eastern religions with their own miraculous powers, as in Buddhism, yoga and Japanese religions like Soka Gakkai. He refers to the "evil spirit world" in this "fourth dimension" that is "under the power and authority of

---

[49]David Martin, Tongues of Fire: The Explosion of Protestantism in Latin America (Oxford: Blackwell, 1990), 140-141.

[50]More than Numbers, 101, 144.

[51]Park, "David Yonggi Cho," 108-120.

[52]*The Fourth Dimension* (Seoul: Seoul Logos, 1979), 10-11; Cho, *Successful Home Cell*, 149.

[53]Fourth Dimension, 173.

[54]Fourth Dimension, vol. 2, 76.

[55]*Fourth Dimension*, vol. 2, 83-85.

almighty God."[56] Although these ideas have brought him severe criticism from evangelical polemicists, Cho is careful to maintain the distinction between the Asian religious world and the Christian revelation. But clearly his experience of this Asian religious spirituality and its element of the miraculous has brought him to the understanding of the "fourth dimension," where visions and dreams are the language and "incubation" or "pregnancy" is the process through which believers receive their requests from God. This "incubation" in the "fourth dimension," he declares, is also the way that miracles happen in other religions.[57] This particular teaching can only be understood by reference to the Asian pluralistic religious background in which Korean Pentecostals are immersed.

Korean Pentecostal scholars are beginning to appreciate the importance of the ancient religious system to Pentecostalism, but they are also aware of its dangers. Young-hoon Lee, one of Cho's most senior ministers, points out that shamanism has influenced Korean Christianity in four ways. Firstly, it "made it easy for Koreans to accept the Christian God and the spiritual world." Secondly, shamanism's "emphasis on the present and on material blessings" made these a "major concern" of Korean Christianity and resulted in indifference to social concerns and a "self-centered Christianity." Thirdly, shamanism "drove Korean Christians to focus on blessings"; and fourthly, it influenced an exclusive and conservative Christianity.[58] Korean Buddhism also influenced Christianity to yearn for present, material blessings and to focus on the other world.[59] Lee says that "Cho's Holy Spirit movement has made the most of the shamanistic background," but that Cho "tries not to be syncretized with shamanism" by his "sticking to the principles of the Bible."[60] He says that the challenge for the

---

[56]Fourth Dimension, 46, 71; Fourth Dimension, vol. 2, 36.

[57]Fourth Dimension, 47-49.

[58]Young-hoon Lee, "The Holy Spirit Movement in Korea: Its Historical and Doctrinal Development" (Ph.D. dissertation, Temple University, 1996), 19-21.

[59]Lee, "Holy Spirit Movement," 25-26.

[60]Lee, "Holy Spirit Movement," 205.

church was that the "shamanistic tendency" of Koreans made them vulnerable to "seeking healing rather indiscreetly" and that they might "focus only on material blessing in the present life."[61] Jeong says that shamanism not only gave Koreans a concept of a High God but through its rituals it offered "help and salvation from worldly suffering and pain of han" (a unique Korean expression roughly translated as bitter grief and despair); and it ensured health, fertility and success. He says that Korean Pentecostalism has a "similar ritual function within the same culture of han."[62] Korea has a "shamanistic environment" that is a "seedbed" for Cho's "contextual ministry." In this unique context, the gospel is interpreted as the healing of han through "this-worldly blessing, material wealth, good health, and other personal and familial well-being which Koreans desperately need."[63] Jeong suggests that the healing of han is achieved through the rituals of Cho's preaching, prayer, worship with dancing and gospel songs, speaking in tongues, and the ministry to women in home cell groups.[64] Another Pentecostal scholar, Dongsoo Kim, has also written of Korean Pentecostalism as the healing of han. He adds the important observation of Cho's calling to the ministry in the midst of personal suffering and a terminal illness from which he was miraculously healed, a similar calling to that of shamans qualifying them to be "priests of *han*."[65] Many African Pentecostal church leaders have been called in similar circumstances, and this too is the way that traditional healers are called. This is another instance of the contextualization of shamanistic culture in Cho's ministry.

Mark Mullins refers to the "shamanistic orientation" that has "undeniably permeated Korean Christianity." He says that the "threefold blessing" theology of Cho Yonggi, the exorcism

---

[61]Lee, "Holy Spirit Movement," 212-213.

[62]Jeong, "Formation and Development," 17, 26-27, 30.

[63]Jeong, "Formation and Development," 235.

[64]Jeong, "Formation and Development," 246-56.

[65]Dongsoo Kim, "The Healing of Han in Korean Pentecostalism," *Journal of Pentecostal Theology* 15 (October 1999), 123-139 (135).

practices of Ki-dong Kim (a Korean Baptist pastor), and the prayer mountain movement are all examples of this.[66] However, I have tried to demonstrate that it is more appropriate to consider Cho's Pentecostalism as a contextual form of Korean Christianity interacting with shamanism. Korean Pentecostals justify their practices of healing and doctrine of blessings by referring to the Bible as their prime source. This tends to confirm Harvey Cox's contention that "primal spirituality now surfacing in Korea…also underlies the original biblical faith as well,"[67] as the main reason for the growth of Pentecostalism in Korea and in other countries of the world. But Cox may not have reflected on the enormous difference between interacting with shamanism (as Korean Pentecostals do) and becoming shamanistic. This is an untenable position for Pentecostals; Cho himself clearly rejects traditional shamanism and says that shamans "serve demons."[68]

Cho's context clearly played an important role in the shaping of his theology. Several Korean scholars have written of the context of the 1950s when Cho was converted from Buddhism to Christianity and the Full Gospel Central Church was founded in the slums of Seoul.[69] This was a time, says Lee Young Hoon, when "most people despaired in emptiness and frustration," and when "Cho's message of salvation in body and spirit gave enormous comfort and hope to the people who were poor and suffering."[70] This message of hope in a good God solved the *han* of people.[71] Cho refers to these years in most of his books; they are a very significant part of his message and the foundation of the theology he developed for a despairing people. He refers to the sufferings created by the Japanese occupation and the Korean War, and his own personal poverty and gradual healing from

---

[66]Mullins, *Made in Japan*, 175-177.

[67]Cox, Fire from Heaven, 226.

[68]David (Paul) Yonggi Cho, *How can I be Healed?* (Seoul: Seoul Logos, 1999), 98-100.

[69]Myung, "Spiritual Dimension," 111, 235-36.

[70]Lee, "Holy Spirit Movement," 179.

[71]Lee, "Holy Spirit Movement," 204; Myung, "Spiritual Dimension," 111.

tuberculosis.[72] This was a time when many were "struggling for existence," when he identified himself with the hundreds of refugees on the streets and became himself "one of the hopeless."[73] He mentions the aftermath of the Korean War when people lost families and businesses, had mental breakdowns, and became "completely possessed by the devil."[74] His ministry began in a poverty-stricken area of suburban Seoul, where he himself was poor and where people were not interested in a message about heaven and hell in their daily struggle for survival. As Myung puts it, in this situation "the gospel had to be reinterpreted and renewed theologically" to meet the needs of people, so a "contextualization of the gospel was needed."[75] Cho's teaching on healing was closely related to the poverty and sickness rampant in Korea at that time.[76] His teaching on blessings and prosperity was his "theological counteraction" to the *han* created by the ravages of the Korean War.[77] For Cho, the message of Christ and the power of the Holy Spirit was a present contextual message that gave hope to a suffering and destitute community. Most of his members in these early years were extremely poor.[78] His views on poverty are clear, again determined by his context:

> Poverty is a curse from Satan. God desires that all His people prosper and be healthy as their soul prospers (3 John 1:2). Yet

---

[72] *Fourth Dimension*, 110; *Solving Life's Problems* (Seoul: Seoul Logos, 1980), 48, 73, 125, 135; *Fourth Dimension*, vol. 2, xi-xviii, 20; *Successful Home Cell*, 3; *More than Numbers*, 24, 97, 118; *Praying with Jesus* (Altamonte Springs, FL: Creation House, 1987), 91.

[73] Fourth Dimension, 9-10.

[74] Fourth Dimension, 14.

[75] Myung, "Spiritual Dimension," 236.

[76] Jeong, "Formation and Development," 216.

[77] Jeong, "Formation and Development," 225.

[78] Fourth Dimension, 172; Solving Life's Problems, 132; Fourth Dimension, vol. 2, xviii, 27; More than Numbers, 23; Salvation, Health and Prosperity: Our Threefold Blessings in Christ (Altamonte Springs, FL: Creation House, 1987), 11; The Holy Spirit, My Senior Partner: Understanding the Holy Spirit and His Gifts (Seoul: Seoul Logos, 1989), 8; Jeong, "Formation and Development," 226-27.

> much of the world has not really seen poverty as I have seen it. Especially in the Third World, people live their lives in despair, struggling to survive for one more day. I am from the Third World. I know first-hand what it is not to have anything to eat.[79]

Elsewhere he writes that it is because of his "oppressed background," he has been able "to understand the plight of many oppressed people who have no hope for a future."[80] It is important to understand that Cho's views on poverty and prosperity come out of his own Korean context of poverty, Japanese occupation, and the Korean War; and should not be interpreted within the context of western wealth and materialism as might be done with the "prosperity" theology of Kenneth Copeland, for example.

5. Cho's Pentecostal Theology

That Cho is a "classical Pentecostal" thoroughly influenced by US Pentecostalism is a feature of his theology that cannot be denied. He is, after all, a minister in the Korean Assemblies of God and Chairman of the World Assemblies of God Fellowship since 1992—thus he is arguably the most influential minister in this denomination globally. He was trained in the denomination's Bible school in Seoul, where he received his own experience of "baptism of the Spirit." Even though he may be regarded in many ways as a theological innovator within classical Pentecostalism (one of the reasons why his books have been so popular in the West), yet his theology is unmistakably Pentecostal. This is especially true of his theology of the Spirit, expressed in his 1989 publication, *The Holy Spirit, My Senior Partner*. The influence of his Assemblies of God background is evident in that Cho stresses the importance of being "filled with the Holy Spirit" and the

[79] *Fourth Dimension*, vol. 2, 137-38.

[80] More than Numbers, 24.

"initial evidence" of speaking in tongues.[81] Cho sees this as an experience subsequent to and distinct from regeneration or conversion,[82] and distinguishes between speaking in tongues as a "sign" and as a "gift."[83] Like all Pentecostals, speaking or praying in tongues is very important to him.[84] Cho sometimes uses the phrase "baptized in the Spirit" in his writings, but distinguishes between being "filled with" and having "fellowship with" the Spirit, between speaking in tongues and being filled with the Spirit,[85] and the latter results in people having an "overflowing blessing" to share with others.[86] The fellowship with the Holy Spirit for every believer is an important emphasis,[87] and perhaps one of the many theological innovations that might place Cho in a pneumatological centre. The Holy Spirit is the "Senior Partner" in his ministry, and Cho says that intimacy or communion with the Holy Spirit is "the greatest experience of my life."[88]

Cho's understanding of evangelism and mission also is typically Pentecostal, motivated by and completely dependent upon the enabling of the Spirit.[89] He says that his preaching is based on the goodness of God, the redemption of Christ and biblical "principles of success," so that meeting the personal needs of people is his priority above "theology, history and politics."[90] His teaching on sickness and emphasis on healing is also typically Pentecostal: physical healing is seen as part of Christ's redemption; sickness is "from the devil" and a "curse"; and God

[81] *Holy Spirit*, 8-9; *Successful Home Cell*, 131, 149. However, Myung, "Spiritual Dimension," 64-65 suggests that Cho does not insist on "initial evidence."

[82] *Holy Spiri*, 100-102.

[83] Holy Spirit, 167-68.

[84] *How to Pray: Patterns of Prayer* (Seoul: Seoul Logos, 1997), 76-83.

[85] Holy Spirit, 111.

[86] Salvation, 49; Successful Home Cell, 119-120.

[87] *Salvation*, 32; *Great Businessmen* (Seoul: Seoul Logos, 1995), 69-75.

[88] Holy Spirit, 13; Successful Home Cell, 131.

[89] Holy Spirit, 21.

[90] Successful Home Cell, 153-56.

wants all people healed.[91] Like most Pentecostal preachers, Cho makes extensive use of personal experience or "testimony" to illustrate his theology. This is particularly noticeable on the subject of healing, when Cho often refers to his own sicknesses and how he was healed,[92] and gives testimonies of people healed during his ministry to them. Cho makes much of the experience of being "born again" and all his books have a strong soteriological and Christocentric tone. His holistic view of salvation is in common with Pentecostals all over the world, and one of the reasons why the Pentecostal message has spread rapidly among people in great need. He even espouses premillenial eschatology like most classical Pentecostals do, complete with end-time apocalyptic predictions about the union of Europe, the revival of Israel, and anti-communist rhetoric.[93] In all these emphases, Cho is a true Pentecostal, clearly influenced by the ideology of the US Assemblies of God.

Hwa Yung, a Chinese Malaysian evangelical, suggests that Cho's theology goes beyond evangelical theology with three distinctives of its own: his ideas of the "threefold blessings" of salvation, the "fourth dimension" of the spiritual realm and "faith incubation."[94] As we have seen, the most contentious criticisms are those that see Cho as a preacher of a North American "prosperity gospel" and on the other hand, those that consider him a "Pentecostal shaman." But his teaching on "prosperity" is based on his emphases, which Cho unashamedly proclaims in true Pentecostal fashion. Following the early Pentecostals who preached a fourfold "full gospel" of Jesus the Savior, Healer, Baptizer with the Holy Spirit, and the Coming King, Cho adds his "threefold blessings." His most often quoted text is 3 John 2 (also

---

[91] *Suffering... Why Me?* (South Plainfield, NJ: Bridge Publishing, 1986), 6, 13, 17, 33-41, 57-62; *Salvation,* 115-56; *How Can I be Healed?* 15-20.

[92] Suffering, 89-93; Successful Home Cell, 41-44.

[93] *Praying with Jesus*, 115-26; *Daniel: Insight on the Life and Dreams of the Prophet from Babylon* (Lake Mary, FL: Creation House, 1990); *Revelation: Visions of Our Ultimate Victory in Christ* (Seoul: Seoul Logos, 1991).

[94] Yung Hwa, Mangoes or Bananas? The Quest for an Authentic Asian Christian Theology (Oxford: Regnum Books, 1997), 206-207.

a favorite with North American "prosperity preachers"): "Beloved, I pray that in all respects you may prosper and be in good health, just as your soul prospers."[95] His teaching on this subject is laid out in several of his books, but most comprehensively in *Salvation, Health and Prosperity: Our Threefold Blessings in Christ*, where he explains that this "aspect of the gospel" was emphasized during a particular time when Korea was "striving to join the ranks of the advanced countries of the world," so that "Korean Christians should have an attitude which is more productive, creative, positive and active."[96] But he was given the message of threefold blessings in the midst of poverty and destitution after the Korean War, and this was to become the foundation of all his preaching and ministry thereafter.[97] The only way to receive the threefold blessings is to believe that God is a "good God" and that salvation includes forgiveness of sins, health and prosperity.[98] His doctrine of "blessings" is not however a selfish, individualistic "bless me" teaching, but one intended to bring "overflowing blessings" to those people who are in contact with each believer.[99]

The threefold blessings doctrine is the most emphasized of all Cho's teachings. The official brochure of the Yoido Full Gospel Church states that the "fivefold message of the Gospel" includes: 1) renewal, or "salvation," expressed in classical Pentecostal terms; 2) the fullness of the Spirit, the doctrine for which Pentecostals are well known; 3) healing, another emphasis of early Pentecostals and one of the main emphases throughout Cho's ministry; 4) blessing, Cho's addition to the "fourfold" gospel, which is declared to be "an abundant life of blessing which would be enough to share with others"; and 5) the Second Coming of Christ. The "threefold blessings of salvation" are further explained

---

[95] *Solving Life's Problems*, 47. Myung Soo Park, "David Yonggi Cho," 108 suggests that this teaching emanates directly from North Americans, especially healing evangelist Oral Roberts.

[96] Salvation, 5.

[97] *Salvation*, 11-12.

[98] *Salvation*, 16-18.

[99] *Salvation*, 49-50.

to include “soul prosperity,” “prosperity in all things” and “a healthy life,” based on the 3 John 2 text.[100] This is clearly a promise of health and prosperity in the present life for Christian believers, but Cho says clearly that happiness does not come from outward wealth (“mere material gain”), but from “solutions to our deep, inner problems,” [101] and he condemns those who think that happiness comes from power and wealth.[102] The fourfold/ fivefold message of the “full gospel” of the Pentecostals is strongly Christocentric and soteriological; and so is Cho’s theology. The focus of page after page of his writings is Jesus Christ and his redemptive work as Savior from sin, sickness, demon possession, poverty, and trouble of every kind. He contrasts his message with that of other denominations:

> I believe it is necessary to preach the full gospel, the total work of Jesus Christ and the Holy Spirit in the life of a believer. The message from our church is about the saving Jesus, the sanctifying Christ, the baptizing Savior, the “blessing” Son of God, the healing Jesus and our soon coming King![103]

It is important to realize that Cho did not develop his teaching on success and prosperity from the context of the affluent West and the North American “health and wealth” preachers. As far as I have been able to ascertain, Cho does not even refer to Kenneth Hagin and other “Word of Faith” teachers in his writings, if we exclude Oral Roberts from this group. In spite of some scholars’ suggestion of a connection between Cho and the “Word of Faith” school of Hagin,[104] I did not find reference to this in any of his writings. However, he does not hide his admiration for and the influence of Roberts (in common with many Pentecostal preachers) and he mentions Robert Schuller, a “possibility

---

[100]Yoido Full Gospel Church, *Yoido Full Gospel Church* (Seoul: Yoido Full Gospel Church, 1993), 1.

[101]Solving Life’s Problems, 15-16.

[102]Praying with Jesus, 26.

[103]Fourth Dimension, 91.

[104]Park, “David Yonggi Cho,” 118.

thinking" preacher with whom Cho has shared platforms, in a favorable light.[105] More controversially, but probably innocently from his perspective, Cho once referred to mind-power writer Napoleon Hill and "positive thinking" advocate Norman Vincent Peale.[106] However this must not detract from the fact that it was in the context of the slums of Seoul among people recovering from the horrors of the Japanese occupation and the Korean War when Cho began to preach that poverty was a curse, and that God was interested in setting people free from this by giving them "the full blessing of prosperity."[107] At the same time, he questioned the motives of those, including preachers, who desired prosperity but did not put God first.[108] For Cho, "prosperity" as an end in itself is evil, for God blesses his people only so that they may meet the needs of the poor and the needy.[109] Because his "contextual theology" is also dynamic, keeping up with the modernization of Korea that occurred from the 1980s onwards, Cho adapted to the changing context and also attracted the emerging middle class with his message of overcoming success in all circumstances, including business ventures.[110] Yet Cho condemns modern western culture with its rapid pace, pleasure-loving activities, and entertainment-centered churches. These things, he declares, hinder people and churches from having "the full blessings of the Lord," as they need time for prayer ("waiting upon the Lord"), worship and the preaching of God's Word, the emphases of Cho's services.[111] He says that many "traditional churches" in the West have "forgotten the vitality of Christianity and have become dead and sterile," and that this is the reason that many western young

---

[105]*Salvation*, 91, 104-105; Park, "David Yonggi Cho," 116.

[106]Successful Home Cell, 160.

[107]*Solving Life's Problems*, 27, 31; Hwa, *Mangoes or Bananas*, 209; Myung, "Spiritual Dimension," 249, 250-51.

[108]Solving Life's Problems, 38.

[109]*Fourth Dimension*, vol.2, 153-54.

[110]Park, "David Yonggi Cho," 120.

[111]*Fourth Dimension*, 33-34, 105-106.

people turn to Eastern mysticism.[112] Early Pentecostals too were a world-denying movement who saw the churches of the day as dry, formal and lifeless, who needed to be restored so that they could experience the power of God. There are passages in Cho's writings that theologically are hard to swallow, such as his teaching that in the kingdom of God there is no poverty.[113] Cho has also been criticized as being unconcerned with social change and structures of oppression, but the YFGC has extensive social care programs.[114] Although the Korean liberation theology known as Minjung theology has espoused the concerns of the poor and oppressed, it is to Pentecostal churches like YFGC that the poor and oppressed have flocked for relief.

Christianity, particularly in its Pentecostal emphasis of the transforming power of the Spirit, purports to offer more than traditional religions like Korean shamanism did. Likewise in Africa, thousands of independent Pentecostal churches have changed the face of Christianity because they have proclaimed a holistic gospel that includes deliverance from all types of oppression like sickness, sorcery, evil spirits and poverty. This central message has often met the felt needs of Africans more fundamentally than that of churches founded by European missionaries, who left a message that is sometimes over-spiritualized and intellectualized.[115] So, if Cho's theology has been born in the context of a deeply suffering nation reeling from the aftermath of Japanese occupation and a devastating civil war, then this message is good news for the poor and oppressed, and provides incentives for people struggling to make a living. Unlike some American "prosperity preachers," Cho does not deny the role of suffering in the purposes of God.[116] The "thorn in the flesh," he says, enables believers to live with "persistent perplexity" and

[112]Fourth Dimension, 2, 76-77.

[113]*Praying with Jesus*, 50-51. A more nuanced teaching on this is given in Cho, *Salvation*, 68.

[114]Lee, "Holy Spirit Movement," 214.

[115]Allan Anderson, *Moya: The Holy Spirit in an African Context* (Pretoria: University of South Africa Press, 1991), 30.

[116]Fourth Dimension, 108-112.

thereby know the grace of God.[117] This is somewhat ambiguous, as Cho distinguishes between suffering and sickness and does not think that sickness is the will of God,[118] but there is no "cheap grace" in his theology. His own experiences of sickness came often and lasted long, but through these he learned to "trust even more," and he was "able to live above despair and continue to walk with God until [his] healing came."[119] He was himself seriously ill for ten years while he preached healing in Christ, and Cho believes that this experience enabled him to be "completely broken" and "helpless" before God.[120] His views on suffering are clear:

> Concerning suffering and endurance of many kinds of trials, we must discipline ourselves to maintain tenacious trust and confidence in the love of God when our lives are shaken by the winds and storms of suffering. Then we will overcome and receive victory. . . . Though everything may look dismal and suffering become worse, God will ultimately cause all these things to work together for good because His Word says so. We must have absolute trust in Almighty God even in times of suffering, because there is no power greater than the power of Almighty God.[121]

It is not clear whether by "suffering" in these and other similar passages include physical sickness, but Cho's ideas here are a world away from the crass statements of the purveyors of a gospel of health and wealth.

---

[117]Solving Life's Problems, 97.

[118]Successful Home Cell, 152; Suffering, 104.

[119]Suffering, 96.

[120]Successful Home Cell, 43.

[121]*Suffering*, 101, 102.

6. Conclusion

Those who censure Korean Pentecostals like Cho for their alleged "shamanism" often fail to see that the parallels with ancient religions in these practices are also continuous with the biblical record. Furthermore, these Pentecostals define their practices by reference to the Bible rather than to shamanism, but see their activities as creative adaptations to the local context. At the same time, Asian Pentecostals might also need a greater appreciation for the rich diversity of their cultural and religious past. Demonizing this past does not explain the present attraction of Pentecostalism for East Asian peoples deeply influenced by their ancient religions and cultures, even though such a demonization might help in the religious competition that is a feature of these pluralist societies. But one conclusion that is incontrovertible is that Korean Pentecostals have found both culturally and Biblically acceptable alternatives to and adaptations from the practices of their ancient religions and are seeking to provide answers to the needs inherent in their own context.

I live in the western world and my understanding of religious phenomena outside my context will always be partial. There are unanswered questions about Cho's theology that are better debated by Koreans themselves. But Pentecostal theology in countries like Korea should not be a reflection of a theology born in the totally different context of the USA, even though cultural radiation from this country has invaded South Korea for over a generation. A theology "made in the USA," whether Pentecostal or otherwise, is a form of cultural colonialism. I believe that Asian Pentecostals must develop a theology that speaks with a different perspective of the voice of the poor, a theology of hope for a suffering people, a genuinely contextual theology. The good news, Cho declares, is that God meets all the needs of believers, including their spiritual salvation, physical healing, and other blessings for material needs. As Hwa Yung has pointed out, Cho is "an excellent example of how the gospel must be appropriately contextualized to address the felt needs of a people."[122] East Asia, like Africa and Latin

[122]Hwa, Mangoes or Bananas, 209.

America, also has the phenomenon of mass urbanization, and the Pentecostal churches have provided places of spiritual security and personal communities for people unsettled by rapid social change. As the Korean church becomes more relevant to their cultural and social context, they become more able to serve the wider society. This is evident in the contextual ministry and Pentecostal theology of David Yonggi Cho.

THEOLOGY OF DAVID YONGGI CHO AS A NEW THEOLOGICAL PARADIGM OF KOREAN THEOLOGY FOR THE NEW CENTURY

Hyeon-sung Bae

1. Introduction

Korean theology has been satisfied with simply introducing western popular theological issues and thoughts into Korea and imitating them without theological reflection. Therefore, Korean theology [1] has been separated from the reality of *sitz im leben.*[2] If theology loses its relevance to the church and society, spending its time in fruitless quarrels over semantics, it may well become a spiritless academic subject. Theology should help the church and society open their eyes to the unlimited potential of God. Though it is an academic field, it recognizes the need to lead contemporary people to the life and truth of Christ.

---

[1]"Korean theology" is a theology that seeks for theological identity of Korea by interpreting and exploring the relationship between the gospel and Korean culture. As a result, Korean theology is a theology which not only represents Christian spirituality in Korea but also conveys cultural and national identity of Korea to Korean Christians. It necessarily asks for new perspective on interpreting the text and the context. According to Chul-ha Han, "Hankuk Shinhaneui Kaenyum" [The Concept of Korean Theology], *Kyohohwa Shinhak* [Church and Theology] 5 (1971), 46-73 (73), Korean theology is "a theology which is expressed by Koreans' intrinsic thought."

[2]As a German term, it indicates essential circumstantial factors on which one's actual reality of life can be formed and based. It is a barometer which evaluates whether one's life operates fairly or not in a society.

It is necessary for Korean Christians to pay attention to David Yonggi Cho's theological contributions given, not only to the Korean church, but also to the global church. Cho is not a theologian but a pastor who has been serving Yoido Full Gospel Church (YFGC) in Korea, the largest single congregation in the world, for 46 years. This noteworthy ministry began as a small tent church in the suburbs of Seoul. As an influential Christian leader, however, he has underlined the role of theology in secular society. He is challenging non-believers to Christian faith by introducing a full-life gospel, which enables people to cope with the issues of life.

It is understood that his successful ministry has already proven his theological potential. The writer has been interested in theologizing Cho's pastoral thoughts and experiences, which have so impacted the world. Known as Youngsan[3] theology, these principles are not for the sake of theology itself but are for the glory of God manifested through his church. The primary purpose of this study, therefore, is to explore the nature of Cho's theology in light of contemporary theological needs.

2. Implications of Cho's Theology and Metaphor of Chopsticks

In order to understand Cho's theology, it is necessary to have an appreciation of the Full Gospel[4] theology that has come forth from Pentecostalism. We can visualize Korean Pentecostal theology through Full Gospel theology. Here, Full Gospel theology is an indigenized form of Pentecostal theology rooted in the historical nature of the Pentecostal movements described as

---

[3]As a pen name of Cho, "Youngsan" (靈山) has a literal meaning of "spiritual mountain."

[4]Here, "Full Gospel" is literally taking and accepting fully and totally all that is in the Bible, to revitalize the faith and fullness of the Holy Spirit as was done in Pentecost. See International Theological Institute (ITI), *Hananimeui Sunghoi Kyohoisa* [The Church History of the Assemblies of God] (Seoul: Seoul Logos, 1998), 249.

"the former rain and the latter rain."[5] Significantly this has not been imported from abroad but is Korean and has become compatible with the Korean mind and spirit through its continual theological reflection and application to the churches in Korea.

Thanks to Cho's contribution to its development, Full-Gospel theology cannot be separated from Cho's theology.[6] It consists primarily of two theological poles: the "Fivefold Gospel"[7] and the "Threefold Blessing."[8] In light of Cho's 46 years of successful ministry, the effective application of Full Gospel theology cannot be underestimated. Cho's ministry has influenced church leaders in Korea and many are following his preaching style, Pentecostal faith, and experience.[9] Cho's theological essence may be delineated as a "holistic salvation" with great attention to the recovery of mankind's intrinsic nature, "The image of God."

Cho's teaching contains various implicitly expressed themes in its theological identity. It is not a theology of the past tense but

---

[5]See Joel 2:23, "He will cause to come down for you the rain, *the former rain*, and *the latter rain* in the first month." All scripture quotations are from the New International Version.

[6]Hyeon-sung Bae, *Sunbokeumshinhak Ihaelulwihan Ipmunseo: Chutgalakkwa Shinhakeui Mannam* [An Introduction to Full Gospel Theology: Meeting with Chopsticks and Theology] (Gunpo, Korea: Hansei University Press, 2002), 34-37.

[7]This is a central issue of Full Gospel theology. It is composed of five essential messages of the Bible: gospel of Christ's redemption, gospel of fullness of the Holy Spirit, gospel of blessing, gospel of healing and gospel of Christ's second coming. See, Yonggi Cho, *Ojungbokeumkwa Samjungchukbok* [Fivefold Gospel and Threefold Blessing] (Seoul: Youngsan Pub., 1983), 49-53.

[8]"Threefold Blessing" has a theological connotation of holistic salvation which entails spiritual, contextual and physical well-being of people based on 3 John 2: "Dear friend, I pray that you may enjoy good health and that all may go well with you, even as your soul is getting along well."

[9]Hyeon-sung Bae, "Comments on Minjung and Pentecostal Movements in Korea," in *Pentecostals after a Century: Global Perspectives on a Movement in Transition*, eds. Allan H. Anderson and Walter J. Hollenweger (Sheffield: Sheffield Academic Press, 1999), 161-63 (161).

the present. His theology is still in process. Jesus Christ never described the kingdom of God without using parables.[10] The same paradigm can be applied to Cho's theology. The writer would like to offer "chopsticks" as a crucial metaphor symbolizing the theological implications of Cho's theology for the following reasons.

First, chopsticks suggest the daily culture of the Korean people. Like cutlery, chopsticks are tools used with meals. So cutlery is to the western food culture what chopsticks are to the Korean. Chopsticks are indispensable. In other words, chopsticks reflect the Korean culture *sitz im leben.* Cho regards *sitz im leben* as an essential factor for doing theology.[11] As the metaphor of chopsticks shows us, Cho's theology reflects the daily culture of Korea.

Moreover, chopsticks entail the profound Korean philosophical principles of harmony. Chopsticks are comprised of one pair. Hence, without inter-action between the two sticks, it is impossible for chopstick users to pick up or hold anything. Harmony is essential. The two sticks function differently in their folding and unfolding. The Chinese letter, 人 (*in*) which means *human being* is composed of two persons. It denotes that one props the other to stand. Human beings cannot live alone without support; just as one chopstick cannot function independently of the other.

One thing we should note is the tension between the two. In spite of this tension, the pneumatological mystery enables us to convert the tension to potential. This tension, therefore, is

---

[10]Matthew 13: 34, "he did not say anything to them without using a parable."

[11]It is the terms that identify the function of theology as active and a dynamic one. It is far from static and a fixed one. Thus, the nature of theology is closer to a verb form rather than a noun. It means that theology is always open to actual reality in order to meet the needs of people. See, John Parratt, *A Guide to Doing Theology* (London: SPCK, 1996).

creative[12] rather than destructive. As harmony and tension are indispensable in using chopsticks, these two elements are essential in understanding Cho's theology. For instance, God's providence and human free will are opposite concepts that have theological tension. In Cho's theology, we can see the holistic theological perspectives that enable these opposite concepts to be harmonized. His theology brings harmony to opposites through creative tension.

In addition, chopsticks require experience and skill to handle them well. Chopstick users should spend time in training to use them properly. If they are used impatiently, disregarding the rules, chopsticks are no longer chopsticks but sticks. Chopsticks are of no use to people who have never used them before. Therefore, to use chopsticks well, people need experience in handling them. Cho emphasizes the point that the Pentecostal experience enables people to cope with the various issues of life in context. As chopstick users need training in their proper use, he challenges today's Christians to receive spiritual training in the ways of Pentecost. As we can see from the above metaphor, chopsticks provide tremendous insight to those who are interested in exploring Cho's theology. In summary, Cho's theology, rooted in a Pentecostal background, is concrete and practical in meeting the actual needs of contemporary people by offering hope and vision.

3. Theology of *Sitz im Leben*

The starting point of theological study is to recover a sense of balance in dealing with people's problems. Considering this, theology needs to address the issues found in their *Sitz im Leben.* Cho's ministry endeavors to heal people's wounds and to restore wholeness. His theology consists of the recognition of *Sitz im Leben* thereby enabling people to experience God's presence and provision. Regarding the role of theology, Cho's position is to

---

[12]James D. G. Dunn, Unity and Diversity in the New Testament: An Inquiry into the Character of Earliest Christianity (London: SCM, 1977), 381.

supply bread to those who come to church asking for it.[13] In this regard, Villa-Vicencio, a leading South African theologian, raises a question on the role of a theology:

> A theology that fails to address the most urgent questions asked by ordinary people (and given the bias of the church in favor of the marginalized people, especially their questions) is not theology at all. It is little more than an academic exercise in uncovering archaic or dying religious beliefs and reified doctrines about God.[14]

Cho ministers to the spiritual being and the natural being. This is the why he underlines a holistic salvation. Cho does not neglect the needs of Koreans' *Sitz im Leben* where various theological motivations emerge. He has raised theological questions from the core of Korean thought and ideology. Moreover, he has a responsibility to seek the healing of the torn and broken minds of the people, not simply in words, but by showing the way. His theological stance is practical and dynamic rather than abstract and static. It aims at solving people's problems and helping them experience God's presence daily by discerning God's will and participating in the historical reality of Korea.

Minjung theology has drawn much attention to the socio-political and economic issues in Korea. According to Harvey Cox Korean Christians invented their own form of liberation theology called "Minjung theology." The Korean term "minjung" describes the ordinary people among whom Christianity first developed.[15] Minjung identifies the grass-roots who are oppressed politically, exploited economically, alienated socially and uneducated in

---

[13]Cho, Fivefold Gospel and Threefold Blessing, 13.

[14] Charles Villa-Vicencio, *A Theology of Reconstruction: Nation-Building and Human Rights* (Cambridge: Cambridge University Press, 1992), 40.

[15]Harvey Cox, Fire from Heaven: The Rise of Pentecostal Spirituality and the Reshaping of Religion in the Twenty-first Century (London: Cassell, 1996), 220.

cultural and intellectual matters. This theology has highlighted the issues of poverty, political violence, deprivation of rights and discrimination against the minjung in their context. During the 1970s and 80s, due to the challenge of Minjung theology, the churches in Korea were awakened from their ignorance of social concerns. In spite of its merits, however, Minjung theology is controversial in that it underestimates the transcendental aspects of godly revelations and relegates them to theories of sociology or ideology. Like liberation theology, it no longer sees itself as an interpretation of the church's traditional doctrine of faith, but as a reflection on praxis, and its critical accompaniment.[16]

Contrary to Minjung theology, Cho's theology satisfies both social and spiritual concerns. While Minjung theology is a socio-political theology seeking to reform an unjust socio-political system and structure, Cho's theology is wholeness-centered seeking holistic salvation. Therefore, it is meaningless and superficial to try to understand Cho's theology without knowledge of the *Sitz im Leben.* In fact, he regards theology as a tool to deepen and broaden opportunities to build people's dignity. He raised the question: How can the gospel meet people's needs who are broken economically, socially, physically and spiritually? Cho states, "God, where are you now? How can I give hope and new life to people who are in a desperate situation lacking of minimum level of clothing and meals?"[17]

Agonizing over this question, he started to pray earnestly. Cho's theological doctrine is found in 3 John 2 forming the hermeneutical tool of "Threefold Blessing." It is a contextual theology gleaned from his reflections on *Sitz im Leben*. It is necessary to develop an expression of truth, faith, and life in Korea by interpreting the *Sitz im Leben* which is relevant to the Korean theological context.

---

[16]Walter Kasper, *Theology and Church*, trans. Margret Kohl (London: SCM, 1989), 133.

[17]Yonggi Cho, *Samjungchukbok* [Threefold Salvation] (Seoul: Seoul Logos, 1989), 18.

4. Theology of Holistic Salvation

Holistic salvation challenges people to live according to the purposes of God's creation reminding us of man's original nature. It is often called "Threefold Salvation" in that it not only signifies salvation from the curse of mankind but also entails blessings in the spiritual, mental and physical dimensions. God enables people to seek holistic salvation wherever they live, and whatever their condition. The word "holistic" (*holos* in Greek) refers to an understanding of reality in terms of integrated wholes, while "salvation" (*soteria* in Greek) implies health and wholeness.[18]

After all, holistic salvation denotes harmonious relationship with God, the self and the world. We live in a society where people are still struggling for their dignity as human beings. Regarding this, Cho suggests the following answers through the "Threefold Blessing":

> Actually, today many people are crying out at the top of their voice due to the problems of purposelessness, a sense of futility, poverty, curse, sickness and fear of death. For them, it is "Threefold Blessing" that is necessary.[19]

Therefore, holistic salvation is living under the reign of God's perfect control. Regarding the ministry of Pentecostal churches in Korea, Harvey Cox points to the three crucial factors of "blessing, wholeness and healing."[20] His comments refer specifically to the theological distinctives of YFGC representing the Pentecostal churches in Korea. Here, blessing, wholeness and healing are central components of holistic salvation.

The kingdom of God is where Cho eventually aims through the concept of holistic salvation. As the kingdom of God has two

---

[18]See, Charles Sherlock, *The Docrtine of Humanity* (Leicester: Inter-Varsity Press, 1996), 212-13.

[19]Cho, Threefold Salvation, 18-19.

[20]Cox, Fire from Heaven, 234.

natures,[21] holistic salvation has both a present-oriented reality and a future-oriented one. While the former is "here and now," the latter carries the eschatological dimension of "there and then." Both are essential in understanding the kingdom of God. Christians, therefore, live between the two realms of the present and the future. The present dimension needs power against sin, sickness, darkness and the curse which prevents us from experiencing God's presence in the here and now. The future looks to eternal life wherein Christians shall be transformed in a place of wholeness without tears, suffering, and death. Cho's theology of holistic salvation concerns meeting people's needs by guiding them to "holistic salvation." It is far from a theology limited to a spiritual satisfaction only or the academic ivory tower. Holistic salvation is an essential element on which the basic frame of Cho's theology is built. Though, it has various theological implications, its main concern is to recover God-given totality, "the kingdom of God" on the various levels. In other words, holistic salvation is restoration of an open relationship with God.

Cho's theology is a theology of holistic salvation which is concerned in meeting the needs of people by guiding them to holistic salvation. It is far from the theology whose boundary is only limited to spiritual satisfaction or an academic ivory tower. Holistic salvation is a crucial theological element on which the basic frame of Cho's theology is built. Though it has various theological implications, its main concern is to recover God-given

---

[21]From the historical perspective, Paul Tillich, *Systematic Theology*, vol. 3 (London: SCM, 1991), 357 views the kingdom of God as both an inner-historical and a transhistorical side. According to him, the former is manifested by the "spiritual presence," while the latter is identical with "eternal life." According to Jürgen Moltmann, *Theology of Hope*, trans. James W. Leitch (London: SCM, 1988), 225, the kingdom of God is in the front line between the present and the promised future. See also J. B. Green, "The Kingdom of God," in *New Dictionary of Christian Ethics and Pastoral Theology*, eds. D. J. Atkinson and D. H. Field (Leicester: IVP, 1995), 530. An African theologian, Justin S. Ukpong, "Christology and Inculturation: A New Testament Perspective," in *Paths of African Theology*, ed. R. Gibellini (London: SCM, 1994), 40-61 (47) describes the two natures of the kingdom of God as a "present reality" and a "reality yet to be consummated."

totality, the kingdom of God, on the various levels. In other words, holistic salvation is the restoration of an open relationship with God.

5. Theology of Pentecostal Experience

The theological foundation of Cho relies on Pentecostal experience as the pivotal element of holistic salvation. As Donald W. Dayton once expressed, Pentecostalism emerged in the midst of unique forms of doctrines and experiences.[22] The most important Pentecostal distinctive in the twentieth century is to acknowledge the works of the Holy Spirit in the lives of ordinary individuals. Pentecostals have sought to articulate their value systems discovered through the experience of the Holy Spirit. In this perspective, we might say that Cho's theology is a theology of Pentecostal experience. Its theological motif relies on the twentieth-century Pentecostal movement whose theological foundations are "firmly planted in the nineteenth century Holiness movement and American revivalism."[23]

The central issue of the Pentecostal movement was the experience of the baptism of the Holy Spirit through which the convictions of Pentecostal faith were strengthened. That is, when speaking of the nature of the Pentecostal experience we cannot help but emphasize the works of the Holy Spirit. Theologians have attempted to understand the Holy Spirit according to their diverse theological perspectives.[24]

---

[22]Donald W. Dayton, *Theological Roots of Pentecostalism* (Metuchen, New Jersey: Hendrickson Publishers, 1996), 16.

[23] R. P. Menzies, "Evidential Tongues: An Essay on Theological Method," *Asian Journal of Pentecostal Studies* 1 (1998), 111-23 (111).

[24]Focusing on Christian faith and revelation, Martin Luther regards the Holy Spirit as a source for understanding God and as a goal for Christian life by experiencing him. According to him, "no one can understand God or God's word unless he has it revealed immediately by the Holy Ghost; but nobody can receive anything from the Holy Ghost unless he experiences it." Quoted in James D. G. Dunn, *Jesus and the Spirit: A Study of the Religious*

The Holy Spirit not only draws our attention to Christ and enables us to open our spiritual eyes, but also works through human beings in history. Furthermore, the Holy Spirit brings an eschatological hope by means of Christ's resurrection and invites us to become children and heirs of God.[25] The Holy Spirit eventually leads one to share Christ's glory. His power is not only for breaking through the walls of human bondage but also for unity embodied in Christ. The experience of the baptism of the Holy Spirit is paramount, whereby Christians are empowered to live under the presence of the Holy Spirit. What is meant by "presence" is the experience of being touched by the Holy Spirit. In a biblical sense, the Pauline term, "new being" or "new creation" (2 Cor 5:17) refers to the state of being grasped by the Holy Spirit. Therefore, the experience of the Holy Spirit is vital to any understanding of Cho's theology.

The early church was established on the foundation of Pentecostal experience. Moreover, members of the early church were Pentecostal in that they were given Charismatic gifts by the Holy Spirit. Thanks to Cho's enthusiasm through his preaching and teaching ministry, these issues in Korea are becoming popular and open even to non-Pentecostals. In this connection, we cannot

---

and Charismatic Experience of Jesus and the First Christians as Reflected in the New Testament (London: SCM, 1978), 175. K. Barth interprets the Holy Spirit in relation to the "Word" by saying: "The Holy Spirit is nothing else than a certain relation of the Word to man." See Karl Barth, *Dogmatics in Outline*, trans. G. T. Thomson (London: SCM, 1949), 138. Arguing the term "Spirit" like all other statements about God, as symbol, Tillich, *Systematic Theology*, III, 111 defines the Holy Spirit "as the actualization of power and meaning in unity." Jürgen Moltmann, *The Church in the Power of the Spirit: A Contribution to Messianic Ecclesiology,* trans. M. Kohl (London: SCM, 1977), 34 attempts to describe the Holy Spirit from the eschatological perspectives by saying, "Eschatologically…the Spirit can be termed 'the power of futurity' for it is 'the eschatological gift,' the beginning (Rom 8:23) and the earnest or guarantee (2 Cor 1:22; 5:5) of the future."

[25] See Hyeon-sung Bae, "Sungryungeui Kwanjumeseobon Bauleui Krisdoron: Rom. 8:1-17" [Paul's Christology from the Pneumatological Perspectives: Rom. 8:1-17] (Th.M. thesis, Seoul Methodist Theological Seminary, 1991), 63.

deny that the rapid church growth in Korea is closely related to Cho's Pentecostal influence.

6. Theology of Healing

The journey towards human wholeness necessarily includes the issue of healing. Healing is an integral part of the Pentecostal message. Cho's "Fivefold Gospel" includes the gospel of healing through a ministry manifested in signs, wonders, and charisma bringing relief from misery and death in individual lives. Accompanied by speaking in tongues, healing is another unique distinctive of Pentecostalism. Throughout the Bible, it was, and is the very nature of God to effect healing. However, churches in Korea seem to entrust healing to the medical doctors. Cho thrust the question of divine healing to the forefront. He placed healing in the theological and systematic order. In this respect, his tremendous achievement in the area of church growth resulted in a Pentecostal-healing ministry.

Jesus Christ never let his patients be sent away when they came to him for healing. Rather, he healed everyone who came to Him. Healing was central to his ministry of teaching and preaching. Jesus' healings were not limited to the physical, but were also holistic in that he linked the cause of the disease to the root of one's being. He demonstrated that the way to reach human wholeness is through healing. It is, therefore, a quest for the divine that has been part of humanity (no matter the cultural and ethnic distinctions) from the beginning of history.

In particular, the issue of healing is closely linked to the eschatological issue that deals with the final history and the kingdom of God.[26] Pentecostals perceive that God's kingdom becomes manifest and transformed into one's actual life toward human wholeness. Therefore, a realized eschatology challenges us to pray for healing. Pentecostals relate physical sickness or

---

[26]As discussed above, the kingdom of God has two natures: an immediate dimension, that is already established here and now; and an eternal dimension, that is not yet come.

material poverty to the spiritual dimension. Consequently, they view the spirit world as a present reality for which the divinely given charism, the discerning of spirits, is essential to any successful encounter with it.[27] Cho regards the cause of disease as a spiritual problem:

> There are many people who become blind or dumb when they are possessed by the devil. . . . Of course there are some who were born without eardrums or some whose eardrums have been ruptured. But there are some who cannot hear because of deaf spirits. And if these spirits are cast out in the name of Jesus, hearing can be restored miraculously and immediately. The Bible says that the devil causes all manner of diseases.[28]

The body is an evident, tangible aspect of a whole human being. A physical disorder not only affects our body, but also our whole life. In the West, people used to understand the cause of disease from the biological perspective. In contrast, traditional Koreans linked it to both biological and spiritual dimensions. That is the reason why traditional Koreans called for doctors as well as shamans when they became sick. In this connection, as Ryu points out, it is to a certain extent possible to consider that the shamanistic nature of Korean culture has somewhat made Koreans accessible to understand biblical truths and value systems.[29]

What makes Cho's understanding of healing distinguishable from evangelicals is that he regards healing not as a selective matter but as a requisite one. His basis for healing ministry is "Christ who has diseases on his back." Christ not only redeemed our sin, but also healed our sickness as well on the cross. In order

---

[27]Jesse Moon, "Power Encounter in Evangelism," in *Power Encounter: A Pentecostal Perspective*, ed. Opal L. Reddin, 2nd ed. (Springfield, MO: Central Bible College Press, 1989), 302-23 (321).

[28]Cho, Praying with Jesus, 246.

[29]Dong-sik Ryu, *Hankuk Jonggyo-wa Gidokkyo* [Korean Religions and Christianity] (Seoul: Korean Christian Literature Society, 1965).

to be healed, therefore, one has to repent of one's sin first and stand firm on the faith that he or she is already healed. He has challenged the believers to rely on the cross of Jesus for it is not only the source of salvation but also the foundation of healing.

The physical body is "a temple of the Holy Spirit" (1 Cor 6:19), a dwelling place of God. God intends that the human body be clean, beautiful, and strong. Accordingly, without physical health we are hard-pressed to maintain human wholeness. Cho seeks physical healing as well as embracing mental and spiritual wholeness through the life in the Spirit. A life of wholeness is a life of health, because healing reconnects people with wholeness. Healing involves making human beings whole.

7. Theology of Holistic Methodology

As shown in the metaphor of the chopsticks, Cho's theology underlines the principle of harmony between opposites. The concepts of good and evil, sacred and secular, heaven and earth, life and death exist in Christian thought. Furthermore, it is true that theology is based on the dual aspects of theory and practice, understanding and doing, loving and knowing, contemplating and acting. These are, however, integrally related and interdependent on one another. In fact, these dualities illuminate, inform, and guide theology in the right direction and into vitality. Therefore, we might say that there is no purely theoretical or critical enquiry that remains detached from involvement with action. When we look back over Christian history, we can find that dualism between theory and practice has been difficult to overcome. Consider Paul Ballard's perspective.

> It is essential for theology to be part of academic enquiry. At the same time, however, the place of theology is at the heart of the Church's life, giving reason for the hope that is within us, making the treasures of Scripture and tradition accessible to the People of God. . . . Theology is

> essentially geared to practice by which was meant the Church's ministry in its widest sense.[30]

Ultimate truth does not lie in a dualistic approach but in an integrative one. Harmony is related to a holistic theological methodology. The Korean church should consider developing a holistic methodology to do theology in an integrative way. Cho's theology stands as such in the "Threefold Blessing."

What then is holistic theological methodology? Above all, it maintains a well-balanced perspective without prejudice or partiality. It guides us to see unity through diversity. Eventually, it is a gateway into the theological world of depth and meaning. Cho integrates the dual aspects of theology by complementary and harmonious factors.

There have been some western scholars who attempted to overcome dualism by turning their faces to East Asian philosophical thought. For instance, Whitehead's theology seems to follow some aspects of East Asian thought more closely than other types of western thought.[31] Thus, even though western methodology has had a great influence on Korean theology, now it has become uncertain of itself and of its basis at least in a Korean context. Korean theology has begun to acquire a new self-confidence and has become a matter of deep concern among Korean Christians over the last two decades.

The holistic theological methodology includes both "theology of orthodoxy" and "theology of praxis." Here, the former needs a cool "mind," while the latter asks for a warm "heart." Regarding these two poles, John Parratt underscores the importance of the balance between two concepts:

> If we concentrate exclusively on the first pole, we shall run the risk of producing an academic theology which is

---

[30]Paul Ballard, "Can Theology Be Practical?" *Contact* 109 (1992), 3-4.

[31]"Introduction," in *Hanism as Korean Mind*, eds. Sang-Il Kim and Young-chan Ro (Los Angeles: Eastern Academy of Human Sciences, 1984), 1-7 (2).

> cut off from the real world in which we live; if we concentrate only on the second, we run the equally dangerous risk of distorting the Christian message. Doing theology, therefore, is something of a delicate balancing act.[32]

It seems clear that holistic theological methodology does not have an “A or B” approach, which forces people to choose a partial understanding of theology, but rather a “both A and B” methodology, which focuses on theological wholeness. Cho encompasses the complementarity of all opposites for the creative integration of the whole.

8. Conclusion

Cho’s theology has dynamic theological elements, which are appreciable to the Korean context. It is necessary to explore his theological concerns with integrity and sincerity in that they allow both the Korean church and society to go forward with maturity. Cho’s theology is wholeness-centered and still developing. He has challenged the Korean church by suggesting a theological paradigm for renewal and revival that cannot be achieved without self-awareness and criticism. To understand Cho’s theology one needs to deal with the broken realities of society as well as the church in a holistic manner: to meet peoples’ needs *Sitz im Leben*. Moreover, his theology is well-balanced and able to critique what is wrong within the church and society.

The Korean church must no longer simply translate western theology into Korean concepts or frames of thought. Rather, it needs theological imagination and vision that can help make both the church and society healthy and strong. As a way of liberating the Korean church from the pitfalls of western theology, the church should develop a holistic theological methodology. Cho’s theology is a form of Pentecostal theology based on his

---

[32]Parratt, A Guide to Doing Theology, 20.

Pentecostal and charismatic background. Furthermore, it seeks to dig out its theological meanings from the creative tension between two opposites through the presence of the Holy Spirit. In this connection, Cho's theology needs to be discussed more openly and deeply as an alternative.

It is becoming an increasing reality that Korean theology needs to look forward to a new paradigm for the new century: one that is relevant to the contemporary theological context. Given this point of view, churches in Korea must begin to consider Cho's theology as an instrument heralding a dynamic paradigm shift of the future.

PRAXIS

A MISSIOLOGICAL EVALUATION OF DAVID YONGGI CHO'S CHURCH GROWTH[1]

David S. Lim

1. Introduction

As the founding and senior pastor of the largest mega-church in the world so far, Rev. Dr. David Yonggi Cho (hereafter, Cho) has clearly been an effective leader of church growth (CG) in Korea and the world. What were the various factors that contributed to such phenomenal growth in Yoido Full Gospel Church (YFGC)? What other factors could have helped make it more effective in terms of evangelism and missions?

This essay critically evaluates six distinct characteristics of Cho's CG model: From missiological (theological and practical) perspectives, what are the positive and negative aspects of Cho's model of CG? My data are collected from published literature, especially Cho's, and includes some interviews with YFGC leaders as reported in Hong.[2]

---

[1]This work is a major revision of a paper entitled "Cho Yonggi's Charismatic Leadership and Church Growth" that was presented at the First Youngsan International Church Growth Conference, Seoul, Korea in August 2003.

[2]Young-gi Hong, "The Charisma of Cho Yonggi and Its Routin-ization in the Yoido Full Gospel Church of Korea," *Journal of Asian Mission* 2:1 (2000), 65-90. Hong is a scholarly participant-observer, being an ordained minister of YFGC who grew up in this church.

2. Definition of Church Growth

"Church growth" (CG) may be defined as "a consciously planned effort to affect increase in membership in a local church." This was popularized by the Fuller School of World Mission,[3] but found one of its best models in the YFGC. But unknown to many, Cho had already established Church Growth International (CGI) as a training and publishing institute in his church campus as early as 1976 to promote and share his CG experience with the global church.

The emphasis of CG is "conversion growth," not "biological growth" nor "transfer growth," as the main means of increasing membership through an ongoing program of evangelism and discipleship in a church.[4] Based on a 1998 survey, the membership increase through "transfer growth" at YFGC was only 52%, lower than that of the average church in Korea (60.7%).[5]

I consider 1964 as the starting point of Cho's mega-church type of church growth based on his creative cell system. He can therefore be considered the first church leader to conceive of and implement such a structure, which has gained global impact, providing the inspiration and a good model for subsequent ones.[6] Cho started his church with five members in a small tent in 1958, which grew to 800 in 1962; 2,000 in 1964; 18,000 in 1973; 200,000 in 1981; 503,000 in 1986; 593,000 in 1990; 671,000 in 1993; 709,070 in 1997; and 720,000 in 1998-99.[7] In the latest

---

[3] Cf. Donald A. McGavran, *Understanding Church Growth* (Grand Rapids: Eerdmans, 1980); C. Peter Wagner, *Your Church Can Grow: Seven Vital Signs of a Healthy Church*, rev. ed. (Glendale: Regal, 1984).

[4] Cf. Wagner, Your Church Can Grow.

[5] Hong, "The Charisma of Cho Yonggi," 86 n. 81. The rates of "conversion growth" and "biological growth" are not given.

[6] Cf. Joel Comiskey, *Groups of 12* (Houston: Touch Publications, 1999).

[7] Hong, "The Charisma of Cho Yonggi," 105. YFGC also branched off two mega-churches: Eunhye wa Chilli Church in 1981, and Full Gospel Inchon Church in 1983.

statistics that I have (1998-99), YFGC had 667 assistant pastors (ordained and non-ordained), 1,159 elders, 80,759 deacons, 831 overseas missionaries, 16,993 home cell groups in 25 large districts and 13 local sanctuaries, and 230,000 regular adult church attenders.[8]

3. Positive Aspects of Cho's Church Growth Model

This study proceeds to show the four positive aspects of Cho's CG model that are worthy of emulation: spiritual leadership, empowering structure, constant renewal and holistic witness.

3.1 Spiritual Leadership

Foremost is the spiritual quality of Cho's leadership that sustained the CG of YFGC. Though only God can read hearts and motives, Cho's integrity may be discerned from the fruit of his life (or lifestyle). Based on the pattern of his life in more than forty years of ministry, he has remained humble in spirit, as evidenced by the simplicity of his lifestyle. Pride has not gone to his head. In spite of the success and popularity gained from his CG, he has remained not just humble and simple, but also teachable and servant-like, open and willing to share his experiences and insights with other colleagues.

It seems clear that Cho has used his gifts with a very spiritual motive: "in the Spirit" for the glory of God and not "in the flesh" for self-glory. He also exercised his leadership in a most spiritual manner: in servanthood for the good of his co-pastors and church members, and not in domination and exploitation for the good of himself and his family.

Though Cho does not directly refer to himself as one possessing "charisma," his church members perceive him to be "spiritual" and "charismatic," that he speaks God's words as God's chosen servant. In fact, according to Hong's 1998 survey,

---

[8]Hong, "The Charisma of Cho Yonggi," 70.

YFGC members rate Cho as more charismatic than how other Korean church members (even of other mega-churches) perceive their senior pastors![9]

His spiritual leadership is seen foremost in his experience of special supernatural endowment. His strong sense of divine calling and mission in life is built on his supernatural experiences,[10] particularly his miraculous healing from a terminal disease and his dramatic conversion.[11] He must have used these events to not just remind himself constantly, but also to repeat them to his constituents and the public. In many of his messages, he claims (and has been seen to have) direct contact with God and given his abilities by God. He proclaims that he ministers with the help of God, and calls the Holy Spirit as his Senior Partner.[12] He always attributes the secret of his fabulous CG to God's sovereign grace and will.[13]

---

[9]Hong, "The Charisma of Cho Yonggi," 72 notes that he compared the charismatic perception, religiosity and CG, with a sample size of 110 from YFGC, 640 from other mega-churches, 265 from large churches and 245 from small and medium-sized churches.

[10]On the significance of spiritual experiences in the emergence of religious leaders, cf. Max Weber, *Economy and Society*, 3 vols. (New York: Bedminster, 1968), 1112, 1117; H. M. Trice and J. M. Beyer, "Charisma and Its Routinization in Two Social Movement Organizations," *Research in Organizational Behavior* 8 (1986), 113-64 (141); L. R. Rambo, "Charisma and Conversion," *Pastoral Psychology* 31:2 (1982), 96-108 (100); Anthony Storr, *Feet of Clay: A Study of Gurus* (San Francisco: HarperCollins, 1996). In the OT cases of Saul and David, cf. Tamas Czovek, "Three Charismatic Leaders: Part One: Saul," *Transformation* 19:3 (July 2002), 169-182 (179-80); and "Part Two: David," 182-98 (196-97).

[11]On Cho's dramatic healing and conversion story, see David (Paul) Yonggi Cho, *The Fourth Dimension*, vol. 1 (Seoul: Seoul Logos, 1979), 9-12; Cho, *The Fourth Dimension*, vol. 2 (South Plainfield, NJ: Bridge Publishing, 1983), xii-xvii; YFGC, *The 30-Year History of Yoido Full Gospel Church* (Seoul: YFGC, 1989), 289-90.

[12]Cho, *The Holy Spirit, My Senior Partner* (Altamonte Springs, FL: Creation House, 1989).

[13]Hong, "The Charisma of Cho Yonggi," 77.

With regards to CG, he also emphasizes the divine dimension: the need for prayer and fasting in bringing revival.[14] He also taught about "visualized" supernatural guidance. When he began to pioneer a church in 1958, he gained a "burning desire" to build the largest church in Korea.[15] In 1960, he started to ask God for 1,000 more members each year; in 1969 for 1,000 more members each month; and in 1979 up to 20,000 more per year.[16] In 1969, he had the assurance or "substance" even before plans were made that he will be able to build a 10,000-seat church sanctuary at $5 million.[17] He recalls that in spite of his hesitance to believe in 1974 that he can build a center for CG International (CGI), his request for a "fleece" of $1million was collected in the exact full amount in just one Sunday.[18]

Then in 1984, he also envisioned to build an additional 15-story building for $10 million, expand the Prayer Mountain for $3 million, and enlarge the existing sanctuary by building a larger church complex around it for another $10 million.[19] In 1988, he visualized the establishment of the nationally circulated *Kookmin Daily* newspaper with a Christian section, which has become the third largest circulation daily in Korea.[20] He also got the assurance in early 1991 that his church will reach 700,000 members soon.[21] In all these, what was visualized looked almost impossible to be achieved, yet they all came to pass!

---

[14]Cho, *More than Numbers* (Waco: Word, 1984), 96-99, 108.

[15]The Fourth Dimension, 31.

[16]The Fourth Dimension, 31.

[17]*The Fourth Dimension*, 34, 191-94. At that time, the Board of elders and 600 deacons objected because the church had only $2,000 in hand; but with his faith and his church's commitment, they moved to the new sanctuary in Yoido in 1973 (*The Fourth Dimension*, 191-94).

[18]*Successful Home Cell Groups* (Seoul: Seoul Logos, 1997), 98-99.

[19]Successful Home Cell Groups, 171-72.

[20]Hong, "The Charisma of Cho Yonggi," 82.

[21]The Fourth Dimension, 36.

Corollary to this is Cho's passion and enthusiasm for his ministry.[22] Leadership requires one to be passionate about what he or she is doing. Such leaders speak enthusiastically and excitedly about their dream and mission in life. They breathe it, study it, talk about it, and teach it.[23] Cho invested time in praying and thinking about his goals and took confident action to be sure that others will share his passions also.

The foundation for spiritual leadership is a person's spiritual discipline. It is the outward measure of one's determination to have integrity of character and fitness for the long haul. Like most Korean pastors and perhaps also exceeding them, Cho has lived a life of strict self-discipline and hard work. Cho himself clearly understands that the pastor's personal, especially his/her spiritual disposition is a key factor that affects the life and growth of his/her church. So he emphasizes this right in the first chapters of his books.[24]

Cho believes in the importance of intimate communion with the Holy Spirit, since the latter is his "senior partner" in ministry; so he teaches this to all his leaders.[25] He claims that he has the habit of rising very early each day and spending at least one hour with God before doing anything else.[26] He has taken periodic prolonged retreats, sometimes to the Prayer Mountain. He also prays and dreams (with 60% of his prayer times) in tongues.[27] This kind of self-discipline extended also to his family time, diet, exercise regimen, etc., and even to the way he learned foreign languages.[28] With such a lived example, he has been able to

---

[22]Hong, "The Charisma of Cho Yonggi," 71.

[23]Stephen R. Covey, *Seven Habits of Highly Effective People* (New York: Simon & Schuster, 1990).

[24]Cf. *The Fourth Dimension*, vol. 2, 1-34; More than Numbers, 15-30; *Successful Home Cell Groups*, 1-12.

[25]Successful Home Cell Groups, 119-34; cf. More than Numbers, 117.

[26]Successful Home Cell Groups, 130-34.

[27]Successful Home Cell Groups, 131.

[28]Successful Home Cell Groups, 131-32.

encourage and teach his members to have similar spiritual experiences. When his members experience such themselves, it adds to their perception of his charisma and intensifies their loyalty to his ministry, thereby contributing to CG.[29]

The most important mark of spiritual leaders lies in their great dedication to serve people. They work hard to serve those whom they lead so that they can develop their talents, grow as persons and work in service themselves. In short, spiritual leadership is also "servant leadership."[30]

Cho believes that love is the highest motivational force in life, which can free people from stress and anxiety, and thus can keep them physically well.[31] This he shows in his preaching: the goal in his sermons is "to introduce Jesus and help people succeed in life."[32] His intention is not to be eloquent, but to turn his pulpit into a counseling room, to meet the needs of his audience and to uplift and encourage them.[33] He has also used proper rituals in the dynamic worship services to provide psychological upliftment for the member's spiritual needs.[34]

---

[29]Hong, "The Charisma of Cho Yonggi," 84-85; cf. Young-gi Hong, "The Backgrounds and Characteristics of Charismatic Mega-churches in Korea," *Asian Journal of Pentecostal Studies* 3:1 (2000), 99-118.

[30]Cf. Covey, *Seven Habits*; Nelson Price, *Servants, Not Celebrities* (Nashville: Broadman, 1989); Lawrence Richards and C. Hoeldtke, *Church Leadership* (Grand Rapids: Zondervan, 1988); Viv Thomas, *Future Leader* (Carlisle: Paternoster, 2002); Walter C. Wright, *Relational Leadership* (Carlisle: Paternoster, 2000).

[31]*The Fourth Dimension*, vol. 2, 147-81; cf. Successful Home Cell Groups, 140-41.

[32]The Fourth Dimension, vol. 2, 147-60.

[33]*The Fourth Dimension*, 156-60; cf. Charles Camic, "Charisma: Its Varieties, Preconditions, and Consequences," *Sociological Inquiry* 50 (1980), 5-23.

[34]Hong, "The Charisma of Cho Yonggi," 84; cf. S. L. Carlton-Ford, "Charisma, Ritual, Collective Effervescence, and Self-esteem," *Sociological Quarterly* 33:3 (1992), 365-87.

Cho also trains his associates and trainees in "authority with love," to not "exercise too much control over their members."[35] The leader's authority is not based on the power of his/her position or on human maneuvering. In YFGC's case, they follow Cho, "because they know I genuinely love them. If I make a mistake, I publicly confess it to them and ask them to pray for me. When a pastor can be open to his congregation like that, they will respect him and obey him. In Christianity all authority must be based on love, just as God's authority over us is based on love."[36] Hence he also teaches, "I never encourage our members to become dependent on the cell leaders, because that would be as bad as Communism or the Moonies. Anything that destroys personal independence and the individual's personality and responsibility is from the devil. God never created us to be puppets."[37]

His servanthood extends to his unselfishness to share the principles and practices that he found to be helpful for CG, without trying to control or strongly influence the decisions of the pastors and churches he ministers to. This is what effective leadership is all about.

Another major mark of spiritual leadership is "simple lifestyle" that reflects their commitment to the cause that they are working for. Unlike many televangelists and pastors, Cho testifies that he lives a "simple yet comfortable lifestyle."[38] Although he receives much donations for personal use in the various conferences and crusades where he had been invited to speak, he has refused to "live like a king." He says, "My heart's desire is to give" to those in need, and the remainder to the church's international outreach ministry funds. He is very conscious that he should set an example to his church about giving, as well as that he should avoid being accused of ill motives in ministry.[39]

---

[35]Successful Home Cell Groups, 93-94.

[36]Successful Home Cell Groups, 94-95.

[37]Successful Home Cell Groups, 94.

[38]More than Numbers, 37, 119.

[39]More than Numbers, 37, 119.

In all these, we can even surmise that in the future, he will remain "broken before the Lord." In the continuous exercise of leadership, there will be limits to CG as has been shown by the cessation of rapid increase in membership, perhaps except for biological and transfer growth, and even the possible decline in YFGC's membership since 1996.[40] He will have to face the growth of nominalism in his church (as is already happening in many Korean churches)[41] and eventual decline in the spiritual quality of his members.[42] He will have to wrestle with the issues that will arise from the limits to the effectivity of his version of "positive thinking" and "prosperity gospel," as expressed in his Fourth Dimension teachings of "The Fivefold Gospel" and "Triple Salvation (Blessings)."[43] His parishioners' ill-health and eventual death will have to be explained by not only spiritual causes (their lack of faith, and sin), but also natural ones (gradual decay of aging, viral attacks, etc.), which may conflict with his present beliefs so far.[44] There may also be a possible decline in "signs and wonders" like in other Pentecostal-charismatic churches. These apparent "setbacks" will serve as checks to possible temptations for him to become proud.

Nonetheless, Cho's spiritual leadership enhanced the productivity of his church, since it elicits greater dedication to the organization and its goals from the constituents.[45] The high quality

---

[40]Cho claims 700,000 members by 1996, *The Fourth Dimension*, 3rd ed., preface.

[41]Young-gi Hong, "Nominalism in Korean Protestantism," *Transformation* 16:4 (1999), 135-141.

[42]Weber, *Economy and Society*, 242 notes, "If proof and success eludes the leader for long, if he appears deserted by his god or his magical or heroic powers, above all, if his leadership fails to benefit his followers, it is likely that his charismatic authority will disappear."

[43]The Fourth Dimension; The Fourth Dimension, vol. 2.

[44]Cf. *Solving Life's Problems* (Seoul: Seoul Logos, 1980); *How Can I Be Healed* (Seoul: Seoul Logos, 1999).

[45]Cf. Robert J. House, "A 1976 Theory of Charismatic Leadership," in *Leadership: The Cutting Edge*, eds. J. G. Hunt and L. L. Larson

of his spiritual leadership has undoubtedly been a major factor in YFGC's growth.

3.2 Empowering Structure

Yet beyond Cho's personal quality is his institutionalization (or routinization) of an organizational structure that may preserve if not outgrow the CG that he has achieved so far.[46] He seems to have solved the problem of possible disintegration that can arise from the inevitable need for succession.[47] In 1964, he found the best possible solution in the lay empowerment model through participatory management by institutionalizing the cell system.[48] He views that home cell groups (HCG) is "the basic part of our church. It is not another church program—it is the program of our church."[49]

(Carbondale, IL: Southern Illinois University Press, 1977), 189-207; Robert J. House, James Woycke, and Eugene M. Fodor, "Charismatic and Non-charismatic Leaders: Differences in Behavior and Effectiveness," in *Charismatic Leadership: The Elusive Factor in Organizational Effectiveness*, eds. J. A. Conger and R. N. Kanungo (San Francisco: Jossey-Bass, 1988), 98-121 (116).

[46]Charismatic leaders and their followers will desire to transform their movements into more permanent institutions. R*outinization* refers to the process by which the dynamism of charismatic leadership is translated into the stability of traditional or bureaucratic organization. This is necessary if the charisma of the leader is to be preserved, be expanded and stand a better chance of survival. See Weber, *Economy and Society*, 241-50, 1112-117 on how the process of structural development takes place.

[47]Cf. Alan Bryman, *Charisma and Leadership in Organizations* (London: Sage, 1992), 71; Jay A. Conger, "Charismatic and Transformational Leadership in Organization: An Insider's Perspective on These Developing Streams of Research," *Leadership Quarterly* 10:2 (1999), 145-79 (168-71).

[48]For a full narrative of this important discovery, read *Successful Home Cell Groups*, 13-29.

[49]More than Numbers, 42.

Through the cell system, he is able to develop a steady stream of leaders for CG and for expansion. Research shows that large churches can maintain high levels of commitment and conformity if they are divided into small homogenous units,[50] and Cho affirms that for CG, "the real secret is home cell groups."[51] And for mission extension, "The expansion of any movement is in direct proportion to its success in mobilizing its total membership in continuous propagation of its beliefs."[52]

Yet perhaps above all, the cell system of home cell groups (HCG) provides a structure in which the issue of succession becomes insignificant. Cho asserts,

> This system of home cell groups does not depend on one person. In our church, it does not depend on me. It depends on the ministry of the Holy Spirit, because He is the one who energizes the leaders. . . . Those members don't depend on me; they depend on one another and on the Holy Spirit.[53]

He also says, "Churches should not have to depend on a single strong pastor,"[54] and "My church is not the church of Paul Yonggi Cho, although I'm the founding pastor. My church belongs to the Lord Jesus Christ and cannot be centered on my personality. With the cell system, the actual ministry is done on the cell level. Although the people hold me in high esteem and are loyal, they can go on without me."[55] He has even empowered each HCG to be

---

[50] Roger Finke, "The Quiet Transformation: Changes in Size and Leadership of Southern Baptist Churches," *Review of Religious Research* 36:1 (1994), 3-22 (8).

[51] Successful Home Cell Groups, vi.

[52] Kenneth Strachan, *The Inescapable Calling* (Grand Rapids: Eerdmans, 1968), 108.

[53] Successful Home Cell Groups, 86.

[54] Successful Home Cell Groups, 52.

[55] More than Numbers, 41.

self-supporting: each cell has its own collection recorded and dispensed by its treasurer.[56]

This empowering structure is nurtured by his "participatory management" style. Cho has had the confidence to delegate, to share power as much as possible. Though effective leaders may be known for being decisive, superior problem-solvers and good at inspiring people to follow their lead, they know that they must share power with their subordinates, allowing them to make their own decisions themselves by helping them to develop judgment skills rather than by making them wait for the leader's decisions. The more power one gives to others, the more he or she will be seen as a visionary leader who is able to focus on strategic issues.

Cho delegates most decisions to his immediate staff, which consists of the assistant pastors and elders. He remains aloof from the routines of the various internal organizations of YFGC. One of his secretaries told Hong, "Cho hardly lectures people. He delegates most administrative affairs to his staff."[57] Cho allows his "fellow-workers to make mistakes and learn from them as God does with me."[58]

Avoiding interference in mundane details actually adds to his charisma: "the separation of administrative concerns from the personal attention of the charismatic helps to preserve his or her aura of extraordinariness."[59] The social distance that evolved because of the increased size of YFGC may have helped to promote his charisma among his members: "Social distance may not have been deliberately created to generate charismatic images, but the product, a sense of distance and awe, may be a result of the creation of a social charismatic image."[60]

In fact, he relates to only a relatively small number of leaders who "have others under them who shepherd the cell leaders, and it

---

[56]More than Numbers, 49.

[57]Hong, "The Charisma of Cho Yonggi," 82.

[58]More than Numbers, 29.

[59]Trice & Beyer, "Charisma and Its Routinization," 144.

[60]Hong, "The Charisma of Cho Yonggi," 75.

is the cell leaders who perform the bulk of the ministry of our church."[61] What he has done was just to turn his church into a training center, investing in his people, the ultimate resource! Without direct knowledge of each leader, he just has to see to it that they are trained in the skills necessary to be effective cell leaders, thereby contributing to his goal of CG!

3.3 Constant Renewal

Cho's CG has not been static, but dynamic; it was constantly being renewed through new initiatives that built on previous achievements. Research show that big organizations find it very difficult to respond to prophetic voices, especially those that will differ from the leader.[62] Catering to mass audiences, mega-churches will also tend to lose their prophetic voices, because their huge assets have to be protected through "compromise" with government and business interests, including those of their own influential upper class members who benefit from the status quo. Their pastors will tend to mainly focus on comforting the afflicted, and hardly on afflicting the comfortable![63] Moreover, in a big bureaucracy, decision-making will be based more on rational thinking and efficiency (which is not always negative) but less on affective action and spiritual guidance.[64] Yet Cho's CG overcame these dangers, and in fact, YFGC has grown into quite an open and creative church!

Even from the start of Cho's ministry among the urban poor of Seoul, his openness to the Spirit gave him the sensitivity to give contextualized teachings to his people. His messages of "positive faith" helped his ailing and destitute members gain a good sense of

---

[61]Successful Home Cell Groups, 65.

[62]Hong, "The Charisma of Cho Yonggi," 87-88.

[63]Cf., Chai Sik Chung, "Beyond Indigenization: Toward a Christian Transcendence in Korea," *Mission Studies* 18:1 (2001), 61-77.

[64]Cf. Margaret M. Poloma, *The Assemblies of God at the Crossroads: Charisma and Institutional Dilemmas* (Knoxville: University of Tennessee Press, 1989), 112, 127-38.

identity and hope of life; they can be delivered from spiritual emptiness and material poverty.[65] He testifies that his "blessings theology" was developed in the context of suffering and devastation of the Korean War.[66] Thereby the poor are able to gain self-confidence and are equipped to labor for the Kingdom of God amidst the needs and hardships of life. They are trained to be leaders, in spite of their low socio-economic and educational backgrounds.

In 1964, he was willing to break Korean church and social tradition: he not only instituted the cell system, but also appointed women to be the cell leaders. He was the first pastor in Korea to actively train and empower women to lead in the church's HCG;[67] in fact, almost all of his first HCG leaders were women.[68] Today, women members still outnumber men by about three to two,[69] perhaps because of the tendency of women to be more attracted to charismatic leaders.[70] But Cho has a correct and better explanation: women are better evangelists than men, and his CG is mainly due to women-to-women evangelism.[71]

Then in 1982, Cho had YFGC start the "Love in Practice" or "Sharing Movement," to provide basic necessities to indigents in the neighborhood, and later to orphanages, homes for the aged and leprosaria. In 1984, the church began to offer free heart surgeries, which later extended to Uzbekistan, Nepal, Cambodia and Ukraine. In 1988, there were three new initiatives: blood donation drive, "Love-Bread Movement" to provide aid to poor neighbors,

---

[65]Young-gi Hong, "The Influence of the Reverend David Yonggi Cho's Church Growth on Korean Society," in *Charis and Charisma* (Carlisle: Paternoster, 2003), 291-318 (294, 298).

[66]Hong, "The Influence," 295.

[67]Hong, "The Charisma of Cho Yonggi," 73.

[68]Successful Home Cell Groups, 21-29.

[69]Hong, "The Charisma of Cho Yonggi," 70.

[70]A. R. Willner, *The Spellbinders: Charismatic Political Leadership* (New Haven: Yale University Press, 1984).

[71]Successful Home Cell Groups, 60-61.

and Elim Welfare Town (with free technical school for poor youth and free nursing home for the aged) in Gunpo City.[72]

There were other initiatives in socio-cultural fronts in the 1980s. A school was started that developed into Hansei University, and Bethesda University grew out of the Full Gospel School of Theology.[73] Cho launched "Invitation to Happiness," the first Christian television ministry in Korea, and the *Kookmin Daily News*, the first Christian daily newspaper in Korea.[74] In 1995, YFGC set up its Environmental Preservation Division, and in 1996, YFGC began the first satellite mission on Korea's communication satellite Moogoonghwa (Rose of Sharon). Later, the church also launched Internet Broadcasting Department for cyber-evangelism and now Video on Demand (VOD).[75] Lately, in 1999, they established "Good People," the first church-based non-government organization (NGO) in Korea, mainly to support holistic "mission to unreached Third World countries...with the love and righteousness of God."[76]

Such constant renewal seems to be institutionalized in Cho's practice of "constant goal-setting." It is not enough to have faith and visions, but these must be translated into goals, strategies, programs and projects. It is through goal-setting that leaders motivate others to achieve their vision.[77] As goals are reached, and feelings of success prevail, one's charisma increases: "success is more important in the initial attribution of charisma"[78] and "nothing succeeds like success."

---

[72]Hong, "The Influence," 304-305.

[73]Hong, "The Influence," 303.

[74]Hong, "The Influence," 305.

[75]Hong, "The Influence," 303.

[76]Hong, "The Influence," 308.

[77]B. Shamir, R. J. House and M. B. Arthur, "The Motivational Effects of Charismatic Leadership: A Self-concept Based Theory," *Organizational Science* 4 (1993), 1-17 (5-8).

[78]S. M. Puffer, "Attributions of Charismatic Leadership: The Impact of Decision Style, Outcome and Observer Characteristics," *Leadership Quarterly* 1 (1990), 177-92.

Cho emphasizes the importance of goal-setting in CG.[79] Here one needs to find a balance of being both realistic and ambitious at the same time. Realism makes one aware of the natural rate of growth, thus not pushing growth beyond the limits of growth: natural growth comes by increments, so one can't force growth against its inherent nature. Yet to inspire, leaders must set goals which are somehow beyond people's grasp, and in spiritual leadership, beyond human capacities, where God's power can be demonstrated.

On setting goals, Cho means the development of five-year plans, with budgets to achieve specific goals.[80] Then these goals and plans are consistently communicated to the people, thus giving the whole church a clear sense of direction. From among the crowd, leaders have to be recruited; hence Cho also has an eye to detect informal leaders "who naturally attract others to themselves. Sometimes people who have a knack for communicating with other people make excellent leaders."[81] Then he sees to it that each leader is trained[82] and has a clear goal and plan; they get this at least through the annual cell leaders' convention.[83] He also knows how to motivate these lay leaders through recognition, praise and caring.[84]

Hence CG leadership requires one to be a constant strategist.[85] Very early in Cho's ministry, in 1964, while almost dying from an unknown disease, he discovered the Exodus 18 formula of structuring his church in a cell system, whereby he can train and

---

[79] *More than Numbers*, 109-11, 161-62.

[80] More than Numbers, 36, 113-15.

[81] More than Numbers, 50.

[82] More than Numbers, 112-13.

[83] More than Numbers, 112-13.

[84] Successful Home Cell Groups, 135-41.

[85] Using David's case, Czovek, "Three Charismatic Leaders," 186 notes, "Charismatic deliverers, if they are to prevail are to be strategists—taking advantage of every opportunity."

use lay leaders (as non-paid assistants!) to lead multitudes.[86] And to keep his church financially sustainable, he organized over 2,000 businessmen into a mission fellowship.[87]

So, Cho and YFGC have seen to it that they are constantly renewed. CG is not static, but dynamic. Given Cho's openness to creative initiatives and use of constant goal-setting, there are grounds for optimism that he will continue to keep YFGC on the path of constant church renewal in the years to come.

3.4 Holistic Witness

A significant distinctive in Cho's CG model has been the "beyond CG" impact that he has made in Korean society and beyond. It appears that through the leadership of Cho, YFGC has been able to not just increase in quantity of church membership, but also in quality of social transformation. The main highlight may be in May 3, 1996, when Cho was awarded the Moogoonghwa medallion, the highest medal given to Korean citizens, primarily for his contributions to the free heart operation movement.[88]

When the concept of CG and phenomenon of mega-churches (not so different from centralized structures of denominations) became popular in the late 1970s, many Evangelical church leaders, especially from the Two-Thirds world have been very critical of it. Most critical are those who see CG as the product of a westernized non-holistic approach to mission that is not concerned for the discipling (or transformation) of societies, viewing evangelism and church development as the main (if not the only) goal of the Great Commission.

Yet as seen in the previous section, it looks like that Cho has successfully led YFGC to move in a more holistic role in society. In many modern cities like Seoul, the main holistic issue is the growing gap between the rich and the poor. It seems that from

---

[86]More than Numbers, 31-35.

[87]Hong, "The Charisma of Cho Yonggi," 81.

[88]Hong, "The Influence," 305.

YFGC's "sharing movement" and its various social ministries from the early 1980s onwards, Cho has developed a CG that has also been able to turn an increasingly materialistic society into a more compassionate and caring one. Through media, especially the *Kookmin Daily News*, the nation (not just the church) has been mobilized to help thousands of boy or girl-led households, donate blood, and volunteer in medical service corps; in 1992, 1,300 civic groups joined in a national "Kind Neighbor, Bright Society" movement to develop kindness as a way of life,[89] and in 2001, a "donation culture" was promoted through feature stories in the newspaper.[90]

Through its two universities, YFGC can develop young people in various professions to provide Christian leadership in society. In 1998, a model "ecological garden" was set up on the banks of Han River in Yoido, which formed "ecological schools" to teach on environmental issues. Since 1999, the church-based NGO "Good People" has sent food, fertilizers and medicine to North Korea; rebuilt schools in India; funded AIDS prevention program in Kenya, sent emergency relief to Kosovo, Turkey, Afghanistan; aided flood victims in Korea; and many other social work with national and global reach.[91]

Cho has shown that CG can lead to holistic ministries, which can outgrow CG goals and can impact society. All that is needed is for church leaders to expand their horizons, equip their members to develop their gifts and empower them to make their dreams come true.

---

[89]Hong, "The Influence," 305-306.

[90]Hong, "The Influence," 307.

[91]Hong, "The Influence," 308-310.

4. Negative Aspects of Cho's Church Growth Model

4.1 Lack of Transformational Contextualization

Most CG advocates, like Cho, have now accepted the Lausanne Covenant formula that both evangelism and socio-political action are parts of the church's mission. As seen above, like many Evangelical and Pentecostal-Charismatic churches, Cho's YFGC has developed many social ministries. Yet like most of them, Cho lacks a stronger prophetic (social and ethical) critique of society. He perpetuates a "false consciousness" that Korea is "the last remaining powerhouse of world Christianity" and that the Korean church is a "house of prayer" when in fact it may be "swollen with pride in thinking that religion is a way to become rich, successful and respectable." [92] His theology of "Threefold Blessings" (or good health and good fortune) seems to be no different "from the contemporary ethos of a crassly materialistic, newly industrializing Korean society that idolizes mammon."[93] Where is the biblical "theology of the cross" in all these?

More recent Pentecostal theologians have raised this issue, too.[94] Of note is:

> Pentecostals must take seriously the critique that, in spite of their significant contributions in areas of social concern within their communities, there has been little conscious effort to provide a horizontal linkage from their experiments in ways of coping with life in their own context to a larger forum where they would have more direct access to the means of cultural production. If Pentecostals are content to form only their own

---

[92]Chung, "Beyond Indigenization," 63-64.

[93]Chung, "Beyond Indigenization," 73.

[94]E.g., Murray Dempster, "A Theology of the Kingdom: A Pentecostal Contribution," in *Mission as Transformation*, eds. V. Samuel and C. Sugden (Carlisle: Paternoster, 1999), 45-75; Douglas Petersen, "Pentecostals: Who are They?" in *Mission as Transformation*, 76-111.

> "substitute societies," they may forfeit the opportunity to participate in radical change or structural transformation.[95]

In many modern cities like Seoul, where "globalization" means the expansion of "consumer societies," the main issue for "mission as transformation" is the growing gap between the rich and the poor. Research should be done to see whether YFGC's various social ministries have been able to truly equip the rich to serve the poor and to empower the poor to serve others.

Moreover there seems to be an absence of dialogue and witness to people and leaders of other faiths, particularly shamans, Buddhists and Confucianists. There appears to be a dearth of interaction with them that can result in models of contextualized witness to religiously inclined people with their own distinct spiritualities. Will YFGC be able to be a transformational witness among the religions in Korea and beyond?

Given YFGC and Cho's presence in civil society and in public media, there may be grounds for optimism that pressing social issues will challenge him and his church to become fully holistic and advocate for truly transformational (or prophetic which may often be counter-cultural) concerns in the future.

4.2 Multiplication Potential

Given the above distinctives of Cho's CG, we can look forward to a greater impact of his ministry. He has shown that there is almost nothing impossible that a spiritual leader can do for CG, church renewal, social transformation and even global impact. As Cho has emphasized, the most critical gift for leadership is "dreams and visions" that are set into goals, which are constantly upgraded as they are achieved! May I show an example of what a possible "vision" that he and other church leaders can consider in our time.

Recent mission practitioners are offering the further "higher goal beyond CG" of church multiplication through "church

---

[95]Petersen, "Pentecostals: Who Are They?" 110-11.

planting movements" (CPM); [96] or "house church networks" (HCN). [97] They view the centralized mega-churches (and their latest forms, like "cell churches" and "Groups of 12" (G-12)[98] to be unable to use the full potential of the whole church to evangelize and transform the whole world, particularly the 10/40 Window.

Theologically, CG perpetuates the "Babylonian captivity" of the church in Christendom structures inherited from centuries of theological emphasis on the "priesthood of a few" (that is, the clergy) rather than the Reformation breakthrough into a servant-church structure based on the biblical teaching of the "priesthood of all believers." CG thinking continues to require hierarchical power centers (best exemplified in the papal system of the Roman Catholic Church) that is opposite to the egalitarian partnership structures of house-churches (or "basic Christian communities," BCC) and facilitative functions of servant-leadership in the New Testament.[99] Unless these mega-forms of CG truly decentralize to

---

[96]E.g., David Garrison, *Church Planting Movements* (Richmond, VA: International Mission Board of Southern Baptist Convention, 1999); David S. Lim, *The Only Way to Disciple Whole Nations: Church Multiplication through Tentmakers* (Quezon City: China Ministries International-Philippines, 2003).

[97]E.g., Robert and Julia Banks. *The Church Comes Home* (Sutherland: Albatross Books, 1989); Wolfgang Simson, *Houses That Change the World* (Carlisle: Paternoster, 2001); cf. Charles Ringma, *Catch the Wind* (Sutherland: Albatross, 1994); C. Rene Padilla, "The Future of Christianity in Latin America: Missiological Perspectives and Challenges," *International Bulletin of Missionary Research* 23:3 (July, 1999), 105-112; Jim Montgomery, *I'm Gonna Let It Shine!* (Pasadena: William Carey Library, 2001).

[98]Cf. Ralph Neighbor, Jr., *Where Do We Go from Here?* (Houston: Touch Publications, 1990); Comiskey, *Groups of 12.*

[99] Cf. Hans Kung, "The Charismatic Structure of the Church," *Concilium* IV: *The Church and Ecumenism* (New York: Paulist, 1965); J. D. G. Dunn, "Ministry and the Ministry: The Charismatic Renewal's Challenge to Traditional Ecclesiology," in *Charismatic Experiences in History*, ed. C. M. Robeck, Jr. (Peabody: Hendrickson, 1985), 81-101; David S. Lim, "The

let each cell function fully as autonomous (self-governing, self-supporting and self-propagating) churches, with their own leaders, budgets and programs,[100] God's church will continue to deprive almost 90% (the unequipped laity) of the church from exercising their priesthood, prophethood and rulership in Christ.

Strategically, the centralized and hierarchical structure of the mega-church type of CG has been disadvantageous to the full growth of the church and its mission. Cho's empowerment model seems to be not empowering enough! In his ideals, each HCG "has limited size, usually not more than 15 families," which is good, but he continues, "It has a definite goal set by my associate ministers and myself. It has a definite plan, given to each cell in written form. It has definite leadership, trained in our school,"[101] which reveals a dependency that hinders their self-developing potential for Kingdom expansion and church multiplication. There is a big difference between training leaders and training followers.[102]

Servant Nature of the Church in the Pauline Corpus" (Ph.D. Diss., Fuller Theological Seminary, 1987) and *The Only Way to Disciple Whole Nations*; Simson, *Houses That Change the World*. Thus there was no need for celebrative worship and governing centers among the people of God in each village or city, except three times a year in the temple in the OT. Yet there were no local shrines nor temples in OT times, just as there were no local church structures in New Testament times. In every city, the "local church" consisted of a fellowship of inter-dependent leaders (usually called "elders") of house-churches, with no central governing body. Our Lord Jesus, Peter, Paul and Apollos were charismatic leaders, but each of them did not build a centralized nor hierarchical structure.

[100] On servant-leadership and servant-structures, cf. Robert K. Greenleaf, *Servant Leadership* (New York: Paulist, 1977); Edgar H. Schein, *Organizational Culture and Leadership* (San Francisco: Jossey-Bass, 1992); Edgar J. Elliston, *Home Grown Leaders* (Pasadena: William Carey Library, 1993); Lim, "The Servant Nature of the Church."

[101] More than Numbers, 42; cf. Successful Home Cell Groups, 113-14.

[102] Paul G. Hiebert, "Training Leaders, Training Followers," *Theology, News and Notes* (June 1989), 23-24; cf. Gene Getz, *Serving One Another* (Wheaton: Victor, 1984).

This lack of full empowerment will necessarily lead to increasing nominalism in the church: there are increasing numbers of YFGC members who join for prestige, success and/or upward social mobility.[103] In a big bureaucracy, decision-making will be based more on rational thinking and efficiency (which is not always negative) but less on affective action and spiritual guidance.[104] The mega-church will also find it very difficult to respond to prophetic voices, especially those that will differ from the leader.[105]

Catering to mass audiences, mega-churches will also tend to lose their prophetic voices, because its huge assets have to be protected through "compromise" with government and business interests, including those of their own influential upper class members who benefit from the status quo.[106] Their pastors will tend to mainly focus on comforting the afflicted, and hardly on afflicting the comfortable!

The major limitation of mega-church type of CG is its hindrance to effective world missions, on at least two counts: a) these big churches model mere addition growth for mega-cities, instead of more church multiplication for national saturation evangelization; and b) they absorb a disproportionate amount of resources (time, money and energy) for church development, and discourage increased spending for holistic cross-cultural missions; they are too expensive to replicate and too heavy to carry elsewhere! If they try, their short-term and resident missionaries have been ineffective to plant contextualized and transformational churches.

---

[103]Hong, "The Charisma of Cho Yonggi," 85-86.

[104]Margaret M. Poloma, *The Assemblies of God at the Crossroads: Charisma and Institutional Dilemmas* (Knoxville: University of Tennessee Press, 1989), 112, 127-38.

[105]Hong, "The Charisma of Cho Yonggi," 87-88.

[106]Cho will find it more difficult to change from his stance on non-involvement in politics as long as there is freedom to preach the gospel (*More than Numbers*, 69-70).

The mega-church model of CG has grown mainly in secularized and urbanized societies which allow religious freedom. But CG has failed and will continue to fail in areas dominated by secularism (western Europe), Communism (Indo-China, North Korea), Islam (Middle East, Central Asia, North Africa, Pakistan, Bangladesh, Malaysia, Brunei), Theravada Buddhism (Sri Lanka, Myanmar), Shinto Buddhism (Japan) and Judaism (Israel). Mega-churches have not been effective in planting indigenous churches and church planting movements in the 10/40 Window nor even in the saturation evangelization of their own nations. Their church constituencies are mostly low quality church-going Christians rather than quality disciples (servant-leaders) who can disciple others!

Actually Cho has begun to do a type of "church multiplication" in more recent years. Though he pioneered only three churches in his first twenty-six years,[107] by 1989 he had already 75 churches and mission work in different parts of the world, like Japan, [108] Australia, U.S.A., Latin America and Europe,[109] and recent reports say that he has about 250 churches in Korea and about 650 churches in the world, including some in "closed countries." If any HCG leader wants to become a licensed minister, Cho pays for her or his Bible School tuition, on condition that he or she serves at least three years in YFGC. If later they want to start their own church, Cho helps them financially for the first six months.[110] He does not provide them anything to give to nationals by teaching them to "depend on God as their total resource"; the nationals are not to depend on foreign funding,[111] so

---

[107]More than Numbers, 10.

[108]Cho chose an ordinary lady minister to plant the YFGC in Japan with a goal of 1,000 members in five years, and she did it! (*Successful Home Cell Groups*, 76).

[109]Successful Home Cell Groups, 47, 79.

[110]Successful Home Cell Groups, 79-80.

[111]Cho himself never asked for financial help from foreign missionaries or churches, even when he was ministering among the poor (*Successful Home Cell Groups*, 179).

Cho's missionaries are told not to give the impression that they are bringing riches to them.[112] And he believes that this kind of church-planting can be done anywhere![113] Hopefully this can be implemented more frequently and more vigorously.

Moreover, Cho also shares the CPM/HCN view that the church meets any time and anywhere: it "meets everyday in factories, schools, offices, homes, restaurants and club buildings." If the Communists take over and kill the pastors, they cannot destroy the 18,000 cells.[114] He sees that such a system is not just persecution-proof, but also poverty/depression-proof![115] Yet in his ministry, in spite of his apparent desire to emphasize the decentralized form of the church, with no need for the presence and ministry of pastors, the focus still flows back to his mega-structure and his personal leadership! Such is the main danger of huge structures: they tend to create high dependency of staff and members on the leaders and especially the top leader.[116]

Yet given his ecclesiology and openness to the Spirit, Cho may be able to lead his church (and the church worldwide) to a multiplication mode. And the global impact will be very great. The evangelistic and transformational impact of one church of 200,000 members (in CG programs) will almost surely be less than that of 500 churches of 400 each (in traditional church-planting programs), and much less than that of 10,000 churches of 20 each (in church multiplication movements). Cho saw this in China,[117] and he can lead in making this replicated all over the world.

---

[112]Successful Home Cell Groups, 175-76.

[113]Successful Home Cell Groups, 174-76.

[114]More than Numbers, 41.

[115]Successful Home Cell Groups, 84-86.

[116]Cf. Jay A. Conger, *The Charismatic Leader: Behind the Mystique of Exceptional Leadership* (San Francisco: Jossey-Bass, 1989); Gary A. Yukl, "An Evaluation of Conceptual Weaknesses in Transformational and Charismatic Leadership Theories," *Leadership Quarterly* 10:2 (1999), 285-305.

[117]Successful Home Cell Groups, 84.

5. Conclusion

As shown in this study, Cho has served our generation excellently with his God-endowed leadership gifts. He has been a charismatic leader *par excellence*, yet he remained humble and simple, a model of mature spirituality and servant-leadership. He has faithfully used his gifts effectively not just for the growth of YFGC, but also for the development of many churches worldwide. And the resultant CG has been of constant internal renewal that has had social impact in Korea and the world!

This study has also shown that most importantly, Cho has effectively moved his mega-church to empower almost 10% of his laity to be HCG leaders and church leaders through the cell system. Perhaps he can lead YFGC to its logical or theological end (empowerment of 100% for NT "priesthood of all believers") and to its practical or strategic end (mobilization of 100% for CPM missions). May his next goal be "church multiplication," not just "cell multiplication." May he train, commission and send most (if not all) of his leaders to plant many more multiplying churches,[118] in Korea and in the non-Christian world! With or without his leadership, the house churches in China are already using the "church multiplication" model as they seek to send 100,000 missionaries across the 10/40 Window in their "Back to Jerusalem" movement.[119]

Or perhaps it is the best that Cho could do in the hierarchical cultural milieu of Korea (his cultural heritage) and the centralized hierarchical system of Christian denominations (his ecclesiastical heritage) in his generation. The challenge for the next generation of those who aspire to church leadership and CG in the post-

---

[118]Most CPMs nowadays believe that it takes a maximum of three years to disciple a believer to become a disciple-maker (servant-leader of a house-church). The discipler just has to be a few steps ahead of his disciple(s), thus 2 Tim 2:2 (cf. John 14:12-14; Acts 20:17-35) can be done in just a few months if not a few weeks!

[119]Paul Hattaway, et al., *Back to Jerusalem* (Carlisle: Piquant, 2003).

modern era should be: are we going to continue to develop more hierarchical and centralized mega-churches or make a "paradigm shift" to more egalitarian and decentralized servant-churches (or HCN) for CPMs in the new millennium? May God use Cho's exemplary leadership to inspire us to obey the Great Commission, to bear explosive witness among the nations, so that "the end will come" (cf. Matt 24:14). Maranatha!

MISSION LEADERSHIP AND CHURCH GROWTH[1]

Chris Sugden

1. Introduction

Dr. Yonggi-Cho's experience in growing the Yoido Full Gospel Church has been described and analyzed in many articles, reviews and discussions. I do not intend to repeat the issues that have been raised in them. The life of his community are testimony to God's blessing on his preaching and teaching of the scriptures. In the Korean context growth has taken place in a situation of war and deprivation. Cho's approach is unique and his community of believers was the instruments whom God chose to use.

My question is: What can we learn from Cho's experience and writings about the role of the leadership of Christian communities in church growth? It is quite legitimate to do this as there are precedents in Christian history to characterize a movement of God by the writings and activities of a leader—there are Lutheran churches and Wesleyan churches. We will reflect on what characterizes a Choian church.

What can we learn about leadership? Leaders lead. They take initiatives and risks and pioneer new territory and methods. They are the first to do things, and determine what must be done first. Leaders appoint others whom they deem fit to carry out the similar vision. They also provide a narrative, the story, the framework for understanding the history and experience of the group over time.

---

[1]An earlier version was presented at the First Youngsan International Symposium on Church Growth and Leadership, Aug 2003, Seoul, Korea.

Cho has clearly done this in his writings. He narrates his own experiences of starting with nothing; of undergoing great anxiety and suffering, and sometimes rejection. This narrative both repeats the experience of Jesus in his ministry of death and resurrection, and illuminates the experience of many of his church members as they go through suffering.

His experiences provide examples of how to respond to suffering and risk in prayer and faith. He builds a theology of faith and prayer based on the Bible and his experiences in interaction with the scriptures. He draws on the Bible as the appropriate justification for his teaching and his action, thus illuminating the meaning of God's word for people in the Korean situation.

2. Leadership in Mission

In our research at the Oxford Centre for Mission Studies (OCMS), our colleagues are studying the leadership roles of a number of contemporary church leaders. A recent doctoral study focused on Archbishop David Gitari, former Archbishop of the Anglican Church of Kenya and his role in giving leadership for justice and truth in a society of declining standards in political life.[2] A current doctoral study is focusing on the role of bishops in Kenya in leading the transition from colonial to independent rule and the factors that shaped the emerging new leadership of the church. These studies found that the leaders of the church have had such a profound influence in Kenyan national life because they provided the role of the old tribal religious leaders—they were the defense of vulnerable people in the community against the extremes of their political leaders. Thus, church leaders had a major role in national life when people saw them fulfilling the expectations they had of religion in their society—to protect the vulnerable.

These leaders provided a narrative for their leadership. In the case of Archbishop Gitari, it was the sacrifice he endured in his

---

[2] Gideon Githiga, *The Church as a Bulwark against Authoritarianism* (Nairobi: Regnum/Uzima, 2001).

opposition to President Moi, in which at least two attempts were made on his life. He provided an example of standing up against injustice in his own culture. He constantly provided biblical justification for his actions in preaching from biblical texts with consistent relevance to his experiences.[3]

Taking these initiatives and taking these risks with justification delivered from the Bible means seeing beyond the horizon and pointing out the direction to others.

Pervaiz Sultan from Pakistan undertook a study on the development ministry of two dioceses in the Church of Pakistan, published subsequently as *The Church and Development.*[4] He examined the approaches to development of two dioceses, one which followed an evangelical ministry in development and one which concentrated on social changes. He discovered that what determined the approach of each diocese was the approach of the leader—one was evangelical and one was ecumenical. But both leaders were similar in exercising an authoritarian approach in giving leadership in the diocese. Essentially, both regarded the people in their dioceses more as objects of their leadership to carry out their agenda.

My own doctoral research in India and Bali focused on the evangelistic and social ministries of churches in South India and Bali among poor people.[5] I studied two leaders, Vinay Samuel in India and Wayan Mastra in Bali. I discovered that what motivated them both was an understanding that central to the development and growth of poor people was for them to recover and discover their own identity and dignity. The heart of this process was the preaching and teaching of the gospel. Poor people, who had been treated as nobodies, were told that through the grace of Jesus

---

[3] David Gitari and Ben Knighton, "On Being a Christian Leader: Story Contesting Power in Kenya," *Transformation* 18:4 (October 2001), 247-62; David Gitari, *In Season and Out of Season: Sermons to a Nation* (Oxford: Regnum, 1996).

[4] Pervaiz Sultan, *Church and Development: A Case Study from Pakistan* (Karachi: Centre for Mission and Development, 2001).

[5] Chris Sugden, *Seeking the Asian Face of Jesus* (Oxford: Regnum Books, 1997).

Christ they could be sons and daughters of God. Though society around treated them as expendable and marginal, they were of inestimable value to God.

It was not enough to leave this new value at an abstract, conceptual or even religious level though it had vital and irreplaceable religious foundations. Both leaders realized that this new identity and dignity had to be expressed and supported in a number of ways. These ways were also informed by their theological understanding of who people are.

Wayan Mastra particularly focused on expressing people's identity in their community culture. He built churches in the local Balinese style and recovered the use of Balinese music in church. He promoted cultural dance in worship. He clearly understood that people need to express their new identity in cultural forms that connect them with their surroundings, their fellows, their past and their community. Dutch culture had replaced all local Balinese culture for the Christians, thus Balinese were known as Black Dutch. He built a theology seeing continuity between what God wrought in nature and what he brought about through grace. As a result, Mastra gave Balinese Christians a new confidence to play a role in their communities, and to provide a lead in some of the important national initiatives such as emigration to less overpopulated parts of Indonesia.

They saw the need to express people's identity and dignity in their calling to be stewards of creation. This was rooted in the Genesis narrative to be fruitful and multiply; to exercise dominion over the creation as the images and representatives of God the absentee landlord to whom all people must give account. Mastra saw this calling in the promise to Abraham to be a blessing to the nations. To be a blessing one needs the strength to hold one's hand out palm down, not palm up to receive a handout. They both saw a particular calling through the gospel to enable poor people to play their role as stewards. Both the Old and New Testament witness to God's special concern for the poor: in liberating the Hebrew slaves from Egypt and in defining the gospel of the kingdom as good news to the poor. Both Mastra and Samuel developed important ministries of micro-enterprise development among poor people to express the calling to be stewards.

They saw the need to model in their leadership the cross-cultural partnership that expressed the gospel as breaking down barriers between races and cultures. They were very aware of their own strong identity and worth as national leaders, yet provided space to Christians from other races and cultures to work closely in partnership with them, a partnership which would be mutually enriching to both parties. This follows the pattern in the New Testament where Paul the Jew had a close partnership with, for example, Luke the Gentile doctor.

We see a biblical understanding of human personhood determining Mastra and Samuel's involvement and leadership in building Christian community: it embraced and expressed the new identity and dignity that people receive through the gospel as sons and daughters of God; the role that expressing people's personhood in their community and cultural context played in affirming their growth and gifts in their culture; the need to enable people to express God's calling to be stewards of creation and provide for their families through enterprise development; and the importance of expressing life and leadership in Christian communities in cross-cultural and international partnership.

We see here how theological and biblical understanding of the nature of human personhood, human flourishing and human community formed the sort of leadership and priorities that both these Asian Christian leaders expressed in their ministries and sought to build into their communities.

3. Leadership for Transformation of Communities

A recently completed doctorate on Pentecostals in the Philippines by Joseph Suico of the Asia Pacific Theological Seminary addressed the image of Philippine Pentecostals as otherworldly and not concerned with or involved in social change. His study finds that their focus on evangelism, prayer and deliverance gives them a tremendous sense of confidence and ability in what can be done in their lives, and families and communities to bring change. They are tremendously empowered to believe change is possible. This is a great resource for poor people.

Suico draws parallels with studies done among Pentecostals in Latin America by Doug Petersen who addressed the same perception.[6] Petersen showed that Pentecostals there did not have a social theology, but their very nature as a community believing in the power of the Spirit in them (not the government nor the church) to bring change was itself a social theology. I noted that Suico, though himself an East Asian, did not draw on any examples or writings of Korean Pentecostals which might reveal the same reflection. I ask whether Cho might give leadership by encouraging similar studies on how Pentecostal faith and practice give dignity, confidence and hope for change to the poor.

These components of mission focusing on human personhood, human flourishing and human community have been brought into a coherent understanding of Christian mission which has been styled "Mission as Transformation." Transformation has been defined by Vinay Samuel as enabling God's vision of society to be actualized in all relationships, social, economic and spiritual, so that God's will may be reflected in human society and his love be experienced by all communities, especially the poor." [7]

Transformation is about a vision of society where God's will is done and his love experienced. Thus "mission is individuals coming to Christ, challenging corrupt and sinful systems, structures and cultures and enabling individuals and communities to experience God's transforming power."[8] How do we see God's transforming power acting in communities today?

---

[6]Doug Petersen, *Not by Might nor by Power* (Oxford: Regnum Books, 1996).

[7]Preface to *Mission as Transformation*, eds. V. Samuel and C. Sugden (Oxford: Regnum Books, 1999).

[8]Vinay Samuel, "Mission as Transformation," *Transformation* 19:4 (October 2002), 243-47 (244).

3.1 Transformation is Focused on Persons

As transformation is focused on persons, the transformation is focused on reorienting their relationships and empowering their choices to develop their character.

Therefore, transformation is about bodies in time and space and therefore in relation to others. Personhood is both ourselves and ourselves in relationships. Transformation is about the development of the self: the substance of the person expressed in the choices we make in relating, receiving and understanding people and situations. Transformation is also about understanding the role we have been entrusted with and about the ability to make moral choices living up to convictions, codes of conduct, standards and guidelines. Transformation is the integrity of a person's belief and actions: that which holds one together and expresses truth, faithfulness and dependability; the ability to be other-regarding: showing love in sacrifice, compassion, acceptance of difference and inclusion, and the ability to resist wrong-doing: with strong ethical resistance, but also able to forgive, heal and rebuild. It is also reconciling and renewing: recognizing that you yourself also have to be cleansed, renewed and reconciled. It is the development of creativity and stewardship: seizing the opportunity, building and taking responsibility. Transformation is also the reality of worship: in worshipping and turning to God in prayer we are really fulfilled and flourish.

As we grow in personhood we become the home where Christ dwells through his spirit. And as we relate to people so that Christ may be formed in them, through our intervention in people's lives be it in medical treatment, teaching, adult literacy, project planning, visiting and having fellowship the Holy Spirit works through us for them.[9]

---

[9]Samuel, "Mission as Transformation," 245-46.

3.2 Transformation is About the Development of Personhood in Community and Thus the Building of Communities.

Such personhood takes shape in community, between people in a covenant relationship. Such communities are moral and marked by freedom, justice, righteousness, order, law, truthfulness, love and grace.

These are creative communities: encouraging stewardship, truthfulness and hope; nurturing people with mercy, forgiveness, patience and long-suffering and building them up; communities that provide security and a sense of belonging. These are places of belonging—where orphaned children and battered women can find themselves in a community that cares as personhood is restored. They are communities that worship—open to the action of God's kingdom and overcome divisions among themselves, unite us and give us energy. They are communities with character—being faithful and honest, compassionate and caring, concerned for justice. The community character reinforces the character of persons; and communities that reflect the kingdom of God—living in anticipation of its reality, especially in worship.[10]

Here is the model and criteria for our churches, and our churches as examples to the surrounding community of what they can be and become.

3.3 Transformation is Through the Action of Communities and Community Institutions. Through Communities We Create the Public Good and Attack Evil Systems.

Through communities we create public good and attack evil systems. We build people's personhood as they engage in public action.

Poverty is virtually eradicated and people are lifted out of poverty through the development of a strong law-governed state with individual freedoms, property rights and civil society institutions. This does not happen through conversion as

[10]Samuel, "Mission as Transformation," 246-47.

conversion produces freedom from the misery and the violence of poverty when men desist work and are committed to their families. It does not occur through ethical change as ethical change produces a lift out of poverty to a level of sustainable growth; but through the development of a strong law-governed state with individual freedoms, property rights and civil society institutions.

Communities are focused on institutions. We cannot access the community as a whole without mediating entities and institutions. These institutions are rooted in the culture. They belong. The church is a mediating institution, part of the community landscape, committed to the community, rooted in the culture. The church is called to be a good civil society institution, a voluntary organization existing for the public good. The church should be holistic.

Transformational development is rooted in communities. Mediating institutions are rooted in the culture of a community. These communities are shaped by their culture. Cultural change is community focused. So transformation must address culture.

Culture is the ideas that people have about people, community, individuals, sin, love, what is or is not important; it perpetuates these ideas through institutions and practices; it is constructed by people. They live with it, seek their profit in it, want to feel good about it; and also change in culture will not come unless people see the advantage in it.

In each culture we have to ask what are the norms that Christian transformation seeks to promote within a culture? Is it possible for culture to be a resource for change rather than a barrier to change?

So we see that there is a large horizon for the mission of the church and thus for the leaders who are called to lead God's church. There is a role for individuals, families, movements and institutions in cultural transformation.

4. Leadership and the Mission of the World Church.

I am therefore minded to ask of David Yonggi Cho at this point in his leadership and in relationship to the mission of the world church, a number of questions in reference to these themes.

4.1 The Gospel in a Context of Poverty and Suffering

We are set in a context where Christianity is moving south. Churches in Africa, Latin America and Asia are growing. Churches in Europe are declining. In Korea, the church has been through poverty and suffering and now has many resources. But the current generation of young people in Korea has not known the struggles that shaped Cho. How will he ensure that his successors in leadership understand the same profound realities of the gospel amidst suffering and trial? What part will the experience of and relationships with the two-thirds world church play in this?

4.2 Partnership in the Gospel

Does the Korean church believe it is qualified to be a leader in the world church through its numerical success? What identity does he see the Korean church having in the world church? What gifts does it bring? To what model of participation in the world church does he see the Korean church aspiring? The following questions need to be raised:

1) Is it the model of being part of the western hegemony through financial resources?
2) Is it a model of being part of the two-thirds world focus on the resources of its people and their eagerness for evangelism?
3) Is it a model of being part of the suffering church because of its recent experience of suffering and trial and the Korean cultural theme of "grudge."
4) In the photograph of the world church, who does he want to be seen standing next to and why?

Would the opportunity to relate as partners with the Two-Thirds World church enable a clear witness to be drawn between the very fruitful alliance of Christianity and Korean nationalism? Studies show that the success of Christianity in Korea related to resistance against the Japanese invasion and identified Christianity with Korean national identity.[11] Studies also show that the policy of the Korean government, kick starting the Korean economic miracle by encouraging people off the land into new giant industries in the cities, has set a cultural pattern making gigantism part of Korean culture and church life. How will Cho lead the Korean churches to face the challenge of being Christians in partnership with those who are Christians in small scattered communities and what enrichment will they bring to the life of the Korean church?

How does Cho relate the financial resources of the Korean church to the financial needs of the church in other parts of the world? What responsibility does he regard the Korean church as having for those churches and for the global witness of the church in those contexts? Churches in Africa and Asia are faced with challenges of disease, poverty, AIDS. They have wonderful resources in their people and their faith. They are thirsty for knowledge to address their problems. For example we at OCMS are working with a college in Kenya to train 25 church leaders over two years to give care and counsel for those infected with and affected by HIV/AIDS. These 25 people will, as part of their post-graduate course, each train 20 people in an area base group. Each of these 500 people will be in touch with 20 people living with or affected by HIV/AIDS. Thus 10,000 people will be impacted by gospel-based care for AIDS. They need $1500 dollars a year each to supplement what they are providing for the costs of this course. For the lack of this, their studies may not go ahead. Given the considerable investment of churches in the United States in the early development of Korean churches, what view does he have of a similar investment in churches in the Two-Thirds World? Why is

---

[11]Mou Youl Choi, "Korean Presbyterianism and Social Work: A Critical Analysis of the Social Work of Four Presbyterian Denominations" (Ph.D, thesis, OCMS/University of Wales, 1996).

it that Korean churches are not currently seen as sources of potential financial support by churches in the Two-Thirds world when seeking for resources? What might be the cultural issues and perspectives that need to be addressed?

Many churches in the US and the UK are encouraging their members to make exposure visits to the Two-Thirds World to build relationships and gain a world perspective on world Christianity. It is now well recognized that Christianity is moving south. Korea is no longer economically in the Two-Thirds World. Are Koreans making exposure trips to the Two-Thirds World not only to build relationships and gain a perspective on world Christianity but also, most importantly, to share their narrative of surviving and growing churches in the midst of poverty with churches in Africa and India?

What is the relationship of Korean personnel to local Christian leadership?

5. Conclusion

I ask these questions in friendship and respect. An international mission symposium and seminar at this important level requires that the respect we give each other include the respect to ask the most important questions. I suggest that the current research being done on leaders who have promoted the growth of the church in other parts of the world prompt these questions of the leadership of the growing church in Korea. I have every expectation of stimulating and exciting answers.

SOCIAL LEADERSHIP AND CHURCH GROWTH[1]

Young-gi Hong

The purpose of this paper is to reflect on the meaning of social leadership and church growth from a missiological perspective and to suggest a future direction for the Korean Protestant church. I will discuss the social participation and church growth of the Protestant church as well as perspectives on church growth and social participation, and their theological bases. Furthermore, I will suggest future tasks of the Korean church, dealing with social leadership, its significance and of Cho as an important case study.

In this paper, social leadership is defined as the influence of the Christian gospel to engender social transformation. Church growth here is considered in terms of the quantitative, qualitative, and healthy growth of a church in the paradigm of the growth of the kingdom of God. Various ministries of the Korean churches during the past century now need to be viewed as a holistic pilgrimage toward the kingdom of God.

1. Perspectives on Church Growth and Social Participation

The conservative evangelical camp and the ecumenical camp have differently interpreted missiological perspectives on church growth. Whereas conservative evangelical churches have asserted that church growth means evangelism, nurturing, and planting new churches, the ecumenical churches have weighed more on social

---

[1]An earlier version of the study was presented at the First Youngsan Conference of Church Growth and Leadership, Aug 2003, Seoul, Korea.

participation as the essential ministry of the churches. The main reason that the conservative evangelical camp has asserted that church growth means evangelism, was the fear that, if evangelism is regarded as merely one aspect among many others of the church's mission, it would gradually be eroded and lose its priority in church mission.[2] The argument was that although non-Christians could and do become involved in many worthy activities on behalf of oppressed and needy people, only the Christian community could firmly proclaim the story of Jesus Christ with conviction.[3] The viewpoint of the conservative evangelical camp has contributed greatly to church growth and world evangelization. However, some held the conviction that such an evangelical understanding of church growth and mission was not adequately interpreting the work of God to transform society.

The churches of the ecumenical camp have stressed the social service and participation of the churches and have contributed greatly to societal development. This has helped Christians to understand the relationship between the Christian gospel and society. However, some progressive groups took the view that the true ministry of the church was "humanization." The concept of *Missio Dei*, that has been developed by Johannes C. Hoekendijk has dealt with humanization as the focus of mission. According to Hoekendijk, "the true nature of the church can be fully prescribed by its function (i.e., participation in the apostolic work of Jesus Christ),"[4] and that God had a prior relationship with the world and His relationship with the church is secondary. Hoekendijk has viewed the identity of the church as needing to become "human." He sees social and political activities as vehicles for true humanization, thus blurring the boundary between the church and the secular world. This viewpoint placed humanization as the first

---

[2] Andrew Kirk, *What Is Mission?* (London: Darton, Longman and Todd, 1999), 56.

[3] Kirk, What Is Mission?, 57.

[4] Johannes C. Hoekendijk, *The Church Inside Out* (London: SCM, 1967), 40.

priority of church mission and obscured the holistic understanding of church mission and the central position of Jesus Christ's ministry.

The difference between the viewpoint of conservative evangelical churches and that of progressive churches had been very acute until the 1970s. This heterogeneous viewpoint existed from the difference in their understanding and emphasis on church growth and mission. However, since the 1970s, both evangelical and ecumenical camps have begun to understand the other's position more and more. The World Council of Churches (WCC) has contributed greatly to the church ecumenical movement and social participation of the church, and its ministerial orientation has significantly changed since the 1980s. The WCC has maintained a theological dialogue with Pentecostal churches and Catholic churches and has shown a greater interest in charismatic ministry or power ministry than ever before. This phenomenon has been also influenced by rapidly growing non-western churches. For the first time in the history of Christianity, the non-western Christians began to outnumber western Christians. The dynamics of non-western Christianity has developed various models of mission and theology, and the WCC has been influenced by this trend. In addition, the WCC must have also been stimulated by the self-awareness and practice of social responsibility of evangelical Christianity.

Evangelical churches were rather passive on societal problems previously. However, their stand began to change in the 1970s when they began voicing their opinion on social problems through the World Evangelical Fellowship (established in 1951) and then the worldwide Lausanne movement (established in 1974). The International Congress on World Evangelization held at Lausanne of Switzerland in 1974 was a landmark congress of various denominations that declared the call for world evangelization and the necessity to participate in remedying social and political problems.

The Grand Rapids Report on gospel evangelization and social participation, published in 1982 by the Lausanne Committee for World Evangelization, states that the primary motive for evangelism and social participation is based on the true nature and character of the Trinity of God.[5] This report proclaims that the church should take on the social responsibility of pursuing relief, justice, and peace as well as the proclamation of the gospel. This report stresses that proclaiming the gospel of Christ is closely related to the social significance of Christianity and that social responsibility has a significant meaning in evangelism.

The International Fellowship of Evangelical Mission Theologians (INFEMIT, established in 1982) based in Oxford, U.K. has suggested a new direction for the ministries and leadership of world churches with the concept of mission as transformation. The INFEMIT has carried out a number of international research seminars and projects, such as mission and modernity, mission and theological education, mission and economy, and mission and politics. The results of the research project on mission and politics were presented in an international conference on Evangelical Christians and Democracy in the Third World, held in Washington D.C., USA, in June 2002. I attended this conference and presented my research paper on Evangelical Christians and the Democratization of Korea since 1987. This conference had merit because case studies of the position and function of evangelical Christianity concerning the politics of each continent were presented at a critical time, soon after the September 11, 2001 terror. The relationship between religion and politics drew great interest, especially at that time. This conference and other activities and phenomena show that evangelical Christians have actively participated in societal problems for the last 15 years.

Regarding the dichotomy between church growth and social participation in mission, Hwa finds historical basis on the traditional dualism of the western world.[6] Dualism views the universe by separating individual reasoning and the outside world, soul and body, spirit and materiality, subject and object, reality and value, religious things and worldly things. According to Hwa,

---

[5]Cf. John Stott, *Bokum Chundo-wa Sahoijok Chaekim* [Evangelism and Social Responsibility], trans. Hwa-ryong Han (Seoul: Tyrannus, 1986).

[6]Yung Hwa, *Mangoes or Barnanas?* (Oxford: Regnum, 1997), 44-55.

western dualism has its root in Greek philosophy, and it gained momentum after enlightenment thought was popularized.

The influence of dualism on Christian mission is clearly seen. Christian mission is not regarded holistically but dually. Is it a spiritual, physical and/or socio-political salvation? Is the soul more important or the body? Is the Christian mission evangelism or humanization? Does God work in the spiritual realm only or in the material realm as well? (If God works in the material realm as well, then we can rightfully expect divine healing and miracles.) Western dualism may have ushered in the problems we now see in Korea between the ecumenical and evangelical church perspectives regarding the essence of Christian mission.

Church growth and social participation may be separated in ministerial concepts but can not be separated in practice. That is because the gospel is not just a general, objective revelation but a concrete realization through the evidence of the church. The true gospel should be significantly proclaimed through the message (words) and the ministry (work) of the church. In this regard, it is noteworthy that a holistic view of church growth has recently come to the forefront, although the gifts and priority of ministry may differ. However, the task of how to practically apply this holistic view to the ministry of the church remains to be accomplished. Then, where does the holistic view on church growth and social participation in relation to church mission have its theological root and place? It is my view that it can be found in the theology of the Kingdom of God.

2. Holistic Connectivity between Church Growth and Social Participation: the Missiology of the Kingdom of God

In order for the church to grow, the gospel message of Jesus Christ should be deeply understood and practiced. Whenever Jesus preached His gospel, He mentioned "the kingdom of God."[7] The

[7]George E. Ladd, "The Gospel of the Kingdom," in *Perspectives on the World Christian Movement*, eds. Ralph D. Winter and Steven C. Hawthorne (Pasadena: William Carey Library, 1981), 51-69.

kingdom of God is the most conspicuous theme of the ministries of Jesus Christ. It is mentioned 117 times in the four gospels of the New Testament and 32 times from the Acts to the Revelation of the Testament.[8] The mission of Jesus Christ was to proclaim and demonstrate the kingdom of God.[9] Jesus said, "The time has come. The kingdom of God is near. Repent and believe the good news!" (Mark 1:15).

The gospel of the kingdom of God was the message of not only Jesus but of the early churches. "But when they believed Philip as he preached the good news of the kingdom of God and the name of Jesus Christ, they were baptized, both men and women" (Acts 8:12). The Apostle Paul also testified of the gospel of God's grace, without regard for his own life, while parting from the elders of Ephesus. It was about the kingdom of God. "However, I consider my life worth nothing to me, if only I may finish the race and complete the task the Lord Jesus has given me--the task of testifying to the gospel of God's grace. Now I know that none of you among whom I have gone about preaching the kingdom will ever see me again" (Acts 20:24-25). While the Apostle Paul was in Rome, he gathered numerous Jews and testified about the kingdom of God from morning until evening. "They arranged to meet Paul on a certain day, and came in even larger numbers to the place where he was staying. From morning till evening he explained and declared to them the kingdom of God and tried to convince them about Jesus from the Law of Moses and from the Prophets" (Acts 20:24-25).

Jesus taught that the kingdom of God exists and is revealed through Him. The kingdom of God was present in Jesus' unique person. Jesus also revealed the power of the kingdom of God and its substance in His ministry through the power of the Holy Spirit.

---

[8]Walter J. Chentry, *Ku-ui Nara-wa Ku-ui Ui* [His Kingdom and His Righteousness], trans. Seong-woong Kim (Seoul: Christian Wisdom Publishing, 1993), 5.

[9]Ron Sider, "What Is the Gospel?," Transformation: An International Evangelical Dialogue on Mission and Ethics 16:1 (1999), 31-34 (29-30).

Jesus proclaimed the new ethical value of the kingdom of God.[10] When Jesus preached about the kingdom of God, He used not only present tense but also future tense for His words (Matt 20:1-16; 22:1-14). Thus, there is a tension between the already revealed kingdom of God and the forthcoming kingdom of God. However, this tension is the mystery of God, and mission and church growth should focus on the work of the Holy Spirit, that is, to realize the kingdom of God on this earth until the Advent of the Lord.

All ministries geared for church growth should be chosen from the perspective of promoting the kingdom of God rather than the self-preservation of the church. For this purpose, the church should recognize the characteristics and features of the kingdom of God on this land. In the kingdom of God, there will be people confessing Jesus Christ is the savior. Thus, evangelism is an important characteristic of the kingdom of God. In the kingdom of God, justice and peace will prevail. Therefore, it is the ministry of the kingdom of God for Christians to work for the realization of justice and peace socially and politically. In the kingdom of God, there will be no mourning or pain. It follows then that it is the ministry of God's kingdom to heal the sick and drive out the demons. In the past, power ministries, such as healing and exorcism, could not join the mainstream in the discourse on mission theology. Those criticisms involving social participation and power ministry as well as their relationship to evangelism should all be understood and unified now in terms of the ministry of God's kingdom.

I have presented the following "kingdom ministry charter" in my book, *God's Kingdom Vision Project*.[11]

---

[10] Graham Cray, "A Theology of the Kingdom," in *Mission as Transformation*, eds. Vinay Samuel and Chris Sugden (Oxford: Regnum Books, 1999), 26-44 (29-30).

[11] Forthcoming. For the basis of the book, see Young-gi Hong, "Evangelical Christians and the Democratization of Korea Since 1987" (A paper presented at the International Conference on Evangelicals and Democracy in the Third World, hosted by the International Fellowship of Evangelical Mission Theologians, Washington D.C., July 2002).

1) Jesus Christ proclaimed the good news of the kingdom of God. Through Jesus Christ, the kingdom of God has arrived on this earth, and the kingdom will be completed with the Advent of Jesus Christ.
2) The Holy Spirit, the master of the church, is the executor of the kingdom of God and anoints the church with power to build the kingdom of God.
3) The church is an agent and sign of the kingdom of God and has been called to build the kingdom.
4) Mission is the effort to realize the character of the kingdom of God on this earth, and its substance is God.
5) In the kingdom of God, everyone will confess Jesus as Christ the Lord. Thus, in season and out of season, we need to make our utmost effort to preach the good news to the ends of the earth.
6) In the kingdom of God, everyone will submit to the absolute sovereignty of God. Thus, we should devote ourselves to nurturing ministry so that every one will become a disciple of Jesus Christ.
7) In the kingdom of God, there will be no one sick and in pain. Thus, we should make the effort to heal the souls, hearts, and bodies of people.
8) In the kingdom of God, people will not just eat and play but serve God with all their responsibility and calling. Hence, we must lead all Christians to develop their God-given gifts so as to serve the church and the world.
9) In the kingdom of God, everyone will worship and praise God wholeheartedly. Therefore, we should develop worship ministry so that every Christian will worship God passionately in their individual lives and public worship.
10) In the kingdom of God, there will be no discrimination based on race, gender, and social status, etc., and everyone will be united in our God. The church, the body of Christ, is one in the world. Thus, we should work on unifying all churches with an ecumenical mind.
11) In the kingdom of God, there will be no war or conflict, and it will be the world of Shalom, the peace of God. Thus, we must endeavor to proclaim the gospel of peace and create peace.
12) In the kingdom of God, the righteousness of God will prevail. Thus, we must have an interest in social service and

social participation so that political, economic, and social justice can be realized.

13) In the kingdom of God, all creatures and the ecological system will be wholly recovered. Therefore, we must take care of our environment and carry out an environmental ministry to preserve and love animals and nature.
14) In the kingdom of God, a world will exist where the love of God prevails and everyone will serve the other. Thus, we must make our effort to transform our community into a community of love, and we need to march forward in the movement for sharing and practicing Christian love in our society.
15) We will carry out all our actions by illuminating them in the will and words of God and in the wisdom of the Holy Spirit.
16) We will maintain a close fellowship with God and sacrificial minds to carry the cross above all in building the kingdom of God. Although this society is not perfect, we will not give up our efforts to transform society and hope for the kingdom of God with our faith and love.
17) We firmly believe that the kingdom of God will arrive eventually on this earth, and we will continue to pray for the Advent.

Church growth should aim to realize the kingdom of God. Church growth with social participation, and the mission of the church with social leadership can find mutually interactive and close relationships only in the mission paradigm of the kingdom of God. Then, how have the Korean churches contributed to Korean society and how is this contribution related to church growth? I will now deal with the case of Korean churches.

3. The Social Contribution of the Korean Protestant Church and Church Growth

Korean Protestant churches have contributed greatly to the development of modern society. Christianity could not grow as well in India or China, because of the prejudice that it is a western colonial religion. However, the Korean Protestant church could strengthen its foundation for growth with the recognition that it was linked with nationalism under the Japanese colonization and with modernization.[12] Korean churches rapidly grew from the 1960s until the 1980s following the Korean War. Protestant Christians numbered about 600,000 in 1960 and increased tremendously to 8,760,000 in 1995. The reason for this rapid growth may be due to the social factor of brisk social change, but the dynamics of the churches that contributed to changing society, also can not be ignored.

Social participation of the progressive churches developed primarily through the organic movement for democracy during the 1970s. Under forced revitalizing reform and the fact that a legal place for the democratic movement was severely restricted, the systematization of the movement through legal church organizations contributed significantly to the democracy movement. Nevertheless, the social participation of the progressive churches and the democracy movement could not secure a broad foundation due to harsh persecution by the military government. Additionally, the movement did not gain the much-needed support of conservative/evangelical Christians. During the 1970s and the early 1980s, the democracy movement of some progressive churches and some Christian students manifested a split characteristic without a firm central point of organization, and it failed to obtain strong support from the evangelical churches.

However, social participation of the progressive churches began to affect the conservative evangelical Christians during the 1980s. The attitude of the evangelical Christians toward society began to change. It was influenced by several factors including cruel military-force brutality during the upheaval at Kwangju, the introduction of social participation theology by evangelical Christians (e.g., the Evangelical Lausanne Covenant, the Grand Rapids Report), the religious oppression by the government (e.g., holding a national civil employee examination on Sunday and the building of a statue of the legendary Korean ancestor, Dangun, an

---

[12] Young-gi Hong, "Dynamism and Dilemma: The Nature of Charismatic Pastoral Leadership in the Korean Mega-churches" (Ph.D. thesis, Oxford Centre for Mission Studies/Wales University, 2000), 20.

idol), etc. We can state that the social attitude of evangelical Christians was not political but rather theological and institutional. The main route for evangelical churches to participate in the democratic movement was through holding a prayer meeting or making a statement.

Social participation of evangelical Christians became more visible after the declaration of June 29, 1987. For example, the Korean Evangelical Fellowship (KEF) made a statement 6 times before the June 29 declaration, but it made 55 declarations between June 29, 1987 and April 1998. Of course, there may be some substantial differences between the declaration and actual action. Nevertheless, the increase of those making a statement is a meaningful social fact. Korean Protestant churches were always the forerunners of the democracy movement protesting against the dictatorial government and have positively led in social service. The political participation of the Protestant churches became significantly more visible in the 1990s. Whether it was a conservative church or a progressive church, many people began to participate and voice their opinion in politics no matter how they differed in their political view. Some Christians led a transparent and rightful election movement for the presidential and congressional elections. As the effective value (voting power) of the Protestant churches in politics increased, the power of the church could no longer be ignored. In the 16th national congress, the ratio of Protestant Christian congressmen was 40% and the ratio of all Christian congressmen including Catholics reached an amazing 65%. In the political area the power of Christianity has increased steadily.

Christian citizen movements were led largely by evangelical Christians in the 1990s. Civil society is a voluntary, self-propagating, self-generating, self-sufficient, and autonomous (from government, politics, and society) organization.[13] Civil society has greater interest in public cause than private purpose. It is involved with social and national matters, but it does not pursue a public position or power. On the contrary, it pursues yielding

---

[13] Larry Diamond, "Toward Democratic Consolidation," *Journal of Democracy* 5:3 (1994), 4-17 (5).

benefit, change in policy and responsibility from the government. Christians have contributed to the attitudinal reform of Korean churches and social reform through the activities of Gyung-sil-yun (The Citizens Committee for Economic Justice), and Giyoon-shil (The Christian Ethics Movement), etc. In the year 2000, Christian NGOs (non-governmental organizations) amounted to 70% of about 1,200 Korean NGOs. The Protestant churches became very active in social services. The number of Christian organizations registered as religious corporations was double the number of all other religious organizations. According to the statistics of the Ministry of Culture and Sightseeing, as of February 2002, the total of religious corporations numbered 407. Among these, 108 foundations and 86 corporations belong to the Protestant church. This amounts to 194, 47.6% of all religious corporations. This is more than double the 92 corporations belonging to Buddhism and the 74 belonging to Catholicism. It may be related to the fact that Christianity has been positively pursuing social activities compared to other religions.

Up to this point, the purpose of both progressive and conservative churches seems to be confrontational as we try to understand the role of the Protestant church in Korean society. However, we have to acknowledge the fact that both camps contributed to Korean society in their own way. When the progressive churches spoke prophetically to society and led the democracy movement, the conservative churches helped many people in despair and under unstable socio-political circumstances through visitation and the message of hope and comfort. If the progressive churches moved in social reform until the 1980s, the conservative churches provided social integration mainly in modern Korean society.

If so, how is the social contribution of the Protestant church related to church growth? The conservative churches grew by providing a refuge to many people facing social and political unrest, through comfort and hope. On the other hand, the progressive churches fought for and devoted themselves to social justice and democracy, thus promoting the social image and credibility of the Protestant church. In this regard, it suffices to say that Korean Protestant churches have grown by filling individual and societal structural needs and by bringing about social reform. We can say that there was a "creative tension," between the church and Korean society, as stated by Robert Bella.[14] However, with the end of a military dictatorship, this creative tension has been greatly eased.

The decline of creative tension makes defining the social role and credibility of the Protestant churches difficult. Many Korean churches, not accustomed to democratic society and not understanding democracy in depth, have had some trouble establishing the coordinates for the role of the church in society. Korean Protestant Christianity has been declining since the mid-1990s. This fact is based on the 1999 Korean social indices survey of the Statistics Bureau. This survey was undertaken with 30,000 people (16-years old and above) as the national survey samples. Even if the statistical errors are accounted for, it has shown that the number of Christians of Protestant churches is clearly decreasing.

The Korean church reached its peak of growth in the early 1990s and began to decline slightly but steadily since 1995. In 1995, the Protestant population amounted to 19.6% of the total population, but dropped to 18.6%, by about 1%, in 1999. It is estimated that about 460,000 people have left the Protestant churches. On the contrary, the number of Buddhists have increased from 19.9% of the total population in 1985, to 23.2% in 1995, and then to 26.3% in 1999. The uptrend is also seen with the Catholics.

The number of Catholics amounted to 4.6% of the total population in 1985 and then increased to 6.6% in 1995, and then again to 7.0% in 1999. The declining trend of the Protestant church is in sharp contrast with other religions such as Buddhism and Catholicism. According to this survey, the Protestant church shows a greater strength in younger and highly educated people living in a metropolitan city compared to other religions. This

---

[14] Robert Bella, *Sahoi Btongdong-ui Sahoi Kuzo* [The Symbolic Structure of Social Change], trans. Young-shin Park (Seoul: Samyoung Press, 1981), 164-75.

survey result is congruent with the government statistical surveys of 1985 and 1995.

This statistical survey also shows where the Christians of Protestant churches are declining. Firstly, the Protestant churches are backsliding in Seoul and Kyunggi-do. Whereas they have increased in traditionally red-spot (under-reached) areas such as Busan (+0.9%), Daegu (+0.4%) and Jeju (+0.6%), they are declining in most other areas. The most conspicuous declining area is Seoul (-2.3%) and Inchon (-3.6%). If the population of Seoul is estimated to be 10 million, this 2.3% is equal to 230,000 people.

Secondly, the number of male Christians is diminishing. The male Christians of the Protestant church was 46.7% in 1995, but it decreased sharply to 40.7% in 1999. This indicates that either many male churchgoers are not satisfied with the Protestant church or that the evangelization of men has become more difficult.

Thirdly, the middle-aged population is leaving the church. In 1995, 20.7% of all people between 35 and 39 years of age were Christians of Protestant churches, but the percentage dropped to 18.7% in 1999. The same trend is shown with people between the ages of 40 and 44. The percentage dropped from 20.5% in 1995 to 19% in 1999. These statistics show that the main populace who leave the Protestant church are males between 35 and 45 years of age, living in a large city.

The quantitative decline of the Korean Protestant church can be explained by multi-faceted analyses. Contextual factors that assisted the earlier rapid growth of the Korean church no longer seem to be at work. New contexts that include religious pluralism, social mobility, and the economic prosperity of Christians, political and social stability, the success of Buddhism, and an increased range of leisure activities, may all have affected the growth of the Korean church. Additionally, materialism and secularism seem to be powerful forces in the Korean church, which has attracted the largest segment of its membership from the middle-class.

When relating these trends to the thesis of this paper, the most essential factors that affect the Protestant churches harshly, are the weakening of social credibility and the problem of nominal Christians.[15]

Based on his investigation of Korean churches during 1945-1960, the study of In-chol Kang, a professor of Hanshin University, suggested that social credibility is related to quantitative church growth in Korea. The most declining populace of Protestant Christians is males in their 30s and 40s, who have a social cognizance. This declined target populace speaks for itself that evangelism has not been effective. It may also mean that their perception of the Protestant churches is not favorable. In spite of the fact that the Protestant churches are engaged in more social service ministry than any other religion, it seems that the public image them is not very positive.

The nominal faith of Protestant Christians has also been a stumbling block for church growth.[16] Presently, among nearly 9 million Protestant Christians, it is estimated that only 6 million regularly attend church on Sundays. Among these regular attendees, it is estimated that about four millions are real, born-again Christians, although there is no empirical data. This may indicate that there are many nominal believers within the Protestant church. They are pseudo-Christians or Christians only in name. This problem of nominal Christians severely weakens the social credibility of the church and the gospel. Social credibility can be enhanced when church leaders and lay Christians lead holy and sacred lives. The problem of nominal Christians in the Protestant church is deeply and inversely related to the spirituality of the church. Therefore, we can see that sociality and spirituality are deeply connected.

---

[15]Young-gi Hong, "Revisiting Church Growth in Korean Protes-tantism: A Theological Reflection," *International Review of Mission* LXXXIX/353 (April, 2000), 190-202.

[16] Young-gi Hong, "Nominalism in Korean Protestantism," *Transformation* 16:4 (1999), 136-41.

It seems that the Korean church is in a very important phase. According to the research of Duke and Johnson,[17] in general, a religion steadily increases, reaches its peak and then a plateau, and then declines gradually. They believe that the activities of the church are influenced by the growth cycle. At the present time, when the growth of Protestant churches is declining, a more devoted dedication is needed for church growth. The Korean Protestant church has the great tasks of developing spirituality and enhancing social credibility. When Christians who have experienced the power of the gospel and its veracity demonstrate the good news in their words and actions, they can enhance social credibility and effect social transformation. I would like to suggest that the Korean Protestant church examine the social leadership of Cho, who has grown the largest church in the world and is highly respected in the world churches.

4. Case Study: David Yonggi Cho's Social Leadership

Cho is the founding pastor of the Full Gospel church and is generally considered conservative. Thus, some people criticize him for not having an interest in social problems or pursuing an undulating faith. However, this is not a valid evaluation.[18] This kind of misconception about Cho is in line with the general image of Full Gospel.

The Pentecostal movement has been perceived as an other-worldly mission movement rather than as a world-transforming mission movement. However, this is not so when we carefully examine the twentieth century Christian mission movements. In Latin America (e.g., Brazil) or Asia (e.g., Philippines), the Pentecostal churches have contributed greatly to social

---

[17] James T. Duke and Barry L. Johnson, "The Stages of Religious Transformation: A Study of 200 Nations," *Review of Religious Research* 30 (1989), 209-24.

[18] Young-gi Hong, *Cho Yonggi Moksa-ui Youngsung-kwa Leadership* [Rev. David Yonggi Cho's Spirituality and Leadership] (Seoul: Institute for Church Growth, 2003), 167.

transformation.[19] The influence of Cho on Korean society has been relatively underestimated, and this may be partly due to the biased viewpoint of some Korean churches, that has illuminated social participation and evangelism with a dichotomous point of view. I will now analyze the aspects of Cho's social leadership and its meaning.

4.1 Cho's Influence on Korean Society

I discussed the following ten points of influence that Cho has had upon Korean society elsewhere.[20] They are summarized and presented here.

4.1.1 Change in the mentality for positive life and hope

Many scholars, who study political democracy, point out that democracy is in the minds of people. In other words, democracy depends on the citizens, who experience a democratic political culture rather than on legal documents guaranteeing human rights or freedom.[21] This point indicates that one of the most important tasks for the development of Korean society is to reform the mentality of people. The message of Cho has influenced the life attitudes of countless numbers of people who suffered from poverty and disease. Cho himself answered in my email interview that his ministry of instilling "a dream and hope for a positive life" in the faith of Christianity was the most important influence on

[19] Douglas Petersen, "Missions in the Twenty-first Century: Toward a Methodology of Pentecostal Compassion," *Transformation* 16:2 (1999), 54-59; Joseph R. Suico, "Institutional and Individualistic Dimensions of Transformational Development: The Case of Pentecostal Churches in the Philippines" (Ph.D. dissertation, OCMS/University of Wales, 2003).

[20] Young-gi Hong, "The Influence of Rev. David Yonggi Cho on Korean Society," in *Charis and Charisma: Rev. David Yonggi Cho and the Growth of Yoido Full Gospel Church*, eds. Sung-hoon Myung and Young-gi Hong (Oxford: Regnum Books, 2003), 197-217.

[21] Sung Moon Pae, *Korea Leading Developing Nation: Economy, Democracy, and Welfare* (Lanham, MD: University Press of America, 1992), 167.

Korean society.[22] It is noteworthy that amidst the challenges of modern Korean society, the message of Cho has inspired common people to have confidence and hope for their lives.

4.1.2 Function of social integration

The ministry of Cho has enabled social integration in religious sociology by integrating Christians in one community. This has happened through the experience of the infilling of the Holy Spirit and a positive outlook on life. While progressive Christianity has absorbed those Christians assenting to its social participation to help remedy troublesome social issues, the ministry of Cho has dealt with sublimating social anxiety in a spiritual way. It has provided a sense of stability and empowerment to the socially, economically and culturally alienated group of people.

4.1.3 Redemption and lift

Cho's ministry helped numerous poor and sick people in the church through material blessing and divine healing. His positive and aggressive message on life produced convictions of faith, and many people became "the have's" socially, economically, and spiritually. We can call these ministerial results, "redemption and lift." A Christian's redemption and lift can be a driving force for missionary devotion and social reform, as Murray Dempster suggested.[23]

4.1.4 Cultural reform

The ministry of Cho has been often criticized as shamanistic. However, this is a mistaken view. Though Korea has a shamanistic environment, which is the seedbed for Cho's ministry, Cho's ministry of healing and blessing through the Holy Spirit can not be

---

[22]David Yonggi Cho, in an email message with the author (October 24, 2002).

[23] Murray W. Dempster, "Evangelism, Social Concerns and the Kingdom of God," in *Called and Empowered: Global Mission in Pentecostal Perspective*, eds. Bryon D. Klaus and Douglas Petersen (Peabody, MA: Hendrickson, 1991), 22-43 (27).

mixed with shamanism. Allan Anderson,[24] Hwa Yung,[25] and others point out that it is wrong to call the ministry of Cho shamanistic. They consider Cho's ministry as a contextual form of Korean Christianity interacting with shamanism. There is an enormous difference between interacting with shamanism and becoming shamanistic. The dimension of Cho's ministry of cultural reform needs to be illuminated in this context anew.

4.1.5 Leadership development

Pentecostalism offers a place for the alienated and women to restore their self-esteem and receive leadership training. Douglas Peterson stated that this is an important social expression of Pentecostalism.[26] Cho's ministry transforms new believers into devoted saints through the experience of the Holy Spirit. He calls church members to serve voluntarily and offers the opportunity for leadership development.

One noticeable point in his ministry is the leadership role of women. In Korean society, where women were not traditionally accepted for leadership positions, Cho acknowledged their leadership potential and provided opportunities for them. The development and application of leadership is based on the Full Gospel doctrine of spiritual gifts. Women, who lacked the opportunity to use their spiritual gifts, were given the responsibilities of evangelism and nurturing and were provided leadership opportunities. This practice is important to human resource development, and can be useful in the development of

---

[24] Allan Anderson, "David Yonggi Cho's Pentecostal Theology as Contextual Theology in Korea" (A paper presented at the First Youngsan International Theological Symposium, Hansei University, Gunpo, Korea, September 2002). A revised version is published in this volume.

[25] Yung Hwa, "Missiological Implications of Dr. David Yonggi Cho's Theology" (A paper presented at the First Youngsan International Theological Symposium, Hansei University, Gunpo, Korea, September 2002). A revised version of the paper is published in this volume.

[26] Douglas Petersen, Not By Might Nor By Power: A Pentecostal Theology of Social Concern in Latin America (Oxford: Regnum Books, 1996), 121.

Korean society. The ministry of Cho, which enhanced the social value of women and instituted the sense of equitable compensation for ability, can be regarded as an important contribution to Korean society.

4.1.6 Interaction with the modernization of Korean society

Cho has been involved in colleges and mass-media ministry which are important carriers of modernity. Pentecostals have built and developed schools as a means to change the lives of people in the process of social change in the beginning. Likewise, Cho has made a sincere effort to nurture the talented through Hansei University, Bethesda University, and the Full Gospel Theological School. In addition, Cho has used TV and radio as a means of mission. Since 1996, Cho's ministry has started global satellite broadcasting. Since the early 1990s, when personal computers began to be widely distributed, Yoido Full Gospel Church (YFGC) established an Internet Broadcasting Division to broadcast the worship service live. The sermons of Cho are also offered to the web users by video on demand. These cases show that Cho's ministry does not ostracize the technological and social value system, but rather utilizes it fully for the effectiveness of Christian gospel.

His ministry has been influenced by the modernization of Korean society and has interacted with this change positively. Grant Wacker described the Pentecostal movement as "the garden of Eden equipped with a satellite dish,"[27] and this description fits the ministry of Cho as well. This is a symbolic example of the spirituality of the Full Gospel grafted onto the modern technology of Korean society.

---

[27] Grant Wacker, "Searching for Eden with a Satellite Dish: Primitivism, Pragmatism, and the Pentecostal Character," in *The Primitive Church in the Modern World*, ed. Richard Hughes (Urbana and Chicago: University of Illinois Press, 1995), 139-166.

4.1.7 Social service activities

Cho and YFGC started the "sharing movement" in 1982, a blood donation drive of love in 1988 and built the Elim Welfare Town in 1988 as a contribution from Christianity to the social welfare service. In addition, free heart surgery operations have been given to the needy since 1984, and the recipients of such free operations totaled more than 3,000 by the year 2001. The subsidy for these operations amounted to 4.14 billion won (approximately 3.3 million U.S. dollars).[28] On May 3, 1996, Cho of YFGC received the highest Medal of Honor given to civilians, the Moogoonghwa medallion, by the government. The merits of Cho and YFGC in such endeavors as the heart operation subsidy program, and the movement to help boys and girls who are head of their households, have been acknowledged at the highest national government level. These cases demonstrate that the ministry of Cho is related to the socialization of Christian faith.

4.1.8 Establishment of The Kookmin Daily News *and its societal impact*

Cho founded *The Kookmin Daily News* in 1988 and through it, started influencing Korean society with the Christian gospel. It is the first Christian daily newspaper published with the Christian spirit, and thus it is historically significant for Full Gospel ministry and Korean society as well. From its inception, it has promoted an awareness of alienated people to the society of Korea. From January 29, 1989, it has helped thousands of boys and girls who are head of their households. Since 1993, it has engaged in the campaign "kind neighbor, bright society." It is a kindness movement for all in Korea. It has also made a sincere effort to help make Korea bright and healthy through campaigns to donate wheelchairs for the handicapped, to improve burial culture, and to send calendars of love, etc. In 2001, it published a study on the donation culture of various nations to challenge Korean Christians to begin their donation habit by sharing simple articles such as

---

[28] "The Social Service Ministries of Yoido Full Gospel Church" (in Korean), *Full Gospel Family News* (February 24, 2002).

used clothes. Recently, it has embarked on a campaign to drive out pornography. Now *The Kookmin Daily News* is faced with the task to develop its professional niche in Christian journalism.

Cho speaks of the significance of *The Kookmin Daily News* as follows:

> The government or society does not pay attention to the cry of the church institution. However, they heed to our voice through a cultural institution of journalism, daily newspaper. Thus, *Kookmin Daily News* is the spokesman of Korean Christianity and the platform for the Korean church to influence the nation or society.[29]

4.1.9 Christian NGO activities

Cho established a Christian NGO, Good People World Family (GPWF), as founder and chairman in 1999. An incorporated body, GPWF is the first church NGO in Korea. It was begun through YFGC, for poor and suffering neighbors in the global village, relying on the words of the Lord, "Go and do likewise" (Luke 10:37). Cho speaks of his mission through GPWF as follows:

> The reason that I founded Good People can be found in the Bible, which says, "The Lord fed me when I was hungry, gave me the clothes when I had nothing to wear, took care of me when I was sick, and visited me when I was imprisoned." I was deeply moved by this passage. Thus, I came to conceive the idea to start a mission work though Good People, with its resemblance to Good Samaritan, in order to deliver the love of Christ directly to those hungry, poorly clothed, sick, and poor people. Through this organization, we would like to extend our helping hands to Africa, the third world, North Korean refugees, those hungry people and children in North Korea, etc. and anywhere our love and help is needed. For example, between 4 million and 5 million North Korean children will die of tuberculosis caused by malnutrition within a year. Because medicine for them must be delivered, our church made special

[29]The author's interview with Rev. David Yonggi Cho, Feb 27, 2003, at YFGC, Seoul, Korea.

> provision for the budget of 4 billion won (approximately 3.4 U.S. million dollars) to send out tuberculosis medicine to North Korea through NGO. And we plan ultimately to send out medicine of 10 million U.S. dollars worth to North Korea. All these efforts are to show the love of Jesus Christ within the Holy Spirit. Korean churches, whether they are small or large, must engage in the movement of love in accordance with their size. I firmly believe that is a way to serve Jesus Christ.[30]

GPWF has engaged in various activities since its inception. As an education and supporting ministry, it has hosted and supported a children's choir, helped poor neighbors, sold Christmas cakes, offered free corn porridge, etc. in 2002. Additionally, GPWF has been sending corn seeds and fertilizer, meals for North Korean children, roasted rice powder, and medicine for tuberculosis every year to North Korea. Moreover, it has continued the ministry of helping the refugees for freedom settle in Korea through Good People College. GPWF has also been undertaking a hospice ministry, helping unfortunate neighbors, supporting foreign laborers, and operating the GPWF service corps of love. The overseas ministries of GPWF include: rebuilding Talegaon school in India, medical care and clothing assistance for the third world, support for Vietnam and the Nanai tribe of Russia, medicine for tuberculosis patients in the Philippines, prevention of AIDS in Kenya, and more. Emergency relief is also an important ministry of GPWF. It has responded swiftly wherever there was suffering due to disaster with relief supplies and medical care. GPWF has a short history, but has achieved remarkable growth.

4.1.10 Participation in the environmental movement

Cho and YFGC established the Christian environmental mission division in 1995 to honor the call of stewardship for the environment and nature. Under the slogan of "nature love, nation love," it has been a forerunner in the environmental preservation movement to spread the need to the Korean people for the

---

[30]The author's interview with Rev. David Yonggi Cho, Feb 27, 2003, at YFGC, Seoul, Korea.

preservation of the environment. GPWF, concerned for environmental issues, started building an ecological garden on the side stream of the Han River in Yoido of Seoul with the support of the city of Seoul and the Green Seoul Citizen Commission. The purpose of this project was to provide an ecological education program to visitors observing the ecological park and developing educational resources that are appropriate for this park.

A full-time staff was placed in the park for continuous monitoring, and greatly helped in the development of educational resources and educational methods. Visitors numbering 8,685 have experienced nature through ecological schools developed for environmental and ecological education. These schools are diverse and include a weekend/seasonal ecological school and one that operates weekdays. There are schools for handicapped boys and girls, for preschool and primary school children and an invitational school for teachers. The important contribution of this ministry is that a model for the operation and management of an urban ecological park has been suggested and developed. Various specialists and experts, as well as city civil servants, participated and cooperated in this project and suggested a cooperative system policy for the urban ecological park.

As we have seen so far, Cho has contributed to the development of Korean society in a variety ways. He has also exercised leadership so that Christians through their churches can contribute to the development of Korean society by holding save-the-nation prayer meetings and by participating in other activities such as the Christian peace forum, etc.

4.2 Analysis of Cho's Social Leadership

What kind of evaluation can be made of the social leadership of Cho? I will analyze the nature of his social leadership in four aspects.

Above all, the foundation of Cho's social leadership came about from the power of church growth. Nyung Kim presents normative power, organizational power, and behavioral power as the institutional power of the church to cause societal and political change.[31]

Normative power here includes prophetic calling and provision of ideology. *Organizational* power includes consolidation in variety, organizational size, a wide range of influence (periodicals, mass media, school, etc.), an international network in addition to material and human resources. *Behavioral* power refers to the ethical authority of the church and societal recognition of public credibility. Cho's social influence has its foundation mainly on the organizational power of church growth. The rapid growth of YFGC greatly enhanced the securing of material and human resources, use of international networks and the power of mass media. Cho's church growth movement gave him the power to influence society in time.

The form of Cho's social leadership is Minjung (populace)-oriented because his social influence was not oriented to the elite, but minjung. Cho himself believes that his pastoral calling is for the common people. His ministry is more minjung than minjung theology. Cho's pastoral message, the fivefold gospel and threefold blessing, was the message of hope that changed so many people. They have met Jesus Christ and found their identity. This contributed greatly to a creative change in modern Korean society, and this aspect makes the character of Cho's social leadership people-transformative. It has a similar contextual setting as the influence of Pentecostalism in Latin America. The Pentecostal movement grew briskly among the poor and alienated people and emerged as a formidable force to change society with time.

Cho's social leadership lies in social transformation through the movement of the Holy Spirit. He understands that his social ministry is an extension of the Holy Spirit ministry. I asked him in an interview how he understands the social significance of the Holy Spirit movement. He said:

---

[31]Nyung Kim, *Hanguk Chungchi-wa Kyohoi Kukga Kaldung* [Korean Politics and Church-Nation Conflict] (Seoul: Sonamu Publsihing, 1996), 20-23.

> The purpose of the fullness of the Holy Spirit is for God to change society and the world. People who are saved and filled with the Holy Spirit must propagate the grace of salvation to those around them. The Bible also says, "But you will receive power when the Holy Spirit comes on you; and you will be my witnesses in Jerusalem, and in all Judea and Samaria, and to the ends of the earth" (Acts 1:8). The Holy Spirit movement must have the power of propagation. There are various ways of mission. There is a movement to save individuals by evangelism and a movement by eradicating the resistance to the Christian gospel and preaching the gospel through changing society culturally. The church should not just stay within its boundary but deliver cultural mission to change society through the Holy Spirit. The gospel of Jesus Christ should be propagated in various ways with the help of the Holy Spirit. It is the Holy Spirit movement that builds a church directly and expands the realm of mission indirectly through education and societal relief.[32]

It is noteworthy that Cho's social ministry is not privatizing but socializing the value of the fullness of the Holy Spirit. We find a link exists between Christian spirituality and sociality through the ministry of the Holy Spirit.

Lastly, the focus of Cho's social leadership is the kingdom of God. Cho's theology of ministry is the theology of hope, and it is to proclaim hope toward the kingdom of God. Cho speaks of the relationship between church growth and the kingdom of God as follows:

> The gospel of the kingdom of God should be preached in all pulpits all over the world on Sunday worship service. Then, people will be excited by the Lord whom we are serving, and will love Him. That's right. If the sinners in your local community realize that God, whom the church worships, is alive and working in us, your church will grow truthfully. God is alive and fills our needs. When people experience heartily life in God, they can see and realize the work of God. And they will

---

[32]The author's interview with Rev. David Yonggi Cho, Feb 27, 2003, at YFGC, Seoul, Korea.

> devote themselves to Him. Among them, the kingdom of God comes. In addition, the changed saints will turn to be witnesses to testify the gospel of the kingdom of God in their society. The kingdom of God may not be visible, but it is working through the power of the Holy Spirit. The church should do all it can to proclaim the gospel of the kingdom of God till the last day of the world. Church growth should have its foundation on the gospel of the kingdom of God through Jesus Christ.[33]

As we have seen, Cho highly esteems the gospel of the kingdom of God. Cho's social leadership can be evaluated in terms of the ministry theology of the kingdom of God as I suggested previously. God's kingdom means ministries of evangelism, discipleship, divine healing, worship, gifting, unity, justice, peace, environment, and love. Cho's ministry manifests itself in almost all of the areas aforementioned. Among these, the ministries of evangelism, divine healing, worship, and gifting seem strongest. On the other hand, it seems that his involvement in the areas of political and economic justice could be increased. However, there has been steady development and progress in these ministries also since the 1990s.

Analyzing Cho's social leadership in light of one's power to cause change in society, his normative and organizational power is very strong, whereas his behavioral power is relatively weak. Since Cho is in a very important position to influence the churches of the world as well as Korean churches, his ministry may require continued interest and self-reflection.

5. The Implications of the Case of Cho for the Korean Church and Future Tasks

Understanding Cho's social leadership style suggests important implications for the Korean church. Above all, it indicates that church growth is relevant to social participation.

---

[33] David Yonggi Cho, "Yoido Full Gospel Church and Rev. Cho's Principles of Church Growth," in *Charis and Charisma*, 35-119 (118-19).

Material and human resources available as a church grows are factors that Korean society should not underestimate. Additionally, the social leadership of the church can enhance the credibility of the church and the gospel. The case of Cho also shows that the Holy Spirit movement is related to the spirituality of social transformation. Social participation should not be a purpose in itself. Any social movements, which are not rooted in the gospel, may not be Christian and may not be able to help the church. Social transformation must be understood in the framework or the paradigm of the Holy Spirit movement to build the kingdom of God on this earth. It must be included holistically within the gospel of the kingdom of God. I believe that the theology of the kingdom of God should be discussed more seriously in the Korean church.

What are the future tasks of the Korean Protestant church as suggested from the case of Cho? Firstly, the Korean church should develop the continuous ministry of the Holy Spirit. Social participation that is not based on spirituality lacks strength. Marxism is the secularized and materialized form of Christian hope for the Advent of the kingdom of God. It was an attempt to build the kingdom of God without social class on this earth, by a reaction to the inconsistency of capitalism. Social change as well as individual change is the ministry of the Holy Spirit. Thus, the social significance of being filled with the Holy Spirit needs to be developed further. For example, charismatic gifts such as divine healing or speaking in tongues must be elevated to the communal and social dimension. The inner change of an individual through the experience of the fullness of the Holy Spirit needs to be developed to effect communal and social change. The fullness of the Holy Spirit can also transform nominal Christians, thus promoting the growth of the Korean church.

Secondly, the sharing movement must be fostered further. Cho and YFGC have contributed greatly so far. Nevertheless, there are millions of people who are suffering from hunger and lack of clothing. There are about 1.2 billion people living on under US$1.00 a day and about 3 billion people under US$2.00 per day.[34] Korean churches need to stress the ministry of the sharing movement more in their theology and faith and it needs to be recognized worldwide in this age of globalization. The gap between the rich and the poor is continuing to widen. Sharing will enhance the public credibility of the gospel and the social influence of the church.

Thirdly, the Korean Protestant church has a rather weak social image in spite of the fact that they provide more social services than any other religion. It seems that Cho's social ministry does not draw proper recognition compared to its contribution. This may be partly due to the fact that the Protestant churches are not united as are the Buddhists and Catholics. Thus, church ecumenism may contribute to the positive image of the church. The Korean church also has to maintain an interest in effective public relations through journalism and mass-media. It has to identify and utilize effective ways to inform society about the church's good deeds.

Fourthly, it is important to develop a theology of social transformation.[35] In Cho's fivefold gospel and threefold blessing, there are powerful implications for social and political change.[36] However, social theology in this area is underdeveloped. There is currently a lack of social and political theology that can explain the new era following minjung theology. This theology should be able to suggest meaningful explanations of such matters as:

- The organic relationship between church growth and social participation,
- The theory and the practice of social participation,
- The significance and tasks of evangelical civil movements,
- Christian alternatives to social issues,

---

[34]Young-gi Hong, *Kingdom Vision Project* (in Korean; Seoul: Korean Christian Literature, 2002), 171.

[35]Cf. Mark A. Noll, *Adding Cross to Crown* (Grand Rapids: Baker, 1996).

[36]David Yonggi Cho, *Ojung Bokgum-kwa Samjung Chukbok* [The Five-fold Gospel and Threefold Blessing] (Seoul: Seoul Logos, 2000).

- The contribution of the church for democratic consolidation.

Lastly, the Korean church must develop the ministry of building leaders. In the theological framework of the kingdom of God, the kingdom is at work not only in the church but also in the world. In order for the Korean church to realize God's kingdom on this earth, it must nurture devoted leaders who live a missionary lifestyle and demonstrate the value system of God's kingdom in the fields of politics, economics, culture, and education. The Korean church must take an interest in identifying leaders with spirituality, intelligence, and social awareness and then train them. "For just as through the disobedience of the one man the many were made sinners, so also through the obedience of the one man the many will be made righteous" (Rom 5:19). When a leader stands upright, his or her influence is immense. It takes time to grow a person; however, in time the social leadership of the Korean church will be promoted and the social transformation of the Christian gospel fostered.

6. Looking to the Future

The Korean church needs to develop social leadership further. For this, it should understand the ministry of the kingdom of God to transform society with the Christian gospel. In the theological framework of the kingdom of God, the social leadership of the church is closely relevant to church growth. The church growth of Cho has helped to develop his social leadership, and this social leadership in turn contributed to the healthy growth of the church, thus developing the kingdom of God. Imbedded within Cho's spirituality is being filled with the Holy Spirit. This has shown us the possibility of individual and societal change. However, these accomplishments are only stepping stones for a leap into the future. The kingdom of God has not yet come upon the Korean church and society. The Korean church should continue her pilgrimage toward the kingdom of God diligently and with humility saying, "We have done just what we had to do."

We are all pilgrims and partners in the kingdom of God. We have to encourage one another and march forward in the kingdom of God as we face this critical time.

PROSPECTS

TOWARD THE FUTURE OF DAVID YONGGI CHO'S THEOLOGICAL TRADITION

Wonsuk Ma

David Yonggi Cho and his ministries stand as a symbol of the explosive expansion of Christianity in the non-western world. As Cho is in the period of his life and ministry to plan for the post-Cho era, the role of Cho and his younger theological disciples becomes critical in charting their future not only for the continuing dynamism in the church or the network of churches, but also the increasing impact to world Pentecostalism and Christianity. In this critical juncture, a reflection similar to what Russell Spittler published decades ago for Pentecostal studies may be needed. Spittler published this piece when any study of Pentecostalism was considered to be neither viable, nor even politically correct not only from those without but also from within. In this seminal essay, titled, "Suggested Areas for Further Research in Pentecostal Studies," he listed with comments suggested areas of study for younger Pentecostals.[1] Although this was not necessarily a profound academic research, its critical importance was well proven in the ensuing decades. It is impossible to find out how many younger Pentecostal scholars have been aided, guided or influenced by this work directly or indirectly.[2] Nonetheless, no one

[1]Russell P. Spittler, "Suggested Areas for Further Research in Pentecostal Studies," *Pneuma* 5:2 (Fall 1983), 39–57.

[2]One concrete fruit may be the upcoming volume dedicated to Spittler himself: Wonsuk Ma and Robert P. Menzies, eds., *Spirit and Spirituality: Essays in Honor of Russell P. Spittler* (London: T. & T. Clark, 2004 forthcoming).

would question the usefulness of such reflective suggestions, and many quietly waited for subsequent revision and expansion of the list either by the same author or others. This essay, in a limited sense, wishes to serve a similar purpose to the future development of the Cho theological tradition.

1. Distinct Role of the Cho Theological Tradition

Cho has never been considered to be a theologian, but more an evangelist and pastor, perhaps more specifically a church growth strategist unusually combining theories and practices. Nonetheless, he has created a powerful theological tradition that has already impacted many churches and Christian leaders in the last four decades, and this seems to be only the beginning. The possibilities are innumerable. However, it all depends on how his theological disciples carry this tradition into the future.

1.1 Cho and Wesley

More than once, Cho was compared with John Wesley, the founder of the Methodist Church in the eighteenth century. In several areas, this comparison appears to be suitable. To begin with, both began a powerful renewal tradition, or spiritual revivals. The tradition Wesley founded was based on the spiritual revival he initiated to Britain during the industrial revolution where social changes were rapid and as a consequence moral decay was rampant. More problematic was the perception that this was part of the package of "development." Cho also came from a similar desperate background, personal and social. Both found the solution to their challenges in spiritual renewal. Thus, both became the founders of powerful spiritual traditions. Second, both were preachers rather than theologians, such as John Calvin and Martin Luther. Cho and Wesley ministered among the ordinary, or more accurately the below-average populace. Third, as a result, their theology is integrated into their sermons, practical teaching, songs and diaries (in Wesley's case), in contrast with John Calvin's voluminous theological treaties. Fourth, by nature of their theological expressions, it is their followers and disciples in the subsequent generations who are left to fully analyze, develop, even refine and present their theologies. It is true that the theological writings of Calvin and Luther also went through a similar process in their subsequent generations, but to a different extent, and in a different way from Wesley's.

The task entrusted to the followers and disciples of Wesley and Cho are in several ways similar to the disciples of ancient prophets including Jesus himself. What they left behind were "legacies" often preserved in memories and some pieces of written records often in the form of narratives (stories). It took another generation or two, in the case of Jesus, for his disciples to have collected, edited and developed written presentations of Jesus' life, teachings and ministry. They are the Gospels. What we have seen is the "mining" of theological "truth" from these deposits of material, these stories.

Cho and Wesley have been able to leave much material (not always written in Cho's case, as there are "tons" of video and audio material available) often in more concrete forms such as sermons and stories. This does not mean that they did not leave "theological" writings at all. However, they are relatively smaller in amount. Thus, the followers of these modern leaders, in comparison with ancient days, benefit from modern technology and availability of writings. More importantly, the modern leaders themselves have left writings, thus, advancing a step further for their followers.

1.2 Potentials of the Cho Theological Tradition

Then what kind of potentials are there for the followers or theological disciples of Cho? The analogy is often made from the Wesleyan tradition as our historical reference.

1.2.1 Possibility of "people's theology"

Cho has the powerful possibility to put theological tasks in the hands of the people in the pew. This is quite unlike the case of Calvin and Luther who developed elite and scholastic theological traditions. Indeed, this is a unique feature of the Pentecostal movement: the creation of people's theology. The source of theologizing is not any theological masterpiece, but sermons, songs, testimonies and diaries. Placing the responsibility of theologization into the hands of the masses is indeed a revolutionary change, truly fulfilling the ideal of the "priesthood of all believers." However, such a right beginning does not always promise "people's theology" as a result. The Wesleyan tradition is a good, but sad example: subsequent generations turned this into an elite and scholastic theological tradition. This is something Cho's theological followers should carefully guard against.

1.2.2 Theology for church renewal

This theology has a potential to serve the church by leading it into the path of renewal. It is true that many theological traditions were born out of a need for renewal (whether it is called "Reformation," "revival" or something else). Their theological systems were either scholastic or "lay" in nature. In an overgeneralizing way, one may argue that the latter, or the pew-orientated theological systems, seem to have a better chance to fulfill its promise. Thus, Methodism had more potential to continue its renewal tradition that the Reformed tradition. However, this potential is not always realized. For instance, the Korean Presbyterian churches are fully alive and kicking with phenomenal growth, explosive missionary impulse, and some "Pentecostal" features in their worship and life. On the other hand, the Holiness Church, which brought a powerful revival tradition with many Pentecostal elements including healing, made a conscious theological choice to be more like existing churches. As a result, their churches have lost distinctive features such as healing, evangelism, prayer traditions and others, which the Korean churches badly need. Of course, the path which the Methodist church has taken is another example. The Cho theological tradition, which has powerful ministry and personal experiences as its basis, can develop a system that will serve the church by providing a firm theological foundation for continuing church renewal. Although institutionalization is an unavoidable life path for an organization pioneered by a powerful charismatic leader such as Cho,[3] many organizations have overcome the trend and begun another cycle of renewal. For instance, the U.S. Assemblies of God began to show various signs of institutionalization and a virtually flat pattern of growth from the late-1950s that lasted for a decade. However, the Executive Presbytery took a bold step by instituting "The Study Committee on Advance" in 1967. The fruit of that endeavor had a dramatic impact on the denomination, resulting in a renewed pattern of growth that lasted into the 1990s.[4] This expansion and growth also gave a strong impetus to the global expansion of the denomination and the wider Pentecostal movement worldwide. In this process, therefore, it is critical for the theological disciples of Cho to guard themselves from any temptation to lead the tradition into a dry and self-serving scholastic path. Without dynamic ministry and church growth, Cho theology does not exist.

1.2.3 Role in the theological formation of "majority church"

The shift of the Christian center from the West and North to the East and South was complete a few decades ago.[5] The explosive growth of the church in the non-western continents and the steady decline of Christianity in the West have contributed to this. This trend coincides with the contrast in the population growth of the non-western world and the decline of the western continent. However, it will take at least several generations before

---

[3]E.g., on the Assemblies of God, USA, Margaret M. Poloma, *The Assemblies of God at the Crossroads: Charisma and Institutional Dilemmas* (Knoxville: University of Tennessee Press, 1989).

[4]William W. Menzies, *Anointed to Serve* (Springfield, MO: GPH, 1971), 399-405. See also, "Report of the General Secretary, 50th General Council, Washington, D.C., July 31-Aug.3, 2003." This report, which can be accessed on the internet (http://Gensec.ag.org) through this address, discloses a pattern of continuing growth.

[5]*World Christian Encyclopedia*, 2 vols., rev. ed., eds. David B. Barrett, George T. Kurian, and Todd M. Johnson (Oxford: Oxford University Press, 2001), vol. 1, 12.

non-western, or "majority world" [6] Christianity develops its indigenous theological infrastructure, including theologians, institution, writings, programs, funds, academic societies, conferences and others. This does not mean that the non-western world does not have some of them. Seminaries and universities are present and so are various initiatives. Yet, most faculty members are still trained in the West, and the theological textbooks used in institutions are heavily western products. Obviously, the theological infrastructure in the non-western world is not commensurate with the size and dynamism of its church.

In this critically formative period of non-western theological systems, theological programs of Cho and his church have been quite impressive. His widely publicized Church Growth International and its wide range of publications are best known. Of course, Cho's own books have been translated into English and other languages (although it seems that less than 10% of Cho's books are available in English). However, less known is the critical work of the International Theological Institute (ITI), the theological brain of Yoido Full Gospel Church. It is because most ITI titles are in Korean: the all too common weakness in Cho study. ITI published many theological books expounding particularly Cho's theology of blessing.

More importantly, however, the Institute organized an annual conference on the Holy Spirit. World renowned scholars such as Jürgen Moltmann, Harvey Cox, Vinson Synan and others were invited, along with Korean theologians representing a variety of theological traditions. This occasion provided instant exposure of Cho's theology and the magnitude of his ministry to participants. Dialogue occurred in a variety of settings and provided an environment conducive to promote mutual understanding and even appreciation of Cho's ministry and theology. As a result, years

---

[6]For this term, e.g., Allan Anderson, "Revising Pentecostal History in Global Perspective" (A paper presented in the International Conference on Asian Pentecostalism, Sept 2001, Birmingham, UK), published in *Asian and Pentecostal: The Charismatic Face of Christianity in Asia*, eds. Allan Anderson and Edmond Tang (Oxford: Regnum Books, 2004 forthcoming).

later, the Presbyterian Church (Tonghap) withdrew its statement labeling Cho as a heretic.[7] The presentations were annually published to provide valuable collections to expound, compare, and evaluate various pneumatological topics. For this important contribution, the leadership and vision of Young-hoon Lee, former director of the Institute, deserves recognition. Currently, under the leadership of Sam-hwan Kim, the Institute is undertaking an ambitious translation project of Cho's books, and already three titles have become available. This project will be a welcome initiative to researchers on Cho's theology and ministry. Two recent theological conferences offering important initiatives are: Youngsan International Theological Conference organized by Hansei University, and Youngsan International Conference on Church Growth and Leadership organized by the Institute for Church Growth. The initiatives of Hyun-seong Bae and Young-gi Hong (respectively) are promising. These efforts and more coming serve as an encouragement and example to fellow "majority world" theologians and church leaders.

1.2.4 Contextual Pentecostal theology

As very well argued by Hwa and Anderson in this volume, the genius of Cho's theology lies in its creative contextual sensitivity. His theology based primarily on his sermons reflects his conscious attempt to make Pentecostal belief, acquired through learning and experience, relevant to the locus of where people are. The relevance of his message is not only to the socio-cultural, but also existential context. His members were going through drastic social changes from post-war devastation, military dictatorship, social unrest, economic hardship and then toward a social and economic upward move in later years. His theology was shaped, reshaped, modified, refined and solidified through his constant learning (as a highly motivated self-taught leader) and interaction with his

---

[7]This decision was made in Sept 1994 in its annual general assembly. Part of the resolution reads, "Cho's sermons and theology accord with the faith of the apostolic universal church. However, it has some problems we had to point out. These problems are related to Pentecostal distinctive doctrines." Reported in *Christian News* (Seoul, Korea), September, 1994.

context. This strong contextual adaptability is further strengthened by the unique nature of "people's theology." In many ways, people have participated in the theologizational process. For example, testimonies are often shared in various gatherings such as cell group meetings, public worship services in the church and in the prayer mountain meetings. They are also published in the monthly magazine *Shinanggye*, his *Full Gospel Family Weekly*, the church website, and sometimes his *Kookmin Daily News.* These spaces for sharing personal experiences have also invited a strong participation by people in the pew in the theologizing process of the Full Gospel tradition.[8] This unique and powerful effort of contextualization can be a model case to many churches in diverse and yet real and challenging contexts.

In order for this creative process to continue, there are several important areas Cho's theological disciples need to keep in mind. First, no theology is final, but temporal. That means, for any theology to be relevant to the changing socio-cultural setting of a new generation even in the same location a constant re-contextualizing effort is required. The church growth theories developed and applied by Cho in the 1970s and 80s, for instance, may need a radical revision as the Korean society has achieved relative prosperity in the 1990s and 2000s. In this way, the Cho theological tradition will have a much longer life than Cho himself. At the same time, this poses a tremendous challenge to his theological disciples. They should not try to fossilize the old glory, but provide new life to the theological tradition. This opens a great potential to creatively contextualize other locales, and Cho's disciples should aid this process to make Cho's theological tradition truly global.

Second, it is important to investigate every possible "root" of Cho's theology. A comprehensive treatment on the "roots" of Cho's theology is yet to be written. It is often suggested that his theology was significantly influenced by his personal experiences in the unique social context. The spiritual tradition of Korean Christianity is also suggested as an important influence on Cho's

[8]In this volume, Myung Soo Park provides this insight.

theological formation.[9] Yet, there seems to be reluctance among Cho's theologians to suggest there has been any influence on Cho's theology. For instance, in the biographies of Cho, the missionaries' role during Cho's theologically formative period is conspicuously minimized or missing, in spite of many suggestions particularly by outsiders.[10] Kang, in addition, also suggests Cho's indebtedness to other influences in this process.[11] When one talks about contextualization, it is primarily the process of application of that which was not locally existent until that point. Otherwise, it is not contextualization but the creation of a new system. Thus, it is inevitable that one must discuss western Pentecostalism, its missionary expansion to Korea, and the missionary influence upon Korean Pentecostal movements, including Cho himself, in the unique social context of the time. If there is even the slightest intention to deliberately downplay "outside" influences on Cho's theology and to project his theology as a unique creation, it is simply an impossible myth. Indebtedness does not diminish its uniqueness, but proves the creativity of the Spirit in the process of constructive application to another living situation. This is the right time for Cho's theological camp to diligently trace the "roots" of Cho's theological tradition.

1.2.5 A word of caution

Even if the YFGC is the largest congregation in the world, it has not been called to develop either a comprehensive theology or church polity. As observed in various historically developed theologies, the YFGC is called to enhance and further develop what has been historically, theologically and practically unique to the church and Cho's ministry: Pentecostalism with the emphasis on holistic blessing. Pentecostalism or more accurately "contextualized Pentecostalism" should be the YFGC's

---

[9]See, for instance, Young-hoon Lee in this volume.

[10]E.g., Myung Soo Park, "David Yonggi Cho and International Pentecostal/Charismatic Movements," *Journal of Pentecostal Theology* 12:1 (October 2003), 107-28.

[11]Chang-soo Kang in this volume.

theological "brand name" applied to every ministry that the YFGC is involved in: church growth, evangelism and mission, leadership development, contextual theologization, social work, Christian education and even environmental stewardship. In addition, it should exert efforts to "Pentecostalize" its unique ministries such as the cell system, the prayer and fasting movement, and the mass media ministry. There have been important studies revealing how much potential there is to be explored.[12] What Cho began is only the beginning of a major theological tradition, and it is to be analyzed, strengthened, expanded and theologized. It is also important to set the whole world as beneficiaries of this theological paradigm. I would like to discuss several specific approaches that the YFGC can take to develop this powerful theological potential.

2. Practical Suggestions

The suggestions are limited to the academic level as the scope of this discussion is theological. The titles are only suggestive.

2.1 "David Yonggi Cho Chairs of Global Renewal Studies"

One of the most lasting and prestigious ways to perpetuate one's life and ministry is the establishment of endowed chairs in universities and seminaries. Donation of a one-time cash gift will establish an endowed chair for an institution. As the name of the honoree is always attached to the title, this is a perpetual honor. The fund can be donated by anyone who wishes to honor an individual, David Yonggi Cho in this case. Depending on the designated area of discipline (e.g., "Global Renewal Studies"), a distinguished scholar can be chosen by the institution in consultation with the donor organization to occupy the chair. His

[12] E.g., Wonsuk Ma, "Yonggi Cho's Theology of Blessing: New Theological Basis and Directions" (Paper presented in the Second Youngsan International Theological Symposium, Hansei University, Goonpo, Korea, May 2003).

or her tenure is determined by the regulations of the institution. During this period, the stipend of the scholar is provided by the endowed fund, as it is placed in an interest-generating financial program by the institution. The individual can be called "Cho Yonggi Scholar of Global Renewal Studies" or so on. He or she can also be available to the YFGC's scholarly actives, such as conferences and symposia. If the church, or a foundation (see below), creates one chair for each major continent, all of them can be called for a conference and other meetings in the church.

Although establishing chairs may take some time, it would be ideal to identify a promising school on each continent and create a "David Cho Yonggi chair." They could be in Asia, Africa, Europe, North America, and Latin America. In addition, it would be appropriate that the Hansei University of Korea also have one Cho Yonggi Chair. My recent dialogue with a prominent Eastern European Pentecostal seminary affirms the significance of this suggestion.

Possibly each Mission Committee of the YFGC could see that a school is chosen and a several-year plan is established to create a chair in the chosen school in their respective areas. Placing one in Asia and another in Africa or Eastern Europe would be a good start with a powerful symbolic value. This would also be an easier practical way to start, as a chair on these continents may cost around US$250,000 each, while in North America, it may cost around US$1.5 million.

On the other hand, establishing a chair in an interdenominational and Evangelical seminary in North America would have powerful symbolic value as well. For instance, a decade or so ago, Fuller Theological Seminary launched the "Cho Yonggi Church Growth Lectureship." This was a rare opportunity to build an important academic structure to promote Cho's unique contribution to modern Christianity. At that time, many believed that the establishment of a "Cho Yonggi Chair" would be a logical follow up. In fact, until recently, leaders of Fuller Seminary continued in their efforts for the chair. Instead, another chair has been created to honor a Korean pastor. Again, this would be a perpetual and conspicuous way to honor Cho.

2.2 "David Yonggi Cho Theological Foundation"

Foundations abound in western society. Many known business establishments have created foundations to promote certain areas of human development. The Carnegie Foundation and the Ford Foundation are some examples from the secular business world, while small and medium academic foundations are rather common around us. In the Christian world, the Pew Trust and the Lilly Foundation are the best known. Unlike the chairs, this is normally founded through the donation of the principle individuals, in this case Cho himself, the institution Yoido Full Gospel Church and/or his friends in the Pentecostal/charismatic communities or mega-churches involved in Church Growth International. How a foundation is established and funded is a secondary issue, however, in comparison with its purposes and specific programs. This is not an evangelistic association, of which the Billy Graham Evangelistic Association may be a good example with its historic Lausanne Consultation of World Evangelization. In contrast, foundations are for a serious advancement of an academic discipline.

Certain scholarly programs such as conferences and publications could be planned by the foundation. However, its main function would be funding worthy programs and research projects. Recently the Pew Trust funded a major globalization project, resulting in a series of epoch-making books. A dissertation scholarship could be provided on selected topics related to Cho's ministry or Pentecostal topics in general. In fact, providing scholarships is a common project of a foundation. Based on interest incomes and free will donations, projects can be submitted for the foundation's consideration. "The Cho Yonggi Annual Award for Pentecostal Studies" could be another possible area to promote academic progress, while significantly increasing this Foundation's visibility. A group of board members would manage the foundation. Once this is realized, it may be the very first of its kind in Asia.

2.3 "International Review of Church Development and Leadership"

It is quite unfortunate that although the church growth movement made a powerful impact on the Christian world for at least a decade, no credible international academic journal has surfaced.[13] To date, there is no active scholarly body devoted to this topic leading the movement through changes and refinement.[14] By nature of the discipline, perhaps it may have been a mistake for scholars to advance and promote the body of knowledge, but the active participation of growing churches was critical. Undoubtedly, YFGC epitomizes this important aspect of the discipline. Both theoreticians and growing churches should have encouraged each other for such a worthy project, but it never happened. However, the bridges have not been burned, and the opportunity is still before us. While in the West, "church growth" has become a sour word; it has been alive and active in many non-western regions. The Institute for Church Growth (Seoul, Korea), established by Sung-hoon Myung, which has served the Korean church for many decades is an encouraging example. Its monthly magazine, *Church Growth*, provides a space for sharing, dialoguing and exploring various church growth programs. Its staff continually develops research as the Korean society constantly changes. As newer church growth/development theories are presented to the church world, a place is needed for scholars and practitioners to interact with one another. In this way, everyone contributes to the refinement of a proposed theory.

---

[13]The most substantial may be *Journal of the American Society for Church Growth*. Some issues are available online (www.ascg.org/journal.htm, checked April 2, 2004). However, its visibility has been rather obscure.

[14]Obviously American Society for Church Growth has been an important academic body promoting the cause. However, its narrow geographical scope (America), and particularly Donald McGavran's "basic and key principles of church growth" appear to be unreasonably limiting (see, for example, the masterhead of the *Journal of the American Society for Church Growth* 10 (Spring, 2000).

Cho and his YFGC are uniquely prepared in several areas to make a significant contribution to the world Christian body. The journal could be an important vehicle of promotion. One is the cell system. Definitely, this could have been a wonderful "trademark" of the church, as Cho expected. The mobilization of laity, and particularly the resources of women, is a tremendously successful, and yet revolutionary anti-cultural program. Now it has been further developed and "marketed" by someone else. Books for an international audience have been written and published by someone else. This can be likened to the microwave technology originally developed by NASA of the USA, but commercially applied by the Japanese as the microwave oven. Americans had to buy microwave ovens from Japan.

Another area of focus for this new publication could be prayer and fasting. Former church growth specialists are now concentrating on this discipline, while deserting their previous sociological theories. YFGC had practiced prayer and fasting long before the scholars started paying attention. For this, the role of the Prayer Mountain, various prayer programs, and particularly the role of the late Rev. Jashil Choi[15] should be seriously studied and published for the world audience.

The third proposed area of concentration is leadership development (in relation to church growth/development). Pastors of mega-churches worldwide, including Cho, could be studied and analyzed. Moreover, although completely unexplored, Cho's mentoring role which has produced more than a dozen big churches throughout Korea, and perhaps still more outside of the country should be studied. Which leader in the world has produced such a group of successful junior mega-church pastors? Also as briefly mentioned, if lay and particularly women's ministry has

---

[15]At long last, a study in English on her has appeared: Julie C. Ma, "Korean Pentecostal Spirituality: A Case Study of Jashil Choi," *Asian Journal of Pentecostal Studies* 5:2 (July 2002), 235-54. A fuller version was presented at the Annual Meeting of the Evangelical Theological Society, Nashville, TN, Nov 2000, and will appear in *The Spirit and Spirituality: Essays in Honor of Russell P. Spittler*, eds. Wonsuk Ma and Robert P. Menzies (London: T. & T. Clark, 2004, forthcoming).

played a pivotal role in the Pentecostal movement in the last century, what happened within the YFGC is a critical example, considering the male-dominant Korean or Asian culture.

There could be many other areas of exploration for this important twice-per-year or even quarterly academic journal. Critical is the nature of any academic publication: this would not be an in-house publication, but one that would provide a credible forum for discussions and interaction by anyone from anywhere in the world as long as the content was worthy of publication. The regular publication, which the Institute for Church Growth is conceptualizing, is therefore encouraging. An international editorial board should be formed and a financial basis should be structured, with an able and willing editor of the journal. By this, the YFGC will finally have its face. The world may then say, as Job did: "I heard of it all these years, but only now I see it." More than one publication could be initiated, of course. A second international journal such as this could come out of Hansei University.

2.4 Theological Symposia and Forums

This is something that YFGC has been good at. The work of ITI was mentioned above. This important tradition continues through Cho's various research arms such as the Institute for Church Growth and Hansei University.

YFGC has shown its exceptional potential in advancing Pentecostal studies in recent important meetings. In 1998 prior to the World Pentecostal Conference in Seoul, the very first full-day academic meetings was organized by Dr. Young-hoon Lee and his friends to deal with unique topics related to Asian Pentecostalism. This significant initiative continued, again through Lee's effort, in the 2001 PWC in Los Angeles. Bethesda Christian University, one of Cho's schools in North America, hosted the International Symposium on Non-western Pentecostalism with participants from Asia, Africa and Latin America. Lee, providentially serving as President of the University again was the key organizer for this conference. In conjunction with the 2004 PWC in Johannesburg, a two-day international conference of Pentecostal scholars is being planned, and this may signal the very first time that a full-scale academic meeting becomes part of this triennial international Pentecostal gathering.

Recently YFGC has been part of the Global Christian Forum. Mainline, Evangelical and Pentecostal churches participate to promote mutual understanding and corporate effort toward the common good. Also the church's participation in the World Council of Churches (WCC) and Pentecostal Dialogue, and hosting the World Alliance of Reformed Churches (WARC) and Pentecostal Dialogue typifies the potential of the YFGC for the future of Pentecostalism, and Christianity for that matter.

2.5 Publication: "Global Renewal Press"

In the past, the Lord has raised up several important publishers in the West to pay attention to Pentecostal/Charismatic titles. Hendrickson has been a steady producer of renewal academic titles, while recently the Sheffield Academic Press has been actively producing theological and biblical studies related to the renewal movement. Regnum International, a division of Paternoster Publishers in UK has been publishing a few titles. Several university presses have produced various Pentecostal titles. Very recently, several major Christian publishing houses including Zondervan, Baker and Eerdmans began to pay attention to renewal titles. More relevantly to the non-western Pentecostal world, the Studies in Non-western Christianity Series of Peter Lang of Frankfurt am Main has produced many valuable titles including several written by Korean theologians. On a popular level, Logos International has been the pioneer in this area, later joined by several Third Wave-oriented publishers including Creation.[16]

[16]For a comprehensive survey, see W. E. Warner, "Publications," *Dictionary of Pentecostal and Charismatic Movements*, eds. Stanley M. Burgess and others (Grand Rapids: Zondervan, 1988), 742-51.

However, new dissertations on renewal titles especially written by Asians, Africans, and Latin Americans rarely find their way to publication. Titles produced by European publishers are priced too high for average Asian readers. For instance, a 250-page hardbound Pentecostal title by Sheffield is US$70.00. As another commercial publisher has bought the Sheffield Academic Press, the prices are rising and their decision for publication now takes longer and has become harder. An example of this difficulty is seen in the book project of *Asian and Pentecostal*, a collection of valuable studies on Asian Pentecostalism originally presented in the Asian Pentecostal Conference in Birmingham, UK in 2001. Due to a high projected retail price, with Asians as the major readership, the editors decided to publish the book through an Asian publishing house. As the growth of the renewal movement is now reaching the non-western continents, a credible publishing house is badly needed. Such a press can be established with an international scope, thus, setting up the operating office outside of Korea.

3. Postlude

In this short study, the critical role that the YFGC can play in the academic area for world Pentecostalism has been discussed. Although there are many other areas to be developed, the theological foundation is the very basis for all areas of ministry. This conviction, however, is more than *self*-serving: now it is time to serve the world. This will require a radical paradigm shift in the operation of every ministry in the church.

The most important paradigm to be shifted is from national to international. Until now, most of the international ministry of the church has been entirely dependent upon Cho himself. His crusades throughout the world and the publication of selected titles of Cho in English are its main activities. As the post-Cho era is approaching, the international contributions of the church and Cho's theology require serious planning and implementation.

It is my hope that Cho's ministry and theology, unique in church history, will continue to develop in future generations. The author's conviction is that now is the time to do so. May the Lord continue to be glorified through what God has began in Cho's life and through the faithful theological and ministry stewardship of his followers.

RESOURCES FOR STUDIES OF DAVID YONGGI CHO

Chang-soo Kang

1. Introduction

David Yonggi Cho was born on February 14, 1936. He was the firstborn of five sons and four daughters. His father was Doo-chun Cho and his mother was Bok-sun Kim. Cho is currently senior pastor of Yoido Full Gospel Church (YFGC) in Seoul, Korea, the world's largest congregation with about 700,000 members. He was raised as a Buddhist, but became a Christian when at the age of 18 he was diagnosed with a terminal case of tuberculosis. He almost totally recovered and then was encouraged by missionary Louis Richards to attend Bible school in Seoul. Finally, at the age of 20, he entered the Full Gospel Bible Institute. Between his conversion event in 1954 and his enrollment at Bible school in 1956, he was greatly influenced by missionary Louis Richards.

After graduating from the Bible school, Cho was encouraged to join a tent church at Daejo-dong, which was initiated by his classmate and future mother-in-law, Jashil Choi in 1958 when he was 22 years old. While he was ministering with Jashil Choi, he was invited to become a preacher of a 1,500-seat auditorium, Full Gospel Revival Center, which was built by missionaries in 1961. In 1962, Cho became the senior pastor of Full Gospel Revival Center. Soon, the name was changed to Full Gospel Central Church. By 1964, the membership increased to 2,000 under the leadership of Cho. In 1966, he became general superintendent of the Korean Assemblies of God at the age of 30. In 1973, a 10,000-seat auditorium was dedicated at Yoido-dong, and the name of the church was changed to YFGC, and then it experienced tremendous growth: 23,000 members by 1974; 100,000 by 1979; and 700,000 by 1992. There were hundreds of assistant pastors and thousands of home cell group leaders, the majority of both groups being women.

With his church's growth, Cho also founded Church Growth International (CGI). He emphasizes positive thinking and positive confession and insists that prayer is the key to church growth. Further, he also stresses being specific in prayer: "one must visualize and specify exactly what is needed."[1] Because of Cho and YFGC's extremely successful ministry, the name of Yonggi Cho and YFGC are well known all over the world. In addition, since Cho is a Pentecostal minister, Korean Pentecostalism has become known to the outside world.

There have been many studies of and about Cho and YFGC. As of 2003, Cho himself has written numerous books and articles.[2] Among them, a number of books have been translated into English, as well as other languages. This bibliographical essay focuses on providing essential sources, written in English, for general readers and researchers with annotations, and is thus confined to studies published in English either by Cho or about him. In a limited way, the study also intends to suggest recommended areas of further study on Cho and YFGC.

In order to understand Cho's life and ministry properly, one cannot ignore the unique context of Korean Pentecostalism, of

---

[1]Young-hoon Lee, "Cho, David (Paul) Yonggi," *The New International Dictionary of the Pentecostal and Charismatic Movements*, eds. Stanley M. Burgess and Eduard M. van der Maas (Grand Rapids: Zondervan, 2003), 522. The Dictionary is indicated as *NIDPCM* hereafter.

[2]Pastor Cho's Resource Center of Yoido Full Gospel Church, ed., *YFGC Pastor Cho's Resource Center, The Index of Resources 2002* (Seoul: YFGC Pastor Cho's Resource Center, 2002). This book, written in Korean, includes all books, articles, photographs, and newspapers of and about Yonggi Cho. It is the most important and valuable resource in order to study about Yonggi Cho and YFGC.

which Cho stands at the center. Currently, Cho's church amounts to about 70% of the Korean Assemblies of God.[3]

This essay is divided into two major sections: Background and bibliography. The former includes three introductory parts: 1) Korean Pentecostalism, to aid the readers in understanding the background of Cho's ministry; 2) The life and ministry of Cho; and 3) Cho's theology. In all the discussions, I have attempted to provide useful, if not comprehensive, bibliographic information for a further study. The second section provides a comprehensive list of studies written in English by and about Cho and YFGC. It is possible that I have overlooked many other works in this discussion, but to the best of my knowledge, this list will provide an exhaustive bibliographical resource for the subject matter.

PART I
BACKGROUND

1. Korean Pentecostalism

It is important to understand Korean Pentecostalism in order to evaluate Cho's theology and ministry properly. I believe that Cho's ministry is in concert with Korean Pentecostal/charismatic traditions. The Pentecostal phenomena in Korea were not introduced by American Pentecostal missionaries or Cho himself, but in reality, some Pentecostal features were already present in

[3]The reason Yonggi Cho can represent Korean Pentecostalism is due to the fact that the other Pentecostal denominations came to Korea after 1963 and their constituencies are not significant in Korean Pentecostalism and that the Korean Assemblies of God occupies about 90 percent of Korean Pentecostals. Their years of coming to Korea are as follows. The Church of God in Korea was introduced in 1963. The Church of God Prophecy missionary came to Korea in 1968. The Church of the Foursquare Gospel in Korea was organized in 1969, in Yeol-soo Eim, "South Korea," in *NIDPCM*, 244-45.

the Korean church since the beginning of the Protestant mission in Korea.[4]

The *New International Dictionary of Pentecostal and Charismatic Movements* (*NIDPCM*) presents the Korean church as Pentecostal/charismatic: with 2,393,749 Pentecostals (32%), 2,020,598 charismatics (27%) and 3,165,652 neocharismatics (42%).[5] Although Cho along with his YFGC is the most influential reason for this development, there are other factors that have contributed. Even though it is almost impossible to extract a direct relationship between the early Korean revival movement and Korean Pentecostalism, many theologians regard the early revival movements and the prayer mountain movement of Korea as the background of Korean Pentecostalism. One example is Young-hoon Lee's study, "Korean Pentecost: The Great Revival of 1907."[6] Here Lee describes the great Pyungyang revival of 1907 as a Pentecostal movement. Yeol-soo Eim's article, "The Roots of Korean Pentecostalism," also traces Korean Pentecostalism from the early revival movement in Pyungyang and the prayer mountain movement.[7] Myung Soo Park's article, "The Korean Pentecost: A Study on the Great Revival of 1903-1907 in the Relationship with Contemporary Worldwide Revival Movement," likewise views the origin of Korean Pentecostal

---

[4]E.g., Chang-soo Kang, "The First Diary of Revival Rallies of Early Korean Protestants in 1915 of Janbong and Kangwha Islands in the Western Sea Area of Korea," (A paper presented in the Sixth Annual Meeting of Asian Pentecostal Society, Nov 2003, Baguio City, Philippines), 62-63; Chang-soo Kang, "The Pneumatology of Ick-Doo Kim" (A paper presented in the 12th William Menzies Annual Lectureship, Jan 12-16, 2004, Baguio City, Philippines); Yeol-soo Eim, "South Korea."

[5]Eim, "South Korea," 239.

[6]Asian Journal of Pentecostal Studies 4:1 (January 2001), 73-83.

[7]A study presented in the 18th Pentecostal World Conference, Seoul, 1998. The revised version is found in Yeol-soo Eim, "South Korea," 239-46.

movement in the Pyungyang revival movement.[8] Jae-bum Lee, who is not a minister of YFGC but a pastor of the Korean Assemblies of God, also wrote a dissertation, “Pentecostal Type Distinctives and Korean Protestant Church Growth.”[9] This study is also in unison with this tradition. Finally, a pastor of YFGC and Pentecostal theologian, Young-hoon Lee, suggests this connection in his dissertation, “The Holy Spirit Movement in Korea: Its Historical and Doctrinal Development.”[10]

There have been four Ph.D. dissertations written on Korean Pentecostalism, including the dissertations mentioned above.[11] Among these four, two were devoted to the study of Pentecostal theology and especially pneumatologies of Korean Pentecostalism. However, in spite of these dissertations, there seems to be a lack of in-depth studies on the Korean Pentecostal understanding of the Holy Spirit. Boo-woong Yoo’s dissertation, the first academic study published on Korean Pentecostalism, is a historical, rather than theological treatment, although the title implies both: *Korean Pentecostalism: Its History and Theology*. At the time when Yoo, a Presbyterian pastor, wrote his dissertation in 1981, Pentecostal churches in Korea were regarded as abnormal or heretical by the Presbyterian churches. Thus, in Yoo’s dissertation, many factors of Korean Pentecostalism were seriously caricatured, and this is

---

[8]A paper presented in the Theological Symposium for Asian Church Leaders, Seoul, 1998.

[9]Jae-bum Lee, “Pentecostal Type Distinctives and Korean Protestant Church Growth” (Ph.D. diss., Fuller Theological Seminary, 1986).

[10]Young-hoon Lee, “The Holy Spirit Movement in Korea: It’s Historical and Doctrinal Development (Ph.D. diss., Temple University, 1996).

[11]Jae-bum Lee, “Pentecostal Type Distinctives and Korean Protestant Church Growth” (Ph.D. diss., Fuller Theological Seminary, 1986); Boo-woong Yoo, *Korean Pentecostalism: It’s History and Theology* (Frankfurt am Main: Verlag Peter Lang GmbH, 1988); Young-hoon Lee, “The Holy Spirit Movement in Korea: Its Historical and Doctrinal Development (Ph.D. diss., Temple University, 1996); Dong-ho Cho, “Intimate Alien: An Immanent Critique of Korean Pentecostalism (Ph.D. diss., City University of New York, 2002).

made clear by the fact that there is no single mention of Cho or YFGC, not to mention their role in Korean Pentecostalism. Surprisingly, he failed to mention any Pentecostal denomination, church or pastor at all. Instead, he substituted Pentecostalism with mysticism and Minjung theology, a Korean version of liberation theology often advocated by Presbyterian theologians. Therefore, this first work on Korean Pentecostalism is full of stereotypical misnomers and thus is misleading to anyone who would like to study Cho or Korean Pentecostalism.[12] Arguably the contributions of Cho and his YFGC to the Korean Pentecostal movement are too important to ignore. Understandably, Yoo's work was criticized by Pentecostal theologians.[13]

Young-hoon Lee, a minister of YFGC, in his dissertation, fills the gap mistakenly left by Yoo, and for this, Lee's work is valuable. Rightly, Lee proves his points through his analysis and evaluation of Yonggi Cho's contributions to the Korean Holy

---

[12]Many theologians relied on Yoo's work and criticized the ministry of Yonggi Cho as the work of a shaman. Further, many theologians followed Yoo's description of Minjung movement as the Holy Spirit/Pentecostal movement in Korea. But the truth is that *Minjung* (people) theology is not a theology of Pentecostals, rather it is a theology of liberal Presbyterians. See, Dong-sik Yoo and others, *Hankuk Kyohoewi Sungryungwoondongkwa Kujo* [A Study on the Pentecostal Movement in Korea: Yoido Full Gospel Church] (Seoul: Korean Christian Academy, 1981); Harvey Cox, *Fire from Heaven: The Rise of Pentecostal Spirituality and the Reshaping of Religion in the Twenty-first Century* (Reading, MA: Addison-Wesley publishing Company, 1995); Jeremy Reynalds, "Shamanistic Influences in Korean Pentecostal Christianity: An Analysis," (www.rickross.com/reference/yoidoyonggi/yoido11.html), checked: Dec 2003; Young-hoon Lee, "The Holy Spirit Movement in Korea"; Hong-jung Lee, "Minjung and Pentecostal Movements in Korea," in *Pentecostals after a Century: Global Perspectives on a Movement in Transition,* eds., Allan H. Anderson and Walter J. Hollenweger (Sheffield, England: Sheffield Academic Press, 1999).

[13]Cecil M. Robeck, Jr., "Review of *Korean Pentecostalism*, by Boo-woong Yoo," *Pneuma* 12:1 (1990), 60-62 (62); Yong-hoon Lee, "The Holy Spirit Movement in Korea," 154-56.

Spirit movement. However, he also overlooks the prayer mountain phenomenon. Subsequently, Yeol-soo Eim argued that the prayer mountain movement is an indigenous Pentecostal movement.[14]

In addition, my study provides additional support for the above argument that Pentecostal features had been part of Korean Christianity. The findings from the dairy are presented as follows:

> Through the characteristics of the diary and their understanding of the Holy Spirit, we can propose that early Christians in the diary were like Pentecostals or charismatics. Thus, I can argue that Pentecostal phenomena continued from the beginning of Korean Protestantism and it became the foundation of the further development of Korean Pentecostalism. In other words, Korean Pentecostalism did not blossom fruitlessly.[15]

Therefore, it is certain that the Korean church had Pentecostal phenomena from the beginning of its history. Pentecostal/charismatic tradition took place in the Korean church way before the coming of foreign Pentecostal denominations in 1952 and the ministry of Cho which began in 1958. Obviously, this is a promising area of further study.[16]

---

[14]See for details, Yeol-soo Eim, "The Roots of Korean Pentecostalism" (A paper presented in the Theological Symposium for Asian Church Leaders, Seoul, 1998), pp. 31-55. A revised version was later published in Yeol-soo Eim, "South Korea," *NIDPCM*, 239-46. According to Eim, Woon-mong Na is the founder of the prayer mountain movement and is an indigenous Korean Pentecostal who actualized, for the first time, the Pentecostal movement by including Pentecostal phenomena. Na wrote influential lecture notes on the Holy Spirit, entitled: "The Gifts of the Holy Spirit," in 1952.

[15]Chang-soo Kang, "The First Diary of Revival Rallies of Early Korean Protestants in 1915 of Janbong and Kangwha Islands in the Western Sea Area of Korea" (A paper presented in the Sixth Annual Meeting of Asian Pentecostal Society, Nov 2003, Baguio City, Philippines), 62-63.

[16]For a general article on Korean Pentecostalism: Wonsuk Ma, "Tasks and Challenges for Korean Pentecostal Churches in the Twenty-First Century," *Australasian Pentecostal Studies* 5 (2002), 63-94.

2. The Life and Ministry of Cho and YFGC

Cho's book *To God Be the Glory* outlines his conversion experience. In addition, the website of YFGC (www.fgtv.org) includes a brief biography of Cho. Yet, the most helpful source on Cho's early life is Karen Hurston, *Growing the World's Largest Church* and Nell Kennedy, *Dream Your Way to Success.*

Concerning the ministry of YFGC, since 1978 the Institute for Church Growth has published *Church Growth,* a monthly magazine that deals with a variety of issues of church growth. It provides a continual river of data, insights and bibliographic tips of Cho and YFGC. However, comparatively less work is available in the area of theological formation of Cho or critical evaluation of his theology or theological assumptions, either in English or in Korean, although there are several written documents about Cho's theological encounters through his early life.[17] The following are several suggested areas for further study.

2.1 The Relationship with Missionaries

First, the life and ministry of Cho must be studied in relation to missionaries. Although Cho came to know Jesus Christ through a girl, "Yongae Kim, the Christian teenage friend of his older sister, Hyesook,"[18] it is evident that he was influenced by a number of missionaries.[19] Louis Richards, the missionary who

---

[17]Yonggi Cho, "Jesus Christ Gives Life," *Pentecostal Evangel,* November 5, 1967; "When Buddha Didn't Answer, Jesus Did!" *The Pentecostal Evangel,* August 26, 1973; Sung-hoon Myung, "Preaching Ministry of Yoido Full Gospel Church" (Th.M. thesis, Fuller Theological Seminary, 1988); Nell Kennedy, *Dream Your Way to Success* (South Plainfield, NJ: Bridge Publishing, 1980).

[18]Karen Hurston, Growing the World's Largest Church, 20.

[19]Concerning this, Myung Soo Park also pointed out in his article, Myung Soo Park, "David Yonggi Cho and International Pentecostal/Charismatic Movements," *Journal of Pentecostal Theology* 12:1 (October 2003), 107-28.

taught the Bible to Cho and encouraged him to enroll in the Full Gospel Bible Institute, says,

> A young girl actually was the one who witnessed to Cho about Jesus Christ. Even though he cursed and rejected her from his sick bed, she was faithful day after day to talk to him about Jesus, and the last day that she saw Yonggi Cho, she left her Bible with him. Her witness stirred faith within him and gave him the desire to know more about Jesus.[20]

Yet, after Cho heard the gospel presentation from the girl, he met Louis Richards and was healed under his ministry, as Richards notes in his payer letter: "Shortly after our arrival in Korea, Evangelist Cho Yonggi and many others found Christ as personal Saviour."[21] Cho spent time with him and engaged in Bible studies for about two years. Cho's letter below, which was mailed to Richards, also proves his influence on Cho:

> I do so very often think of you! How the time flies so quick. How the time flies so quick. Now I am already 59 years old! But still I think of the World Mission in Pusan and the blessed time of Worship under your ministry! . . . but yet in my heart I am your boy and your sheep. . . . I am still your son in Jesus.[22]

Mr. and Mrs. Louis P. Richards also outline their ministry as follows in their prayer letter of June 9, 1974:

> During the fourteen years we served in Korea, we established the Full Gospel Radio broadcast, the Correspondence School and an extensive literature program. Soul-winning Seminars were conducted throughout South Korea during this period of ministry. Shortly after our arrival in Korea, Evangelist Cho

---

[20]Rosemary Jackson, "God Will Direct Our Steps," *Spirit* (spring 1997), 3.

[21] Louis Richards, "Prayer Letter of June 9, 1974," at Flower Pentecostal Heritage Center.

[22]Yonggi Cho, "Letter" to L. Richards, quoted in Rosemary Jackson, "God Will Direct Our Steps," *Spirit*, Spring, 1997, 4.

> Yonggi and many others found Christ as personal Saviour. This work soon became entirely indigenous and according to our last report, twelve of the original converts were in full-time ministry. For five years I served as an evangelist to the Korean Army, ministering to thousands of Korean soldiers.[23]

The influence of missionaries on Cho is not only limited to Louis Richards. It can also be found in other words of Cho, as follows:

> When asked how God had led him into this ministry, Brother Cho replied, "Brother John Stetz was my Pentecostal father in Bible School. His teaching in Pentecostal truths concerning the apostolic power that is available today was the beginning of my ministry."[24]

Furthermore, John Hurston played a significant role in Cho's ministry. He ministered with Cho at the Full Gospel Center and invited him to be a pastor of the church in 1961. The church later became Full Gospel Central Church, and there is no doubt that this was one of the most important times in Cho's life and ministry. Hurston was the first senior pastor of the church, but in 1962 as Cho was ordained, he became the senior pastor, while Hurston became a missionary advisor to Cho and ministered with him between 1960 and 1970.[25]

These three examples clearly show the important role that missionaries played in relation to Cho. Due to the increasing importance of Cho and YFGC, however, the role of missionaries has been minimal in the studies on Cho. We, however, cannot devaluate the role of missionaries. In various ways, Pentecostal

---

[23] Louis P. Richards, "Prayer Letter," June 9, 1974, at Flower Pentecostal Heritage Center.

[24] "Victory below The 38th," *The Pentecostal Evangel*, November 12, 1962.

[25] Karen Hurston, *Growing the World's Largest Church* (Springfield, MI: Charism, 1994), 24-26; "Missionary file of Hurston John W," in Flower Pentecostal Heritage Center.

missionaries paved the way for the unique ministry of Cho as well as other national Pentecostals. More importantly, missionaries provided a Pentecostal theological orientation for the Pentecostal movement in Korea.[26]

2.2 The Relationship with Jashil Choi, Cho's Mother-in-law

In addition, it is worthwhile to note the relationship between Cho and Jashil Choi, his mother-in-law, in order to understand Cho's life and ministry. There are several pertinent factors, which we must be aware of, to comprehend the role of Jashil Choi.

First, when Cho was seriously ill while studying in the Full Gospel Bible Institute in 1957, Jashil Choi took care of him for several months. Although Cho had been healed, he still retained tuberculosis and had to sleep out of the dormitory for many days; he usually slept in a church. In these lonely hours, Jashil Choi became Cho's best friend and spiritual mother. Through this close kinship, Choi and Cho developed a parent-child relationship. Their close affinity was further developed as Choi became Cho's mother-in-law. Jin-hwan Kim, a former General Superintendent of the Korean Assemblies of God, said that no one can deny the role of Jashil Choi in Cho's early ministry. Although, Yonggi Cho was a senior pastor from the beginning, Jashil Choi was a spiritual leader in Cho's early ministry.[27]

Second, indubitably, Cho's ministry began because of Jashil Choi. Choi initiated and prepared the tent church by herself. She purchased a U.S. army tent in order to start a church on her property and invited Cho to preach at its first service. As the ministry proceeded, Choi became a faithful and helpful supporter of Cho. Cho notes about his mother-in-law as follows:

---

[26]Concerning this issue, see also Myung Soo Park, "David Yonggi Cho and International Pentecostal/Charismatic Movements." *Journal of Pentecostal Theology* 12:1 (October 2003), 107-28.

[27] Jin-hwan Kim, interview by the author, December 9, 2003, Angeles City, Philippines.

> Pastor Ja Shill Choi, who was my Bible school classmate and later became my mother-in-law, is a supreme example in the ministry of prayer and sacrificial devotion to God. During my years of ministry, Sister Choi has remained close by my side, and I have learned to know, love, and appreciate her greatly. In both word and deed, she devoted her life entirely to serving the Master.[28]

Third, Choi was the initiator and founder of the prayer mountain of YFGC in 1974. This prayer mountain, now formally called Osanri Choi Ja-sil Memorial Fasting Prayer Mountain, was founded immediately after the construction of YFGC in 1973, and contributed greatly to the growth of YFGC. During this time, the prayer mountain movement was popular amongst Korean Christians. Many Christians experienced Pentecostal phenomena—mostly speaking in tongues and divine healings—in prayer mountains and continued to visit prayer mountains for their spiritual needs. This unique spiritual tradition in Korea began in the 1950s. If YFGC had not had its own prayer mountain, it is hard to imagine what would have happened to YFGC today.

Concerning the ministry of Jashil Choi, Yong-hoon Lee notes, “Many miracles and divine healings followed her co-ministry with pastor Yonggi Cho, which lasted for about 30 years.”[29] Pastor Yong-rae Park, who was once an assistant pastor of YFGC also notes, “We cannot think about Yonggi Cho without Jashil Choi. She was a great help in Cho’s ministry.”[30] Even if Park overemphasized the role of Choi, still we cannot ignore Choi’s influential contributions to Cho’s ministry.

---

[28] Yonggi Cho’s forward to Jashil Choi, *Korean Miracles* (La Canada, CA: Mountain Press, 1978), v.

[29] Young-hoo Lee, “Choi, Jashil,” in *NIDPCM*, p. 522.

[30] Yong-rae Park, interview by Chang-soo Kang, August 20, 2002, Baguio, Philippines. Concerning Jashil Choi, see in detail, Julie C. Ma, “Korean Pentecostal Spirituality: A Case Study of Jashil Choi,” *Asian Journal of Pentecostal Studies 5:2* (July 2002), 235-54; Nell Kenneday, *Dream Your Way to Success*; Yong-hoon Lee, “Choi, Ja-shil,” *NIDPCM*, 522.

2.3 Cho's International Ministry

Yonggi Cho led countless revival rallies in Korea as well as abroad. There is no disputation of Cho's influence in Korean churches,[31] but there are only a few studies on Cho's influence in the world. Cho's international ministry began with his participation in the World Pentecostal Conference in 1967. In the following years, Cho preached in several nations, and after the construction of YFGC, he often led overseas revival rallies. Furthermore, through the Church Growth International (CGI), conferences are conducted each year to train leaders and laity from abroad, and CGI published books, brochures, and the Church Growth Magazine are distributed in some 125 countries.[32] In this area, only one study is represented, and that concerns Cho's role in Japanese Christianity.[33]

3. Theological Studies on/about Cho and YFGC

The primary resources for any theological inquiry on Cho's life and ministry are several books of Cho available in English and his sermons. For instance, through Cho's *Jesus the Son*, we can understand his Christology; *Salvation, Health and Prosperity: Our Threefold Blessings in Christ* provides a valuable theological foundation for his theology of blessing. *The Holy Spirit, My Senior Partner* defines Cho's pneumatology, while his *The Nature of God* delineates his understanding of God. Through his books on Revelation and Daniel, we can grasp Cho's eschatology. The

[31] For example, see Chang-sup Shim, "Assessing the Impact of Pentecostalism on the Korean Presbyterian Church in Light of Calvin's Theology," *Chongshin Theological Journal* vol. 3 (1998), pp. 115-31.

[32] Peggy Kannaday, "The World Largest Church," *Pentecostal Evangel*, Feb 6, 1994, 13.

[33] Mark Mullins, "The Empire Strikes Back: Korean Pentecostal Mission to Japan," in *Charismatic Christianity as a Global Culture*, ed. Karla Poewe (Columbia, SC: University of South Carolina Press, 1994).

following are a few areas in which I feel that further reflections are urgently needed.

3.1 Theological Reflection

There are several theological studies about Cho: e.g., Hsieh-Kan Christian Wei, "The Analysis and Criticism of the Theology and Methodology of Paul Yonggi Cho" (Ph.D. diss., Bob Jones University, 1992) and Philip Douglass, "Yonggi Cho and the Korean Pentecostal Movement: Some Theological Reflections," *Presbyterian* 17 (Spring 1991). However, most of them are often not well balanced, or highly selective in their treatment. One example is the first controversy surrounding Cho's book, *The Fourth Dimension*, as discussed below. Also Boo-yoong Yoo's misrepresentation of Korean Pentecostalism further contributed to some misunderstandings on Cho.

3.2 Theology of Blessing: Three-fold Blessing

The first critical studies on Cho began with Cho's theology of blessing. Much of the criticism derived from Cho's book, *Fourth Dimension*, as we can see in Dave Hunt and T. McMahon's book, *The Seduction of Christianity: Spiritual Discernment in the Last Days* (Eugene: Harvest House, 1985). Here, Hunt and McMahon criticize Cho's teachings as "the seduction of the Church." Sung-hoon Myung defends Cho: "Cho does advocate that, in general, it is God's will for every believer to be prosperous in wealth and health as well as in spirituality."[34] The weakness of Hunt and McMahon is their overdependence on just one book. Here, Myung's advice shines: we have to understand Cho's theology in a general context, not merely depending on one book, *Fourth Dimension*.[35]

---

[34]Sung-hoon Myung, "Preaching Ministry of Yoido Full Gospel Church" (Th. M. thesis, Fuller Theological Seminary, 1988), 94.

[35]Myung, "Preaching Ministry of Yoido Full Gospel Church," 94-113.

There are other studies on the same issue. Some of them are: Soo-young Kim, "A Biblical Critique on the Prosperity Gospel of Paul Yonggi Cho" (Th.M. thesis, Dallas Theological Seminary, 1989); Richard Nelson, "The Self-improvement Gospel of David Yonggi Cho: A Critique of Self-help Theology" (Th.M. thesis, Lincoln Christian Seminary, 1998); Sam-hwan Kim, "The Question of Good and Evil in Full Gospel Faith: A Study of the Theological Foundation for the Threefold Blessing of Dr. Yonggi Cho" (paper presented at 2002 Youngsan International Theological Symposium, September, 2002, Goonpo, Korea).

3.3 Contextualization/Indigenization

The next debate has taken place in contextualization issues. Studies in this area include: Won S. Hwang', "Contextualization of the Gospel by Paul Yonggi Cho in the Korean Context" (Th.M. thesis, Trinity Evangelical Divinity School, 1994); Daniel J. Adams, "Reflections on an Indigenous Movement: The Yoido Full Gospel Church," *Japan Christian Quality* 57 (Winter 1991); and Allan Anderson, "The Contribution of David Yonggi Cho to a Contextual Theology in Korea," *Journal of Pentecostal Theology* 12:1 (2003).

3.4 Leadership of Cho and Growth of YFGC

Most studies are devoted understandably to this area because of the tremendous growth of YFGC, and two areas stand out, Cho's leadership and various aspects of church growth. Their related areas include cell-based ministry, church planting, the policy and strategy of supporting the pioneering works of YFGC, prayer movement, leadership of Cho, preaching ministry of YFGC, etc. Most studies are affirmative on Cho and YFGC, and try to adapt the church growth principles of YFGC as a church growth model *par excellence*. In this area, Sung-hoon Myung's Ph.D. dissertation, "Spiritual Dimensions of Church Growth as Applied in the Yoido Full Gospel Church" (1990) is the most recommendable work. Myung describes and evaluates the growth of YFGC using four "Spiritual dimensions: the work of the Holy

Spirit, prayer, preaching and the leadership of the church." Myung also outlines the manifestations of the Holy Spirit at YFGC, thus his study best deals with Cho's pneumatology by comparing it with other academic writings. Moreover, the First Youngsan International Church Growth Conference, which was held in 2003, provided fruitful studies on the leadership of Cho.[36] See the bibliography for related works.

3.5 Sociological Studies

A recent social case study of Cho and YFGC is Dong-ho Cho's dissertation, "Intimate Alien: An Immanent Critique of Korean Pentecostalism" (Ph.D. diss., City University of New York, 2002). This work deals with YFGC from the viewpoint of social value. Another study also included in this area is Vincent Beng Leoh's "Ethics and Pentecostal Preaching: The Anastatic, Organic, and Communal Strands" (Ph.D. diss., Southern Baptist Theological Seminary, 1990). A serious attempt is needed to study Cho's life and theology in the socio-political and cultural context of Korea.

3.6 Pneumatology of Cho

Regarding the pneumatology of Cho, the 2003 Youngsan International Theological Symposium provided several meaningful articles. Among the five presenters, four delved into Cho's understanding of the Holy Spirit. Although their viewpoints are different from one another, this conference provides a starting point for further study of Cho's pneumatology.

3.7 Concluding Remarks

Most studies on or by Cho have focused on the growth of YFGC. Sometimes, however, theological studies are collapsed into

---

[36]Yong-gi Hong, ed., The Role of Leadership in Church Growth: 1st Youngsan International Church Growth Conference (Seoul: Institute for Church Growth, 2003).

the church growth aspects of Cho's ministry, and such related topics are Cho's positive thinking, theology of blessings, contextualization and others.

In the academic world, most affirmative writings about Yonggi Cho come from his own disciples: Sung-hoon Myung, Young-hoon Lee, Yonggi Hong, Mun-hong Choi, Dong-sung Lee and others. On the other hand, we have seen critical assessments of Cho's theology and ministry. It is unfortunate that most of the critical studies appear not to have full information on Cho and YFGC. Thus, in a manner of speaking, both groups are biased. This situation made it urgent to see the third category of scholars who are not "obligated" to affirm Cho, and yet have good knowledge of his theology and ministry. It is encouraging, therefore, to see new studies by such scholars, and this volume contains some. We may see more studies by this third category of scholars with appreciation and affirmation of Cho's theology and ministry, and yet with critical assessment and recommendations for future developments.[37]

In collecting resources by or on Cho, it has become apparent that early material, particularly prior to 1973, was extremely difficult to locate. Until recently, primary sources, especially from the crucially important pre-1973 years, the year when the YFGC building was completed, there is a critical deficiency in relevant material, and this situation is worse for English resources. Thus, there is a need for Korean Pentecostal theologians to devote their attention to this formative stage of Cho's theology and ministry, as a comprehensive and scrupulously objective biography of Yonggi Cho has yet to be written.[38]

---

[37]Recently, beginning in 2002, Hansei University organized Young-san International Theological Symposium (YITS) and produced studies on David Yonggi Cho. If this conference continues annually, it will provide more theological studies on and about Cho. The 2002 YITS focused on Cho's theology in general and the 2003 YITS devoted its issue to Cho's pneumatology.

[38]Regarding American Pentecostal leaders, there have been several studies about their lives. David Edwin Harrell, Jr., *Oral Roberts: An American Life* (Bloomington, IN: Indian University Press, 1985); Edith

The following section provides possible resources of and on Yonggi Cho, available in English. The resources come mainly from the library of Asia Pacific Theological Seminary, Baguio, Philippines, ATLA religion database, Internet research and *YFGC Pastor Cho's Resource Center: The Index of Resources 2002.*[39] Outside of Korea, the Logos International and later, Bridge Publishing provided a handy outlet, while in Korea it has been the in-house publishers such as Seoul Logos, International Theological Institute (ITI) and the Church Growth International (CGI). Due to the lack of a worldwide distribution network, most of Cho's works published in Korea have not been widely circulated.

PART II
BIBLIOGRAPHY OF AND ON DAVID YONGGI CHO

1. Books and Articles by Cho

1.1 Books

70 Unique Illustrations. Seoul: CGI, 1989.

A Bible Study for New Christians. Seoul: Seoul Logos, 2002.

A Call in the Night, Sermon Series 1. Seoul: Seoul Logos, 2002.

Answers to Your Questions. Seoul: CGI, 1984.

Born to Be Blessed. Seoul: Seoul Logos, 1993.

Daniel: Insight on the Life and Dreams of the Prophet from Babylon. Lake Mary, FL: Creation House, 1990.

Great Businessmen. Seoul: Seoul Logos, 1995.

Blumhofer, *Aimee Semple McPherson: Everybody's Sister* (Grand Rapids, MI: William B. Eerdmans Publishing Company, 1993). In a similar way, Cho's life, ministry and his contribution to world Christianity, deserves a serious study.

[39]Pastor Cho's Resource Center of Yoido Full Gospel Church, ed., *YFGC Pastor Cho's Resource Center, The Index of Resources 2002.*

Home Cell System. Seoul: CGI, 1987.

How Can I Be Healed? Seoul: Seoul Logos, 1999.

How to Pray: Patterns of Prayer. Seoul: Seoul Logos, 1997.

March Forward to Hope, Sermon Series 2. Seoul: Seoul Logos, 2002.

More than Numbers. Waco, Texas: Word Books, 1984.

Prayer That Brings Revival. Altamonte Springs, FL: Creation House, 1998.

Prayer: Key to Revival. Waco. Texas: Word Books, 1984.

Praying with Jesus. Seoul: Seoul Publishing, 1993.

Revelation: Visions of Our Ultimate Victory in Christ. Seoul: Seoul Logos, 1991.

Salvation, Health and Prosperity: Our Threefold Blessings in Christ. Altamonte Springs, FL: Creation House, 1987.

Solving Life's Problems. Plainfield, NJ: Logos International, 1980.

Spiritual Leadership for the New Millennium. Seoul: Seoul Logos, 2003.

Successful Home Cell Groups. Miami, FL: Logos International, 1981.

Successful Living. Seoul: Youngsan Publications, 1977.

Suffering...Why Me? South Plainfield, NJ: Bridge Publishing, 1986.

The Apocalyptic Prophecy. Altamonte Springs, FL: Creation House, 1998.

The Concept of Love Growth. Seoul: CGI, 1984.

The Fourth Dimension, vol. 1. South Plainfield, NJ: Bridge Publishing, 1979.

The Fourth Dimension, vol. 2. South Plainfield, NJ: Bridge Publishing, 1983.

The Fourth Dimension, 3rd ed. Seoul: Seoul Logos, 1996.

The Holy Spirit My Senior Partner: Understanding the Holy Spirit and His Gifts. Altamonte Springs, FL: Creation House, 1989.

The Homecell Group Study Guide 1. Seoul: Seoul Logos, 1997.

The Homecell Group Study Guide 2. Seoul: Seoul Logos, 2000.

The Leap of Faith. South Plainfield, NJ: Bridge Publishing, 1984.

The Nature of God: Who Is God...Really. Watchung, NJ: Charisma House, 2001.

To God Be the Glory. Seoul: Seoul Publishing, 1973.

When I Am Weak, Then I Am Strong. Seoul: Seoul Logos, 2002.

1.2 Coauthored Works

With Florence Biros, Richard Halverson, and Robert Schuller. *Expand Your Horizon: How to Make Your Faith Work!* Melbourne, FL: Dove Christian Books, 1988.

With Harold Hostetler. *Successful Home Cell Groups*. Plainfield, NJ: Logos International, 1981.

With John W. Hurston. *Largest Korean Church's Home Cell Units: Asian Perspective* 26. Taipei, Taiwan: Asia Theological Association, n.d.

With John W. Hurston. "Ministry Through Home Cell Units." In *Korean Church Growth Explosion*. Ed. Bong-rin Ro and Martin L. Nelson. Seoul: Word of Life Press, 1983, 270-89

With John W. Hurston and Karen Hurston. *Caught in the Web: The Home Cell Unit System at Full Gospel Central Church, Seoul Korea*. La Canada, CA: Mountain Press, 1978.

With Ken Gaub. *Answers to Questions You've Always Wanted to Ask*. Green Forest, AR: New Leaf Press, 1994.

With Robert Gee Witty. *Divine Healing*. Nashville, TN: Broadman Press, 1989.

With Wendell Smith. *Great Faith: Making God Big*. Portland, OR: City Bible Publishing, 2001.

1.3 Articles and Chapters

"A New Image . . . through the Cross of Jesus." *Pentecostal Evangel*, April 16, 1995, 8-9.

"Active Faith." *South East Asia Journal of Theology* 23:2 (1982), 121-25.

"Celebration of Power, Message from 2000 Celebration." *Pentecostal Evangel*, October 6, 2000, 6-9.

"Forward" to Jashil Choi, *Korean Miracles*. La Canada, CA: Mountain Press, 1978.

"Holy Spirit and Church Growth." In *1989 Philippine Church Growth International Conference*. Manila: Cover & Pages Corporation, 1989.

"Home Cell System: A Key to Church Growth." In *Church Growth Manual, No. 4*. Seoul: CGI, 1992.

"Letter" to L. Richards. Quoted in Rosemary Jackson. "God Will Direct Our Steps." *Spirit*, Spring 1997, 3-4.

"Prayer: One Key to Church Growth." In *Church Growth Manual, No. 4*. Seoul: CGI, 1992.

"Sunday Night at the General Council: God Gave Me a Dream." *Pentecostal Evangel*, November 4, 1979, 8-12.

"Testimony Given by Cho Yonggi, Korea." *Pentecostal Evangel*, November 5, 1967, p. 10.

"The Evangelist and the Life of Faith." Address to the International Conference for Itinerant Evangelists, Amsterdam, Holland. July 12-21, 1983.

"The Holy Spirit: A Key to Church Growth." In *Church Growth Manual, No. 4*. Seoul: CGI, 1992.

"The Power of Prayer." *Pentecostal Evangel*, October 6, 1994, 6-7.

"The Secret behind the World's Biggest Church." In *Azusa Street and Beyond: Pentecostal Missions and Church Growth in the Twentieth Century*. Ed. L. Grant McClung, Jr. South Plainfield, NJ: Bridge Publishing, 1986, 98-108.

"When Buddha Didn't Answer, Jesus Did!" *Pentecostal Evangel*, August 26, 1973, 8-12.

"Church Ministry, Taking Steps with the Holy Spirit: Interview by Sung-hoon Myung." In *Charis and Charisma: David Yonggi Cho and the Growth of Yoido Full Gospel Church*. Ed. Sung-hoon Myung and Yong-gi Hong. Oxford. Regnum Books International, 2003, 3-12.

2. Books and Articles about Cho and YFGC

"150 Years of Evangelism." *Pentecostal Evangel*, August 5, 1979, 6-7.

"An Interview with Cho Yonggi." *Pentecostal Evangel*, November 5, 1967, 8-9.

"World Assemblies of God Congress and 2000 Celebration, Conversation with David Yonggi Cho and Thomas E. Trask." *Pentecostal Evangel*, March 12, 2000, 6-7.

Adams, Daniel J. "Reflections on an Indigenous Movement: The Yoido Full Gospel Church." *Japan Christian Quality* 57 (Winter 1991), 36-45.

_____. "The Life and Ministry of Cho Yonggi: A Theological Inquiry." *Chinese Theological Journal* 3:1 (1988): 31-57.

Allan Anderson, "The Contribution of David Yonggi Cho to a Contextual Theology in Korea," Paper read at the First Youngsan International Symposium at Hansei University, Goonpo, Korea, September 2002, and subsequently published under the same title in *Journal of Pentecostal Theology* 12:1 (2003), 87-107.

Bae, Hyeon-sung. "Response of Minjung and Pentecostal Movements in Korea." In *Pentecostals after a Century: Global Perspectives on a Movement in Transition*. Eds. Allan H. Anderson and Walter J. Hollenweger. Sheffield, England: Sheffield Academic Press, 1999, 161-63.

_____. "The Theological Implications of a Korean Pentecostal Identity: Reflecting on Full Gospel Theology of Korea." Paper presented at the International Conference on Asian Pentecostalism, The University of Birmingham, September 2001.

Blair, William Newton. *The Korean Pentecost and the Sufferings Which Followed*. Edinburgh: Banner of Truth Trust, 1977.

Burnett, Cordas. "We Saw Revival in Seoul Korea." *Pentecostal Evangel*, September 7, 1969, 8-9.

CGI. *Church Growth Manual, No. 1*. Seoul: CGI, 1986.

_____. *Church Growth Manual, No. 2*. Seoul: CGI, 1987.

_____. *Church Growth Manual, No. 3*. Seoul: CGI, 1990.

_____. *Church Growth Manual, No. 4*. Seoul: CGI, 1992.

_____. *Church Growth Manual, No. 5*. Seoul: CGI, 1993.

_____. *Church Growth Manual, No. 6*. Seoul: CGI, 1994.

_____. *Church Growth Manual, No. 7*. Seoul: CGI, 1995.

_____. *Church Growth Manual, No. 8*. Seoul: CGI, 1996.

_____. *Church Growth Manual, No. 9*. Seoul: CGI, 1998.

_____. *Church Growth Manual, No. 10*. Seoul: CGI, 2000.

_____. *Church Growth Manual, No. 11*. Seoul: CGI, 2001.

_____. *Church Growth Manual, No. 12*. Seoul: CGI, 2002.

_____. *Church Growth Manual, No. 13*. Seoul: CGI, 2003.

Chan, Simon. "The Pneumatology of Dr. Paul Yonggi Cho." Paper presented at 2003 Youngsan International Theological Symposium, Hansei University, Goonpo, Korea, May 2003.

Cho, Dong-ho. "Intimate Alien: An Immanent Critique of Korean Pentecostalism." Ph.D. diss., City University of New York, 2002.

Cho, Il-koo. "Healing in the Context of Korean Pentecostalism, 1950s to the Present: Historical and Ethnographic Approaches." Ph.D. diss., Claremont Graduate University, 2002.

Cho, Paul Yonggi. "Yonggi Cho Changes His Name." Interviewed by C. Peter Wagner, *Charisma & Christian Life* (November 1992).

Choi, Ja-shil. *Korean Miracles*. La Canada, CA: Mountain Press, 1978.

Choi, Kilhak. "A Study on the Effective Policy and Strategy of Supporting the Pioneering Church of Yoido Full Gospel Church." Th.M. thesis, Oral Roberts University, 1998.

Choi. Mun-hong. "Dr. Yonggi Cho and the Holy Spirit." Paper presented at 2003 Youngsan International Theological Symposium, Hansei University, Goonpo, Korea, May 2003.

Church Growth International (http://Churchgrowthint.homestead.com).

Church Growth Magazine. A quarterly published by CGI, Seoul, Korea.

Comiskey, Joel. "His Cell Groups and Dynamics of Church Growth." In *Charis and Charisma: David Yonggi Cho and the Growth of Yoido Full Gospel Church*. Eds. Sung-hoon Myung and Yong-gi Hong. Oxford. Regnum Books International, 2003, 143-58.

Commiskey, Joel Thomas. "Cell-based Ministry: A Positive Factor for Church Growth in Latin America." Ph.D. diss., Fuller Theological Seminary, 1997.

Coote, Robert T. "The Gospel and Urbanization." A workbook for participants in a seminar held April 23-27 and April 30-May 4, 1984, at the Overseas Ministry Study Center, Ventnor, New Jersey.

Douglass, Philip. "Yonggi Cho and the Korean Pentecostal Movement: Some Theological Reflections." *Presbyterian* 17 (Spring 1991), 16-34.

Genet, Harry. "Big Trouble at the World's Largest Church." *Christianity Today* 26 (January 22, 1982), 30, 39.

Gunter, Paul Stewart. "A Case Study of the Prayer Ministry of Yoido Full Gospel Church." Th.M. thesis, Dallas Theological Seminary, 1987.

Han, Sang-ehil. "A Response to Dongsoo Kim." *Journal of Pentecostal Theology* 15 (October 1999), 123-39.

Hong, Yong-gi. "The Charisma of Cho Yong-gi and Its Routinization in the Yoido Full Gospel Church of Korea." *Journal of Asian Mission* 2:1 (March 2000): 65-90.

_____. "The Influence of His Church Growth on Korean Society." In *Charis and Charisma: David Yonggi Cho and the Growth of Yoido Full Gospel Church*. Edited by Sung-hoon Myung and Yong-gi Hong. Oxford. Regnum Books International, 2003, 197-217.

_____. "Revisiting Church Growth in Korean Pentecostalism: A Theological Reflection." *International Review of Mission* 89/353 (2000), 190-202.

_____. "The Impact of Charismatic Pastoral Leadership on Religious Commitment and Church Growth in the Korean Mega-churches." *Mission Studies* 18:2 (2001), 22-49.

Horn, Ken. "South Korea: A Fortress of Prayer." *Pentecostal Evangel*, August 6, 2000, 6-17.

Hunt, Dave and T. McMahon. *Beyond Seduction: A Return to Biblical Christianity*. Eugene: Harvest House, 1987.

_____. T*he Seduction of Christianity: Spiritual Discernment in the Last Days*. Eugene: Harvest House, 1985.

Hurston, John and Karen L. Hurston. *Caught in the Web: The Home Cell Unit System at Full Gospel Central Church*. Seoul: Mountain Press, 1978.

Hurston, Karen. *Growing the World's Largest Church*. Springfield. Missouri: Charism, 1994.

Hwa, Yung. "Missiological Implications of Dr. David Yonggi Cho's Theology." Paper presented at the First Youngsan International Theological Symposium, Hansei University, Goonpo, Korea, September 2002.

Hwang, Won S. "Contextualization of the Gospel by Paul Yonggi Cho in the Korean Context." Th.M. thesis, Trinity Evangelical Divinity School, 1994.

Im, Hyung-geun. "Dr. Yonggi Cho's Understanding of the Holy Spirit: Centering on Fellowship with the Holy Spirit." Paper presented at 2003 Youngsan International Theological Symposium, Hansei University, Goonpo, Korea, May 2003.

International Theological Institute, ed. *Yoido Full Gospel Church: Its Faith and Theology*. Seoul: Seoul Logos, 1993.

Jung, Jong-hee. "The Formation and Development of Korean Pentecostalism from the Viewpoint of a Dynamic Contextual Theology." Th.D. thesis, University of Birmingham, 2001.

_____. "The Korean Charismatic Movement from the Perspective of Indigenous Pentecostalism." Paper presented at the International Conference on Asian Pentecostalism, The University of Birmingham, September 2001.

Kang, Chang-soo. "An Analytical Study on the Life of Woon-mong Na, Indigenous Korean Pentecostal." Th.M. thesis, Asia Pacific Theological Seminary, 2003.

_____. "The First Diary of Revival Rallies of Early Korean Protestants in 1915 of Janbong and Kangwha Islands in the Western Sea Area of Korea." Paper presented in the Sixth Annual Meeting of Asian Pentecostal Society, Nov 2003, Baguio City, Philippines.

_____. "The Pneumatology of Ick-Doo Kim." Paper presented in the 12th William Menzies Annual Lectureship, Jan 12-16, 2004, Baguio City, Philippines.

Kannaday, Peggay. "The World's Largest Church." *Pentecostal Evangel*, February 2, 1994, 12-13.

Kennedy, Nell L. *Dream Your Way to Success: The Story of Dr. Yonggi Cho and Korea*. Plainfield, NJ: Logos International, 1980.

Kim, Dong-soo. "The Healing of Han in Korean Pentecostalism." *Journal of Pentecostal Theology* 15 (October 1999), 123-39.

Kim, Il. "A Study of Full Fukuoka Church of Japan as Model Church Revival through the Prayer Movement: An Application of Dr. Cho's Prayer Pattern (Yonggi Cho)." Th.M. thesis, Regent University, 1999.

Kim, Sam-hwan. "The Question of Good and Evil in Full Gospel Faith: A Study of the Theological Foundation for the Threefold Blessing of

Dr. Yonggi Cho." Paper presented at 2002 Youngsan International Theological Symposium, Hansei University, Goonpo, Korea, September 2002.

Kim, Sooyoung. "A Biblical Critique on the Prosperity Gospel of Paul Yonggi Cho." Th.M. thesis, Dallas Theological Seminary, 1989.

Korea Assembly of God, ed. *Yoido Full Gospel Church*. Seoul: Korea Assemblies of God, 1996.

Landrus, Heather. "Hearing 3 John 2 in the Voices of History." *Journal of Pentecostal Theology* 11:1 (November 2002), 53-69.

Lee, Dongsung. "Exploration of the Leadership of David (Paul) Yonggi Cho and Its Influence on Growth of Yoido Full Gospel Church (Korea)." Th.M. thesis, Regent University, 2001.

Lee, Hong-jung. "Minjung and Pentecostal Movements in Korea." In *Pentecostals after a Century: Global Perspectives on a Movement in Transition*. Eds. Allan H. Anderson and Walter J. Hollenweger. Sheffield, England: Sheffield Academic Press, 1999, 138-60.

Lee, Jae-bum. "Pentecostal Type Distinctives and Korean Protestant Church Growth." Ph.D. diss., Fuller Theological Seminary, 1986.

Lee, Larry. *Could You Not Tarry One Hour?* Rockwell, TX: Church on the Rock, 1985.

Lee, Sang-hwan. "Korean Pentecostal Response." *Pnuema* 23:1 (Spring 2001), pp. 54-60.

Lee, Soong-kyo, Hae-koon Kuak, and Joong-wook Yoon, Eds. *Ordeal and Glory through the Thirty Year History of Yoido Full Gospel Church*. Seoul: YFGC, 1989.

Lee, Young-hoon. "Korean Pentecost: The Great Revival of 1907." *Asian Journal of Pentecostal Studies* 6:1 (2003), 73-83.

_____. "The Case for Prosperity Theology." *Evangelical Review of Theology* 20:1 (January 1996), 26-39.

_____. "The Holy Spirit Movement in Korea: Its Historical and Doctrinal Development." Ph.D. diss., Temple University, 1996.

_____. "The Korean Holy Spirit Movement in Relation to the Pentecostal Movement." Paper presented at the International Conference on Asian Pentecostalism, The University of Birmingham, September 2001.

Leoh, Vincent Beng. "Ethics and Pentecostal Preaching: The Anastatic, Organic, and Communal Strands (Anastatic strands, organic strands, social ethics)." Ph.D. diss., Southern Baptist Theological Seminary, 1990.

Lim, Donghwan. "A Study of Yoido Full Gospel Church: Its Evangelism and Nature." Th.M. thesis, Regent University, 1999.

Ma, Julie C. "Korean Pentecostal Spirituality: A Case Study of Jashil Choi." *Asian Journal of Pentecostal Studies* 5:2 (July 2002), 235-54.

Ma, Wonsuk. "Tasks and Challenges for Korean Pentecostal Churches in the Twenty-First Century." *Australasian Pentecostal Studies* 5 (2002), 63-94.

_____. "The Effect of His Sermon Style for Church Growth on the Development of Theology." In *Charis and Charisma: David Yonggi Cho and the Growth of Yoido Full Gospel Church*. Eds. Sung-hoon Myung and Yong-gi Hong. Oxford. Regnum Books International, 2003, 159-71.

_____. "Yonggi Cho's Theology of Blessing: New Theological Basis and Directions." Paper presented at 2003 Younsan International Theological Symposium, Hansei University, Goonpo, Korea, May 2003.

McClung, Lloyd Grant, Jr. "The Church Growth: Church Planting Study Guide." Ph.D. diss., Fuller Theological Seminary, 1985.

Menzies, William W. "Yonggi Cho's Theology of the Fullness of the Spirit: A Pentecostal Perspective." Paper presented at 2003 Youngsan International Theological Symposium, Hansei University, Goonpo, Korea, May 2003.

Mullins, Mark R. "The Empire Strikes Back: Korean Pentecostal Mission to Japan." In *Charismatic Christianity as a Global Culture*. Ed. Karla Poewe. Columbia, CA: University of South Carolina Press, 1994, 87-102.

Myung, Sung-hoon. "Preaching Ministry of Yoido Full Gospel Church." Th.M. thesis. Fuller Theological Seminary, 1988.

_____. "Spiritual Dimensions of Church Growth as Applied in the Yoido Full Gospel Church." Ph.D. diss., Fuller Theological Seminary, 1990.

_____. "The Influence of His Leadership on the Churches of Korea." In *Charis and Charisma: David Yonggi Cho and the Growth of Yoido Full Gospel Church*. Eds. Sung-hoon Myung and Yong-gi Hong. Oxford. Regnum Books International, 2003, 123-42.

_____ and Yonggi Hong, eds. *Charis and Charisma: David Yonggi Cho and the Growth of Yoido Full Gospel Church.* Oxford: Regnum Books International, 2003.

Nelson, Richard Dean. "The Self-improvement Gospel of David Yonggi Cho: A Critique of Self-help Theology." Th.M. thesis, Lincoln Christian Seminary, 1998.

Nickel, Ruth D. and Thomas R. Nickel. *Dying Korean Buddhist: The Cho Yonggi Miracle*. Hanford. CA: Great Commission International, 1973.

Oak, Han-hum. "Message of Hole: Interview by Sung-hoon Myung." In *Charis and Charisma: David Yonggi Cho and the Growth of Yoido Full Gospel Church.* Eds. Sung-hoon Myung and Yong-gi Hong. Oxford. Regnum Books International, 2003, 13-20.

Park, Moon-ok. "An Eschatological Understanding of Dr. Yonggi Cho's Idea of Divine Healing." Paper presented at 2002 Youngsan International Theological Symposium, September 26, 2002, Goonpo, Korea.

Park, Myung Soo. "A Study of Him and the Growth of Yoido Full Gospel Church." In *Charis and Charisma: David Yonggi Cho and the Growth of Yoido Full Gospel Church*. Eds. Sung-hoon Myung and Yong-gi Hong. Oxford. Regnum Books International, 2003, 173-96.

_____. "David Yonggi Cho and International Pentecostal/Charismatic Movements." *Journal of Pentecostal Theology* 12:1 (October 2003), 107-28.

Reynalds, Jeremy. "Shamanistic Influences in Korean Pentecostal Christianity: An Analysis." (http://www.rickross.com/reference/yoidoyonggi/ yoido11.html), checked: Dec. 23, 2003.

Ritter, Preston James. *The Bible and Dr. Paul Yonggi Cho*. Seoul: Korea Christian Information Center, 1983.

Robeck, Cecil. "The Influence on the Churches in the World: Interview by Yong-gi Hong." In *Charis and Charisma: David Yonggi Cho and the Growth of Yoido Full Gospel Church*. Eds. Sung-hoon Myung and Yong-gi Hong. Oxford. Regnum Books International, 2003, 27-34.

_____. Review of *Korean Pentecostalism: Its History and Theology*, by Boo-woong Yoo. *Pneuma* 12:1 (Spring 1990): 60-62.

Rodman, Williams, J. and Vinson Synan. *The Holy Spirit and Church.* Seoul: Yoido Full Gospel Church, 1997.

Shim, Chang-sup. "Assessing the Impact of Pentecostalism on the Korean Presbyterian Church in Light of Calvin's Theology." *Chongshin Theological Journal* 3 (1998), 115-31.

Sizer, Stephen. "Spiritual Warfare and David Yonggi Cho." In *The Toronto Blessing and the Prosperity Gospel Faith Movement.* (http://www.christchurch-virginiawater.co.uk/articles/articles.html #Toronto), checked: Dec 26, 2003.

Stetz, John. "Sharing the Peacegiver in Korea: Full Gospel Central Church, Seoul." *Pentecostal Evangel*, March 7, 1976, 6-7.

_____. *Gleanings from Korea's Harvest.* Springfield. MI: Colorweb, 1965.

Strang, Stephen. "Cho's Problems with Prosperity." *Charisma & Christian Life*, March, 1988.

Strohmer, Charles. "God as Servant, Man as God." *Alpha*, Feb. 1995.

Synan, Vinson. "The Yoido Full Gospel Church." *Cyberjournal for Pentecostal/Charismatic Research* 2 (July 1997, http://www.pctii.org/cybertab.html), checked: Dec 26, 2003.

Vaughan, John N. *The Large Church: A Twentieth Century Expression of the First Century Church.* Grand Rapids, MI: Baker Book House, 1985.

Wagner, Peter. "Leadership and Communication: Interview by Yong-gi Hong." In *Charis and Charisma: David Yonggi Cho and the Growth of Yoido Full Gospel Church.* Eds. Sung-hoon Myung and Yong-gi Hong. Oxford. Regnum Books International, 2003, 21-26.

Wei, Hsieh-Kan Christian. "The Analysis and Criticism of the Theology and Methodology of Paul Yonggi Cho." Ph.D. diss., Bob Jones University, 1992.

Widjaja, Sutrisna. "The Concept of the Church According to David Yonggi Cho" (http://eapi.admu.edu.ph/eapi00/Sutrisna.htm), checked: Dec 23, 2003.

Widjaja, Sutrisna. "The Theology of Salvation of David Yonggi Cho and Its Pastoral Challenges to Indonesian Christian Ministers." M.A. thesis, East Asian Pastoral Institute, Philippines.

Yoo, Boo-woong. *Korean Pentecostalism: Its History and Theology.* Frankfurt am Main: Verlag Peter Lang GmbH, 1988.

_____. "Response to Korean Shamanism by the Pentecostal Church." *International Review of Mission* 75 (January 1986), 70-74.

INDEX

SCRIPTURE INDEX

AUTHOR INDEX